D1336917

Renault 12 Owners Workshop Manual

by J H Haynes
Member of the Guild of Motoring Writers

and Tim Parker

Models covered

All Renault 12 models, 1289 cc
Saloon L, TL, TS and TR
Estate TN and TL

Covers manual and automatic transmission versions

ISBN 0 85696 503 0

HAYNES PUBLISHING GROUP
SPARKFORD YEOVIL SOMERSET ENGLAND
distributed in the USA by
HAYNES PUBLICATIONS INC
861 LAWRENCE DRIVE
NEWBURY PARK
CALIFORNIA 91320
USA

Acknowledgements

The late David Stead should be acknowledged first. David Haynes kindly loaned his Renault 12 for us to work on and take the photographic sequences.

Thanks are due to Regie Renault, particularly to their organisation in the United Kingdom, for their assistance with technical material and illustrations.

The Renault franchise garages should not be forgotten. Many have supplied more than adequate answers to many seemingly irrelevant and 'suspicious' questions and given many a secret away. They have really been most helpful particularly those garages in Cambridge and Yeovil.

Castrol Limited have again assisted with lubrication details.

About this manual

Its aims

The aim of this Manual is to help you get the best value from your car. It can do so in several ways. It can help you decide what work must be done (even should you choose to get it done by a garage), provide information on routine maintenance and servicing, and give a logical course of action and diagnosis when random faults occur. However, it is hoped that you will use the Manual by tackling the work yourself. On simpler jobs it may even be quicker than booking the car into a garage, and going there twice to leave and collect it. Perhaps most important, a lot of money can be saved by avoiding the costs the garage must charge to cover its labour and overheads.

The manual has drawings and descriptions to show the function of the various components so that their layout can be understood. Then the tasks are described and photographed in a step-by-step sequence so that even a novice can do the work.

Its arrangement

The manual is divided into twelve Chapters, each covering a logical sub-division of the vehicle. The Chapters are each divided into Sections, numbered with single figures, eg 5; and the Sections into paragraphs (or sub-sections), with decimal numbers following on from the Section they are in eg 5.1, 5.2, 5.3 etc.

It is freely illustrated, especially in those parts where there is a detailed sequence of operations to be carried out. There are two forms of illustration: figures and photographs. The figures are numbered in sequence with decimal numbers, according to their position in the Chapter: eg Fig. 6.4 is the 4th drawing/illustration in Chapter 6. Photographs are numbered (either individually or in related groups) the same as the Section or sub-section of the text where the operation they show is described.

There is an alphabetical index at the back of the manual as well as a contents list at the front.

References to the 'left' or 'right' of the vehicle are in the sense of a person in the driver's seat facing forwards.

Whilst every care is taken to ensure that the information in this manual is correct, no liability can be accepted by the authors or publishers for loss, damage or injury caused by any errors in, or omissions from, the information given.

Introduction to the Renault 12

The story of the Renault 12 is long and involved and unfortunately this introduction is not the proper place for its telling. However, any brief introduction to this model must look further than France to catch the first glimpse of the car. Before the 12 saloon was marketed in France which was again some time before it reached the English shores, there was a very similar looking car for sale in Brazil with a Ford badge on its bonnet and the 'proper' Renault engine under it. However there seems to be little doubt that the 12 was designed in France and was intended as a car to replace the rear engined Renault models which were sadly dating. Its introduction enabled Regie Renault then to describe themselves as the world's largest manufacturer of front wheel drive cars.

The Renault 12 first appeared in England in May 1970 as one of two versions of the saloon, the TL and L. It has very little similarity in design to any of the other front wheel drive models in the Renault range although it does use many familiar components. Whereas the Renault 4, 6 and 16 have the engine placed behind the transmission and independent rear suspension, the 12 has its engine in front of the transmission and non-independent rear suspension by beam axle. The Renault 12 is of monocoque construction similar to the 16 but not to the 4 and 6.

In January 1971 an estate version was introduced in the United Kingdom and in October 1972 an increased performance version of the saloon, the TS. All models available to UK customers are fitted with the well known 1289 cc 'Sierra' engine taken from the Renault 10 and a four speed manual gearbox. Unfortunately the 16 and 16TS engined versions available as the Gordini in France and the normal versions in America are not imported.

On analysis the Renault 12 is non-conventional but is one of the most reliable cars Renault UK have ever imported. It provides very comfortable economic and safe motoring which can be endorsed by the fact that Paris uses them for her taxis and that Renault have re-launched into the fast growing sport coupe market with the 15 and 17 which use the same running gear.

Renault designations of models covered by this manual:

R1170 TL and L
R1171 Estate (designated TN until 1974)
R1330 Estate (1975 on)
R1177 TS saloon
R1177 Automatic saloon (designated TR until 1974, then 12 Auto)

Contents

Renault 12TL Saloon

Renault 12TR Saloon

Renault 12TS Saloon

Renault 12 Estate

Vehicle identification and ordering spare parts

Buying spare parts

Spare parts are available from many sources. Renault have many dealers throughout the UK and USA, and other dealers, accessory stores and motor factors will also stock Renault spare parts.

Our advice regarding spare part sources is as follows:

Officially appointed vehicle main dealers — This is the best source of parts which are peculiar to your vehicle and are otherwise not generally available (eg complete cylinder heads, internal transmission components, badges, interior trim etc). It is also the only place at which you should buy parts if your vehicle is still under warranty. To be sure of obtaining the correct parts it will always be necessary to give the storeman your vehicle's engine and chassis number, and if possible, to take the 'old' part along for positive identification. Remember that many parts are available on a factory exchange scheme — any parts returned should

always be clean! It obviously makes good sense to go straight to the specialists on your vehicle for this type of part, for they are best equipped to supply you.

Other dealers and auto accessory stores — These are often very good places to buy materials and components needed for the maintenance of your vehicle (eg oil filters, spark plugs, bulbs, fan belts, oils and greases, touch-up paint, filler paste etc). They also sell general accessories, usually have convenient opening hours, charge lower prices and can often be found not far from home.

Motor factors — Good factors will stock all of the more important components which wear out relatively quickly (eg clutch components, pistons, valves, exhaust systems, brake cylinders/pipes/hoses/seals/shoes and pads etc). Motor factors will often provide new or reconditioned components on a part exchange basis — this can save a considerable amount of money.

OVAL PLATE AND LOSENGE PLATE

A - Vehicle type number
B - Equipment number
C - Fabrication number
D - Chassis number
E - Version number

* The paint code is stencilled adjacent to the oval plate.

Prefix S means synthetic paint is used.
Prefic C indicates cellulose

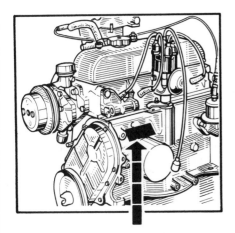

Engine number - includes engine type number (see specifications
(Chapter 1) and engine number

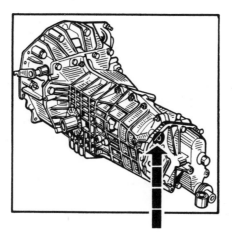

Gearbox number - includes type and number (see specifications
(Chapter 6)

Tools and working facilities

Introduction

A selection of good tools is a fundamental requirement for anyone contemplating the maintenance and repair of a motor vehicle. For the owner who does not possess any, their purchase will prove a considerable expense, offsetting some of the savings made by doing-it-yourself. However, provided that the tools purchased are of good quality, they will last for many years and prove an extremely worthwhile investment.

To help the average owner to decide which tools are needed to carry out the various tasks detailed in this manual, we have compiled three lists of tools under the following headings: *Maintenance and minor repair, Repair and overhaul,* and *Special.* The newcomer to practical mechanics should start off with the *Maintenance and minor repair* tool kit and confine himself to the simpler jobs around the vehicle. Then, as his confidence and experience grows, he can undertake more difficult tasks, buying extra tools as, and when, they are needed. In this way a *Maintenance and minor repair* tool kit can be built-up into a *Repair and overhaul* tool kit over a considerable period of time without any major cash outlays. The experienced do-it-yourselfer will have a tool kit good enough for most repair and overhaul procedures and will add tools from the *Special* category when he feels the expense is justified by the amount of use these tools will be put to.

It is obviously not possible to cover the subject of tools fully here. For those who wish to learn more about tools and their use there is a book entitled *How to Choose and Use Car Tools* available from the publishers of this manual.

Maintenance and minor repair tool kit

The tools given in this list should be considered as a minimum requirement if routine maintenance, servicing and minor repair operations are to be undertaken. We recommend the purchase of combination spanners (ring one end, open-ended the other): although more expensive than open-ended ones, they do give the advantages of both types of spanner.

Combination spanners - 8, 10, 11, 13, 14, 17 mm
Adjustable spanner - 9 inch
Engine sump/gearbox/rear axle drain plug key (where applicable)
Spark plug spanner (with rubber insert)
Spark plug gap adjustment tool
Set of feeler gauges
Brake adjuster spanner (where applicable)
Brake bleed nipple spanner
Screwdriver - 4 in long x ¼ in dia (flat blade)
Screwdriver - 4 in long x ¼ in dia (cross blade)
Combination pliers - 6 inch
Hacksaw, junior
Tyre pump
Tyre pressure gauge
Grease gun (where applicable)
Oil can
Fine emery cloth (1 sheet)
Wire brush (small)
Funnel (medium size)

Repair and overhaul tool kit

These tools are virtually essential for anyone undertaking any major repairs to a motor vehicle, and are additional to those given in the *Maintenance and minor repair* list. Included in this list is a comprehensive set of sockets. Although these are expensive they will be found invaluable as they are so versatile - particularly if various drives are included in the set. We recommend the ½ in square-drive type, as this can be used with most proprietary torque wrenches. If you cannot afford a socket set, even bought piecemeal, then inexpensive tubular box spanners are a useful alternative.

The tools in this list will occasionally need to be supplemented by tools from the *Special* list.

Sockets (or box spanners) to cover range in previous list
Reversible ratchet drive (for use with sockets)
Extension piece, 10 inch (for use with sockets)
Universal joint (for use with sockets)
Torque wrench (for use with sockets)
'Mole' wrench - 8 inch
Ball pein hammer
Soft-faced hammer, plastic or rubber
Screwdriver - 6 in long x 5/16 in dia (flat blade)
Screwdriver - 2 in long x 5/16 in square (flat blade)
Screwdriver - 1½ in long x ¼ in dia (cross blade)
Screwdriver - 3 in long x 1/8 in dia (electricians)
Pliers - electricians side cutters
Pliers - needle nosed
Pliers - circlip (internal and external)
Cold chisel - ½ inch
Scriber (this can be made by grinding the end of a broken hacksaw blade)
Scraper (this can be made by flattening and sharpening one end of a piece of copper pipe)
Centre punch
Pin punch
Hacksaw
Valve grinding tool
Steel rule/straight edge
Allen keys
Selection of files
Wire brush (large)
Axle stands
Jack (strong scissor or hydraulic type)

Special tools

The tools in this list are those which are not used regularly, are expensive to buy, or which need to be used in accordance with their manufacturers' instructions. Unless relatively difficult mechanical jobs are undertaken frequently, it will not be economic to buy many of these tools. Where this is the case, you could consider clubbing together with friends (or a motorists' club) to make a joint purchase, or borrowing the tools against a deposit from a local garage or tool hire specialist.

The following list contains only those tools and instruments freely available to the public, and not those special tools produced by the vehicle manufacturer specifically for its dealer network.

You will find occasional references to these manufacturers' special tools in the text of this manual. Generally, an alternative method of doing the job without the vehicle manufacturers' special tool is given. However, sometimes, there is no alternative to using them. Where this is the case and the relevant tool cannot be bought or borrowed, you will have to entrust the work to a franchised garage.

Valve spring compressor
Piston ring compressor
Balljoint separator
Universal hub/bearing puller
Impact screwdriver
Micrometer and/or vernier gauge
Carburettor flow balancing device (where applicable)
Dial gauge
Stroboscopic timing light
Dwell angle meter/tachometer
Universal electric multi-meter
Cylinder compression gauge
Lifting tackle
Trolley jack
Light with extension lead

Buying tools

For practically all tools, a tool factor is the best source since he will have a very comprehensive range compared with the average garage or accessory shop. Having said that, accessory shops often offer excellent quality tools at discount prices, so it pays to shop around.

Remember, you don't always have to buy the most expensive items on the shelf, but it is always advisable to steer clear of the very cheap tools. There are plenty of good tools around at reasonable prices, so ask the proprietor or manager of the shop for advice before making a purchase.

Care and maintenance of tools

Having purchased a reasonable tool kit, it is necessary to keep the tools in a clean serviceable condition. After use, always wipe off any dirt, grease and metal particles using a clean, dry cloth, before putting the tools away. Never leave them lying around after they have been used. A simple tool rack on the garage or workshop wall, for items such as screwdrivers and pliers is a good idea. Store all normal spanners and sockets in a metal box. Any measuring instruments, gauges, meters, etc., must be carefully stored where they cannot be damaged or become rusty.

Take a little care when tools are used. Hammer heads inevitably become marked and screwdrivers lose the keen edge on their blades from time-to-time. A little timely attention with emery cloth or a file will soon restore items like this to a good serviceable finish.

Working facilities

Not to be forgotten when discussing tools, is the workshop itself. If anything more than routine is to be carried out, some form of suitable working area becomes essential.

It is appreciated that many an owner mechanic is forced by circumstances to remove an engine or similar item, without the benefit of a garage or workshop. Having done this, any repairs should always be done under the cover of a roof.

Whenever possible, any dismantling should be done on a clean flat workbench or table at a suitable working height.

Any workbench needs a vice: one with a jaw opening of 4 in (100 mm) is suitable for most jobs. As mentioned previously, some clean dry storage space is also required for tools, as well as lubricants, cleaning fluids, touch-up paint and so on which become necessary.

Another item which may be required, and which has a much more general usage, is an electric drill with a chuck capacity of at least 5/16 in (8 mm). This, together with a good range of twist drills, is virtually essential for fitting accessories such as mirrors and reversing lights.

Last, but not least, always keep a supply of old newspapers and clean, lint-free rags available, and try to keep any working area as clean as possible.

Spanner jaw gap comparison table

Jaw gap (in)	Spanner size
0.250	¼ in AF
0.275	7 mm
0.312	5/16 in AF
0.315	8 mm
0.340	11/32 in AF; 1/8 in Whitworth
0.354	9 mm
0.375	3/8 in AF
0.393	10 mm
0.433	11 mm
0.437	7/16 in AF
0.445	3/16 in Whitworth; ¼ in BSF
0.472	12 mm
0.500	½ in AF
0.512	13 mm
0.525	¼ in Whitworth; 5/16 in BSF
0.551	14 mm
0.562	9/16 in AF
0.590	15 mm
0.600	5/16 in Whitworth; 3/8 in BSF
0.625	5/8 in AF
0.629	16 mm
0.669	17 mm
0.687	11/16 in AF
0.708	18 mm
0.710	3/8 in Whitworth; 7/16 in BSF
0.748	19mm
0.750	¾ in AF
0.812	13/16 in AF
0.820	7/6 in Whitworth; ½ in BSF
0.866	22 mm
0.875	7/8 in AF
0.920	½ in Whitworth; 9/16 in BSF
0.937	15/16 in AF
0.944	24 mm
1.000	1 in AF
1.010	9/16 in Whitworth; 5/8 in BSF
1.023	26 mm
1.062	1 1/16 in AF; 27 mm
1.100	5/8 in Whitworth; 11/16 in BSF
1.125	1 1/8 in AF
1.181	30 mm
1.200	11/16 in Whitworth; ¾ in BSF
1.250	1¼ in AF
1.259	32 mm
1.300	¾ in Whitworth; 7/8 in BSF
1.312	1 5/16 in AF
1.390	13/16 in Whitworth; 15/16 in BSF
1.417	36 mm
1.437	1 7/16 in AF
1.480	7/8 in Whitworth; 1 in BSF
1.500	1½ in AF
1.574	40 mm; 15/16 in Whitworth
1.614	41 mm
1.625	1 5/8 in AF
1.670	1 in Whitworth; 1 1/8 in BSF
1.687	1 11/16 in AF
1.811	46 mm
1.812	1 13/16 in AF
1.860	1 1/8 in Whitworth; 1¼ in BSF
1.875	1 7/8 in AF
1.968	50 mm
2.000	2 in AF
2.050	1¼ in Whitworth; 1 3/8 in BSF
2.165	55 mm
2.362	60 mm

Recommended lubricants and fluids

COMPONENT	TYPE OF LUBRICANT OR FLUID	CASTROL PRODUCT
ENGINE SUMP (1)	Multigrade engine oil 20W/50	GTX
TRANSMISSION (2)	SAE 80 EP	Hypoy Light
DISTRIBUTOR AND GENERATOR BUSHES (3)	Light oil/Engine oil	GTX/Everyman
FRONT AND REAR HUB BEARINGS (4)	Lithium based grease High melting point	LM GREASE
HYDRAULIC SYSTEM (5)	SAE J1703e	Castrol Girling Universal Brake and Clutch Fluid (do not mix)
BRAKE MECHANISMS (ADJUSTER CAM AND SHOES TO BACKPLATES)	High melting point white grease	PH Grease
COOLANT (6)	Glycol based antifreeze and distilled water	Antifreeze

Additionally Castrol 'Everyman' oil can be used to lubricate door, boot and bonnet hinges, and locks, pivots, etc.

DISTRIBUTOR CONTACT BREAKER CAM AND BATTERY TERMINALS	Petrolum jelly	
HYDRAULIC PISTONS	Rubber grease	
INNER DRIVE SHAFT JOINTS	Specific Renault lubricant	

Routine maintenance

Although any car will probably 'go' for a considerable time without doing anything to it in the way of maintenance, there is no doubt that prevention is certainly less costly than cure. Those who boast that they never lift the bonnet and never have any trouble are probably spending a fortune in fuel and oil and driving an unsafe vehicle with no performance.

Maintenance tends to get less frequent and less regular as the car gets older and changes owners more frequently.

Modern cars — the Renault 12 included — are designed and built with a large percentage of components which have a certain life and are then renewed. Consequently the approach to maintenance is no longer a matter of wading in with the oil can and grease gun. In fact on the Renault 12 there are no grease nipples at all.

Modern maintenance can be divided into two categories, one part for safety, the other for performance and economy. The former requires inspection and perhaps action. The latter requires regular checks and action. The maintenance routines given below give frequency on a time basis. The intervals are minimum for a mileage of 1000 miles or less per month on average. Consistent mileage in excess of 1000 per month might call for a shorter maintenance interval. Where necessary the maintenance procedures are explained after the schedules. Otherwise the relevant chapter in the book giving the details is referred to.

Safety maintenance schedule

STEERING
Front suspension arm ball joints - Check for wear	3 months
Steering tie-rod ball joints - Check for wear	3 months
Steering gear - Check wear in steering rack	3 months
Front wheel bearings - Check looseness with drive shaft	
	3 months

BRAKES
Hydraulic fluid reservoir in level - Check	1 month
Handbrake efficiency - Check and adjust	3 months
Brake pad and shoe lining material thickness - Check	6 months
Hydraulic lines, hoses, master cylinder and wheel calipers - Examine for leaks or corrosion	6 months
Renew hydraulic fluid in system by bleeding right through	3 years
Rear brakes - adjust (as necessary)	3 months

Note: A significant drop in the fluid reservoir level or any other indication of fluid leakage is a danger signal. A complete and thorough examination of the hydraulic system should be made.

SUSPENSION
Tyres - Inflation pressure check	Weekly
Tyres - Wear and damage check	As suspect
Shock absorbers - Check for leakage and malfunction	3 months
Front and rear suspension arm pivot bushes	6 months

Drive shafts - Check for universal joint wear	3 months
Rear hubs - Check for end float	3 months

Safety maintenance procedures

STEERING - See Chapter 10.

BRAKES
Hydraulic fluid reservoir level. Raise the bonnet. The hydraulic fluid reservoir is mounted on the bulkhead. Clean round the filler cap before removing it and top up to the indicated level with the approved fluid if necessary. (See recommended lubricants schedule). For other brake matters see Chapter 8.

SUSPENSION
See Chapter 10.

Efficiency and performance maintenance schedule

ENGINE
Lubricating oil - Top up to level	Weekly
Drain, renew filter and refill with fresh oil	3 months
Fan belt - Check tension and adjust if necessary	1 month
Battery - Electrolyte level check	Weekly
Distributor - Check contact points gap	
Adjust or renew	3 months
Lubricate	3 months
Air cleaner Renew paper element	6 months
	(If dusty
	atmosphere
	more often)
Valve clearances - Check and adjust	6 months
Spark plugs - Remove, clean and reset	3 months
Renew	12 months
Carburettor - Check throttle cable linkage and lubricate	6 months
Clean jets and filters	6 months

FRONT AND REAR SUSPENSION
See Chapter 10.

GEARBOX
Check oil level and top up if necessary	3 months
Drain and refill with fresh oil	6 months

CLUTCH
Check pedal free travel	6 months

Efficiency and performance maintenance procedures

ENGINE
Lubricating Oil
When the engine has been stopped for at least 2 minutes, and

is standing on level ground, remove the dipstick. The level mark should be between 'Min' and 'Max'. Add oil through the filler in the valve rocker cover, allowing time for the oil to drain down before checking the level again.

When changing the oil the engine should be warmed up first. Then unscrew the sump drain plug and drain the oil into a container which should hold at least a gallon or 4 litres to avoid overflow.

The filter cartridge is located at the left front of the engine. To remove the filter cartridge use a chain wrench which can be improvised from a length of chain and a screwdriver. Grease the rubber seal of the new filter cartridge and screw it home firmly but no more than hand tight.

Clean and replace the sump drain plug making sure the washer is in good condition. Refill the engine with 5.25 Imp. pints/3 litres of fresh oil. Run the engine to check that the filter seal does not leak and recheck the oil level again later.

Fan belt - See Chapter 2.
Battery - See Chapter 9.
Distributor - See Chapter 4. For lubrication put one or two drops of engine oil into the hole just below the spindle cam.

Air Cleaner - See Chapter 3.
Valve Clearances - See Chapter 1.
Spark Plugs - See Chapter 4.
Carburettor - See Chapter 3.

FRONT WHEEL BEARINGS
See Chapter 10.

GEARBOX
Lubricating Oil

With the car standing level and having been at rest for at least 2 - 3 minutes remove the level plug on the right hand side of the gearbox casing. The oil should be level with the hole and the easiest way to check this is to add oil from an oil gun or dispenser pack until it overflows. When draining the oil warm the gearbox up with a good run first and then remove the level plug and the drain plug from the bottom of the casing. Let it drip for at least 15 minutes. Replace the drain plug and refill with 3 Imp. pints/1.64 litres of the recommended oil.

CLUTCH PEDAL FREE TRAVEL
See Chapter 5.

RM1. Location of engine oil dipstick

RM2. Use a chain wrench on the oil filter

RM3. Gearbox drain plug

RM4. Use a 'flexitop' to fill the gearbox

RM5. Do not overfill the brake fluid reservoir

RM6. Look after the bodywork. Lubricating hinges doubles their life

Chapter 1 Engine

Contents

Specifications

Engine - general

Type ... ...   4 cylinder, in line, overhead valve, pushrod operated. Cast iron block with removable cylinder liners. Aluminium cylinder head. 'Sierra' engine

Bore	73 mm (2.874 in)	
Stroke	77 mm (3.031 in)	
Cubic capacity	1289 cc (78.7 cu in)	
Renault type number	810—02 (all models)	810—05 (R1177)
Bhp (SAE)	60 at 5250 rpm	68 at 5500 rpm
Torque (SAE)	70.2 lb ft at 3000 rpm	72.3 lb ft at 3500 rpm
Compression ratio	8.5 to 1	9.5 to 1
Firing order	1 3 4 2 (No. 1 at flywheel end)	
Idling speed	750 to 800 rpm	
Oil sump capacity - Max	5.25 Imp pints/3 litres*	
Min	3.5 Imp pints/2 litres*	

* Plus ½ pint (0.25 litre) for filter renewal

Cylinder head

Adjusting the rocker arm clearances:

when cold:	Inlet	0.15 mm (.006 in)
	Exhaust	0.20 mm (.008 in)
when hot:	Inlet	0.18 mm (.007 in)
	Exhaust	0.25 mm (.010 in)

Cylinder head depth:

Nominal	73.25 mm (2.884 in)
Minimum repair size	72.95 mm (2.872 in)
Maximum bow of gasket face	0.05 mm (.002 in)
Combustion chamber volume	37.81 cc (2.307 cu in)

Valve guides

Internal diameter	7 mm (.276 in)
External diameter: Nominal	11 mm (.433 in)
Repair sizes: With 1 groove	11.10 mm (.437 in)
With 2 grooves	11.25 mm (.443 in)

Valve seats

Seat widths:

Inlet	1.1 to 1.4 mm (.043 to .055 in)
Exhaust	1.4 to 1.7 mm (.055 to .067 in)

Valves

Head diameter: Inlet	33.5 mm (1.319 in)
Exhaust	30.3 mm (1.193 in)
Stem diameter	7 mm (.276 in)

Valve springs

Free length (approx)	42 mm (1.21/32 in)
Length under a load of 36 da N (80 lb)	25 mm (63/64 in)
Wire diameter	3.4 mm (.134 in)
Coil internal diameter	21.6 mm (.850 in)
Colour	Light green

Tappets

External diameter: Nominal	19 mm (.748 in)
Repair size	19.2 mm (.756 in)

Pushrods

Length	176 mm (6.15/16 in)
Diameter	5 mm (.197 in)

Valve timing

	All models	(R1177)
Inlet valve opens	20° BTDC	22° BTDC
Inlet valve closes	60° ABDC	62° ABDC
Exhaust valve opens	60° BBDC	65° BBDC
Exhaust valve closes	20° ATDC	25° ATDC

Camshaft

Number of bearings	4
End play	0.06 to 0.11 mm (.001 in to .005 in)
Valve maximum lift (all models) Inlet	7.43 mm
Exhaust	7.43 mm
(R1177) Inlet	7.726 mm
Exhaust	7.764 mm

Crankshaft

Number of bearings	5
Bearing material	White metal
End play	0.05 to 0.23 mm (0.002 to 0.009 in)
Thrust washer thicknesses	2.28 — 2.38 and 2.43 mm (.090 — .094 — .090 in)
Crankpins	Roll hardened
Nominal diameter	43.98 mm (1.731 in)
Regrind size for repair size bearing shells	43.75 mm (1.722 in)
Regrinding tolerances	0 (.0 in)
	0.020 mm (.001 in)
Main bearing journals	Roll hardened
Nominal diameter	46 mm (1.811 in)
Regrind size for repair size bearing shells	45.75 mm (1.801 in)
Regrinding tolerances	0 (.0 in)
	0.020 mm (.001 in)

Liners

Bore	73 mm (2.874 in)
Diameter of bottom centering location	78.5 mm (3.091 in)
Liner protrusion	0.04 to 0.11 mm (.002 to .0045 in)
Box seal thicknesses available:	
Blue mark	0.08 mm (0.003 in)
Red mark	0.10 mm (0.004 in)
Green mark	0.12 mm (0.0047 in)

Connecting rods

Bearing material	White metal

Pistons

Gudgeon pin fitting	Force fit in the small end free turning in the piston
Direction of fitting	Arrow towards the flywheel end
Gudgeon pin length	62 mm (2.7/16 in)
Gudgeon pin diameter	20 mm (.787 in)

Piston rings

Number	3
Ring gap	Pre-set

Oil pump

Oil pressure: At 600 rpm	0.7 bar (10 psi)
At 4000 rpm	3.5 to 4 bars (50 to 55 psi)

Torque wrench settings

	lbf ft	Nm
Cylinder head bolts (cold):		
Stage 1	25	34
Stage 2	40	54
Stage 3	50	68
Rocker shaft nuts and bolts	15	20
Main bearing cap bolts	50	68
Big-end cap bolts	35	48
Camshaft sprocket bolt	20	27
Manifold nuts	10	14
Flywheel bolts	35	48

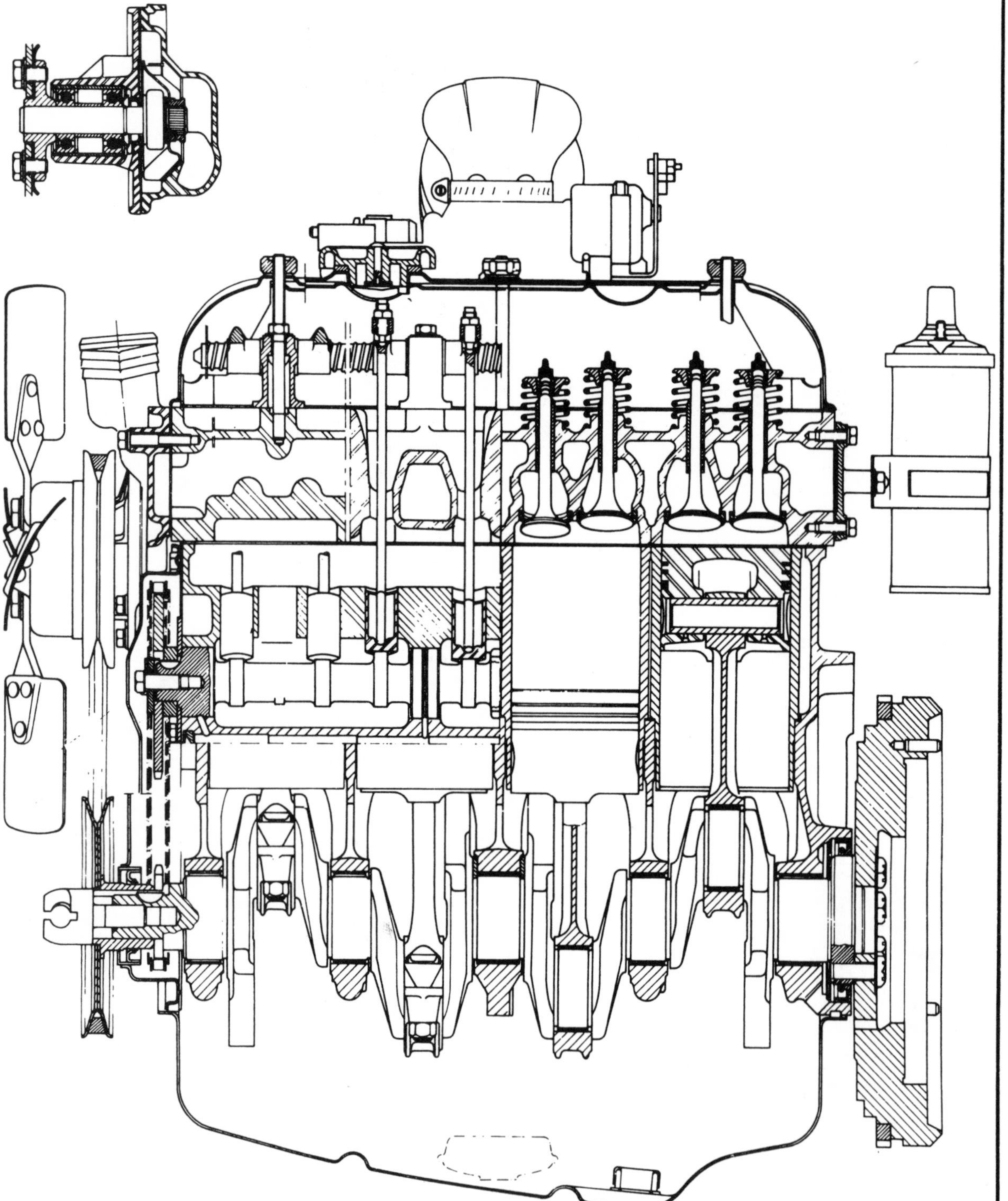

Fig. 1.1. Longitudinal cross-section of the engine; FRONT to the left

PART 1 — REMOVAL AND DISMANTLING

1 General description

The engine fitted to the Renault 12 is similar to that fitted to the last model of the rear engined Renault 10. The capacity is 1289 cc. There is little difference between the engines of the 12 saloon and estate and the 12 TS. Details of type identification are given in Ordering Spare Parts.

The engine is a water cooled overhead valve-in-line four cylinder design. The block is of cast iron while the cylinder head is of an aluminium alloy. The overhead valves are pushrod operated from a chain driven camshaft located on the side and halfway down the cylinder block. The crankshaft runs in five main bearings. The aluminium three ring pistons run in removable cast iron cylinder liners, which sit vertically in the cylinder block and are held in place by the cylinder head.

The oil pump and distributor drive are driven by skew gear from the camshaft which runs directly in the cylinder block. Removable shell bearings are used for the big end and main bearing journals. Although the engine is indeed conventional in design it is positioned unusually for a front wheel drive car, for the gearbox and drive is placed behind the engine.

It is a strong engine, which is neither difficult to remove, disassemble nor repair.

2 Special maintenance

All routine maintenance tasks have been dealt with in the appropriate section. This section deals with particularly important aspects of the maintenance of the engine. Never run the engine without a fan belt even for a few miles, for the water pump will not function. Head gasket failure and possible seizure will result before very long!

Always make sure the heater system is properly bled and that the seals on the cooling system are efficient.

These engines are fairly high revving units and are necessarily designed to be well lubricated. Do not be unduly alarmed that they use oil. Not excessively, but you will have to top up between changes, particularly if their full performance is used.

It is therefore wise to check the oil level more frequently than normal.

3 Major operations which may be carried out with the engine in place

1 The following work may be conveniently carried out with the engine in place:

Removal and replacement of the cylinder head assembly
Removal and replacement of the sump
Removal and replacement of the connecting rod big end bearings
Removal and replacement of the pistons, connecting rods and cylinder liners (after removal of the cylinder head and sump)
Removal and replacement of the engine mountings
Removal and replacement of the timing chain cover, timing chain and sprockets
Removal and replacement of the oil pump.

2 It is possible to do most work on the engine with it still in the car but such is the work needed to remove other parts of the car that it is hardly worth considering. For example, in theory, it is possible to replace the flywheel with the engine still in place but it would mean the removal of the transmission unit. As this is more difficult to do than just to remove the engine by itself or with the transmission unit, it is considered as not possible. Therefore the next Section deals with those tasks which are more economically done with the engine out of the car.

4 Major operations for which the engine must be removed

Although most of these are not impossible with the engine still in the car it is certainly easier in the long run to remove the engine.

Removal and replacement of the camshaft
Removal and replacement of the crankshaft and main bearings.

5 Engine - removal

1 Engine removal is a very similar procedure whether it accompanies the gearbox or not. For light weight leave the gearbox in the car. This Section will describe both contingencies. To remove the engine complete with gearbox refer to paragraph 30 of this Section.

2 For extra lightness remove as many components from the engine before starting. Their removal is described in other Sections of this Chapter. Consequently this Section will describe the simple removal.

3 Disconnect the battery, both positive (first) and negative terminals. Remember to remove the earth strap direct from the battery to the bellhousing when you get to it. (photo)

5.3 Disconnect the positive terminal first.
Don't use tools on the terminals.

4 Remove the bonnet complete with hinges. Undo the two hinge pin bolts. An assistant is necessary. See Chapter 11. Place the bonnet in a safe place. (photo)

5 Place protective sheets of cloth, blanket or paper over the wings of the car.

6 Drain the engine oil.

7 Drain the cooling system. See Chapter 2. Use the cylinder block drain plug too, near the bulkhead.

8 Remove the air cleaner from the carburettor. See Chapter 3. (photos)

9 Remove the top and bottom radiator hoses completely. Retain the thermostat but throw away the original hose clips if they are of the 'cotter pin' type. Disconnect the twin hoses to the expansion bottle at the radiator. (photos) Remove the radiator but retain the rubber buffers on which it sits. See Chapter 2. (photo)

10 Disconnect the heater hoses along the rocker cover, both inlet and outlet pipes. (photo)

11 Disconnect the alternator - recording the wiring sequence and then remove it. See Chapter 9.

12 Remove the fan belt. See Chapter 2.

5.4a It's easier to remove the bonnet so.

5.4b The other end of the bolt in the previous photo.

5.4c Two people are necessary.

5.8a. This is a captive bolt

5.8b. The air cleaner is heavier than it looks

5.9a Top hose removal. Note 12TS radiator cowl.

5.9b 'Overflow' pipe.

5.9c Clear the fan blade. Note the paint code number on the right.

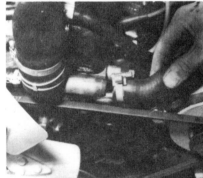

5.10 The heater hose being pulled off.

5.11a The alternator leads cannot be muddled.

5.11b Loosen the pivot bolt.

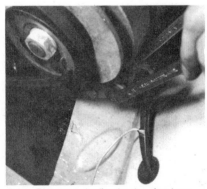

5.11c The slotted adjusting bracket here.

5.11d Slip off the fan belt carefully.

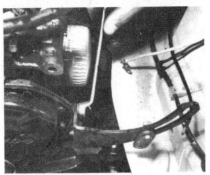
5.11e Once the alternator is away remove the mounting bracket from the cylinder head.

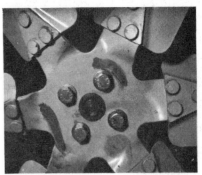
5.12 Mark the position of the fan bolts, fan and shaft.

5.13 The pulley is located by the fan.

5.14 Fuel input pipe is thicker, overflow to tank is thin.

5.15 Remove the coil mounting bracket with the coil.

5.16a The heat shield nuts may be seized.

5.16b The large and small starter motor cables.

5.16c Removing the starter is nasty.

13 Remove the fan and pulley from the water pump, fixed by a locking tab on four setscrews once the alternator has been removed. See Chapter 2.

14 Pull off the inlet and outlet fuel pipes from the fuel pump, and the vacuum pipe from the distributor.

15 If the engine and gearbox are being removed together, remove the ignition coil noting its connections. See Chapter 4.

16 Disconnect the feed wires to the starter motor and tie aside, once the heat shield from the exhaust manifold has been removed. Remove then starter motor securing bolts and the motor itself if the engine is being removed without the gearbox.

17 Pull off the water temperature gauge wire at the cylinder head and the oil pressure gauge wire from the left side of the cylinder block.

18 Disconnect the accelerator and choke cables from the carburettor (see Chapter 3) and unhook the outer cable of the accelerator (throttle) which is sprung to a bracket on the rocker cover. R1177 has a special rod mechanism which can remain on the rocker cover.

19 Remove the starting handle dog from the crankshaft by hitting with a sharp blow first, then unscrew. Remove the crankshaft pulley located with a Woodruff key. Retain the key.

20 Undo the centre clamps and swing the front suspension anti-roll bar away (see Chapter 10) and then undo the two fixing bolts of the crossmember and remove it.

21 Access is now available to undo the exhaust clamp between the manifold and down pipe (or at the manifold for engine removal alone).

22 For engine removal alone proceed as follows: (See paragraph 30 for engine and gearbox removal continued). Remove the three top bolts securing the engine to the gearbox.

23 Remove the five clutch shield and two bottom bolts securing the engine to the gearbox.

24 Now place a sling around the engine to just take its weight, one loop at the front just in front of the sump and one at the rear between the sump and the flywheel.

25 Place a trolley jack (possibly a scissor jack) or some supporting wood under the gearbox.

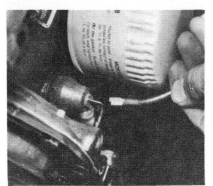

5.17 The oil pressure sender. The water temperature sender unit is on the rear of the cylinder head

5.18a This is the 12TS throttle control at the carburettor. The 12L/TL is simpler.

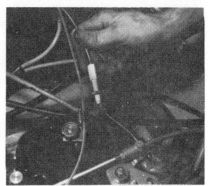

5.18b Pull the adjuster for outer cable away carefully. It breaks easily.

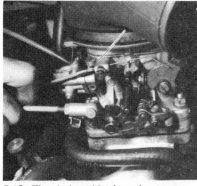

5.18c The choke cable clamp locates on the outer. The notch in the inner indicates its fixing.

5.20 The engine cross member below. Don't lose its bolts.

5.21a Disconnection from below. Arrows show exhaust points for work.

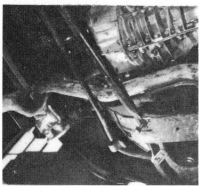

5.21b The exhaust pipe at the manifold has been released. 12TS twin pipe.

5.23 Bell housing to engine shield.

5.29a Hoist in position. Try to have room to move.

5.29b The starter dog is still on this engine as it is lifted without the gearbox. Note location of sling.

5.31 Engine rests on cross member. Exhaust down pipe has gone.

5.32 Use a parallel pin punch if the 'real' tool is not available.

5.33a Speedometer cable. The clamp
screw just appears.

5.33b The gearshift mechanism bolt.

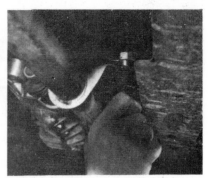

5.34 That last exhaust mounting. This
one is flexible.

5.35 The clutch pivot bracket removed
from the bell housing.

5.40a Note the angle of the engine (with
the gearbox).

5.40b You need the room, its a steep
angle.

26 Remove the four bolts on each engine side mounting (one in the mounting centre and three securing the mounting centre bracket to the bodyshell). The engine is now "free".

27 Lift the engine hoist until the top of the gearbox just touches the underside of the steering crossmember and build up the gearbox support to hold it in this position.

28 Remove the two loose engine mountings from either side of the engine - these should each consist of the mounting bracket, the mounting and its re-inforcement.

29 Slowly pull the engine forward on the hoist making sure the primary shaft of the gearbox takes NO strain and then up and out. Place on wooden support blocks or a bench or on the floor.

30 For removal of engine and automatic transmission, refer to Chapter 12. To remove the engine and manual gearbox as a unit, complete paragraphs 1 to 22 inclusive then drain the gearbox oil. Temporarily refit the crossmember removed in paragraph 20, and proceed as follows.

31 Remove the gearbox rear mounting by first removing the three bolts which secure the gearbox to the mounting and then the two nuts securing the crossmember to the bodyshell side mounting pads. Carefully lower the gearbox onto the front engine crossmember just replaced.

32 Punch out the two drive shaft roll-pins and then very carefully lever the gearbox from side to side to release the drive shafts from the splines on the gearbox. Once each one is released carefully place the drive shaft to one side to avoid it jamming in the gearbox.

33 Disconnect the speedometer drive cable from the gearbox and the gearshift control lever bolt (see Chapter 6).

34 Loosen the exhaust clamp which will have been undone when the gearbox crossmember was removed.

35 Disconnect the clutch cable at the release lever on the gearbox (see Chapter 5).

36 Remove the cable pad securing screw on the outer cable stop to the clutch housing.

37 See paragraph 24 and fit the sling.

38 See paragraph 25, support the gearbox and remove the engine crossmember again.

39 See paragraphs 26, 27 and 28 but do not build up the gearbox support. Instead lower it, simply so that the gearbox 'tail' will not drag on the ground.

40 Pull the engine and gearbox forward and then up and out at a steep angle, protecting the gearbox 'tail' at all times. This must be guided by an assistant.

41 Lower the engine and gearbox together to the ground and proceed to remove the gearbox from the engine. Support both on wooden blocks.

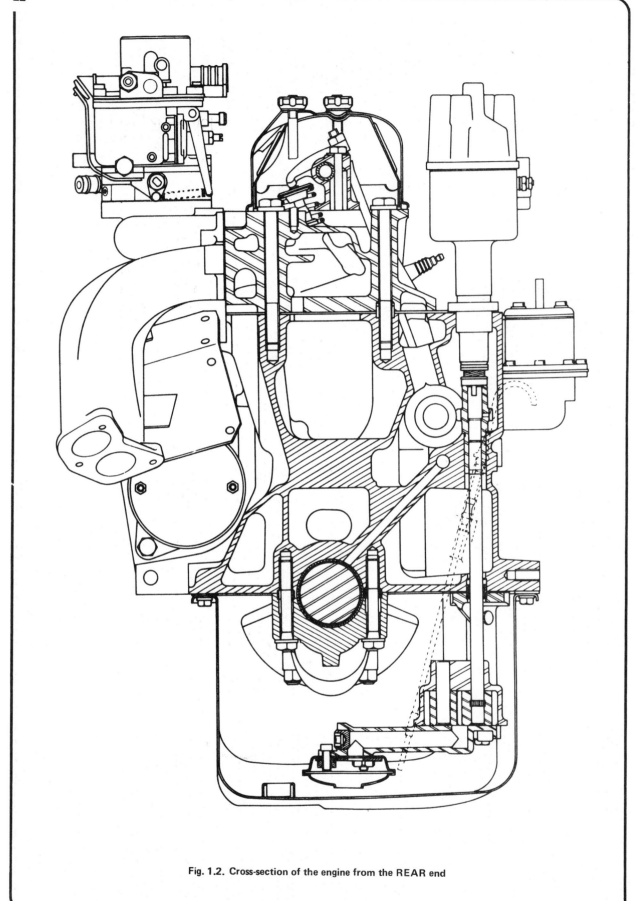

Fig. 1.2. Cross-section of the engine from the REAR end

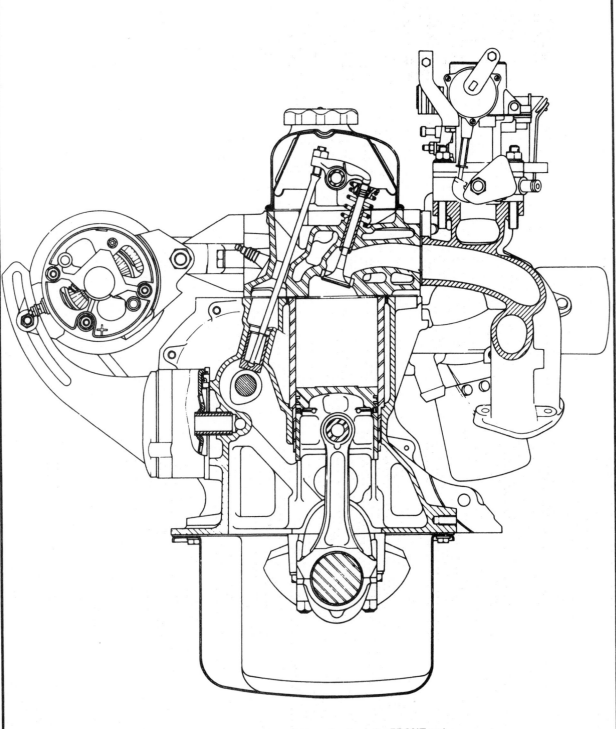

Fig. 1.3. Cross-section of the engine from the FRONT end

6 Engine dismantling - general

1 Owners who have dismantled engines will know the need for a strong work bench and many tools and pieces of equipment, which make their life much easier when going through the process of dismantling an engine. For those who are doing a dismantling job for the first time, there are a few 'musts' in the way of preparation which, if not done, will only cause frustration and long delays in the job in the long run. It is essential to have sufficient space in which to work. Dismantling and re-assembly is not going to be completed all in one go and it is therefore absolutely essential that you have sufficient space to leave things as they are when necessary. A strong work bench is also necessary together with a good engineer's vice. If you have no alternative other than to work at ground level, make sure that the floor is at least level and covered with a suitable wooden or composition material on which to work. If dirt and grit are allowed to get into any of the component parts all work which you carry out may be completely wasted. Before actually placing the engine wherever it is that you may be carrying out the dismantling, make sure that the exterior is now completely and thoroughly cleaned.

2 Once dismantling begins it is advisable to clean the parts as they are removed. A small bath of paraffin is about the best thing to use for this, but do not let parts which have oilways in them become immersed in paraffin otherwise there may be a residue which could cause harmful effects later on. If paraffin does get into oilways every effort should be made to blow it out. For this it may be necessary to carry the particular part to a garage fitted with a high pressure air hose. Short oilways such as there are in the crankshaft can be cleared easily with wire.

3 Always obtain a complete set of gaskets when the engine is being dismantled - no gaskets on an engine are re-usable and any attempt to do so is quite unjustified in view of the relatively small cost involved. Before throwing any gaskets away, however, make sure that you have the replacements to hand. If, for example, a particular gasket cannot be obtained it may be necessary to make one, and the pattern of the old one is useful in such cases.

4 Generally speaking, it is best to start dismantling the engine from the top downwards. In any case, make sure it is firmly supported at all times so that it does not topple over whilst you are undoing the very tight nuts and bolts which will be encountered. Always replace nuts and bolts into their locations once the particular part has been removed, if possible. Otherwise keep them in convenient tins or pots in their groups, so that when the time comes to reassemble there is the minimum of confusion.

7 Engine dismantling - ancillaries

1 A word of warning at this stage is that you should always be sure that it is more economic to dismantle and overhaul a worn engine rather than simply exchange it with a Renault Factory Exchange Unit.

2 If you are intending to obtain an exchange engine complete, it will be necessary first of all to remove all those parts of the engine which are not included in the exchange. If you are stripping the engine completely yourself with the likelihood of some outside work to be done by specialists, all these items will be taken off anyway.

3 Short engines are not available from Renault Limited. It is as well to check with whoever may be supplying the replacement exchange unit what it is necessary to remove, but as a general guide the following items will have to be taken off. Reference is given to the appropriate Chapter for details of removal of each of these items:

Generator - Chapter 9
Distributor - Chapter 4
Thermostat - Chapter 2
Carburettor - Chapter 3
Inlet/exhaust manifold - Chapter 1
Fuel pump - Chapter 3
Engine mounting brackets - Chapter 1
Distributor/oil pump drive - Chapter 4
Gearbox - Chapter 6
Ignition coil - Chapter 4
Clutch - Chapter 5
Dipstick
Fan and its pulley - Chapter 2
Starter motor - Chapter 9
Temperature and oil pressure sender units - Chapter 1
Sender units - Chapter 1

Always clean the engine before exchanging.

8 Inlet/exhaust manifold - removal

1 To take the engine out of the car it is necessary to remove the inlet/exhaust manifold. This is described in Section 5.

2 The inlet/exhaust manifold should be removed before the cylinder head is removed.

9 Valve rocker gear - removal

1 It is not necessary to remove the valve rocker gear from the cylinder head in order to remove the cylinder head from the engine, either in or out of the car.

2 Remove the rocker cover by undoing the three retaining nuts and lift off. Lift off the rocker cover gasket.

3 Breather pipes etc. will differ from model to model and should be extracted with care. All lift off easily.

4 The rocker gear is attached to the cylinder head by four fixings - two bolts and two longer studs and nuts (these longer studs act as locating points for the rocker cover). Undo the four fixings with the appropriate spanners and then lift off the rocker shaft and pedestals. Make sure that the pushrods do not 'stick' to the rocker arms.

5 The rocker shaft can be further dismantled by taking off the arms, pedestals and springs. DO NOT try to extract the two press-fit end plugs.

6 Unclip the end retaining clips and after noting the order, slide all the parts off the shaft.

10 Cylinder head - removal

1 The cylinder head may be removed with the engine either in or out of the car.

2 If the engine is to remain in the car, the following must be done first:

Remove the air cleaner and carburettor, the exhaust manifold and cable connections (see Chapter 3). Drain the cooling system and remove the fan and pulley, fan belt and water pump (see Chapter 2). Remove the heater top hose (see Chapter 2). Disconnect the fuel outlet pipe to the carburettor at the fuel pump and the distributor vacuum pipe. Disconnect the HT lead from the coil and the plug caps from the spark plugs. Remove the generator and its support bracket.

3 With the engine out of the car the majority of these tasks will have been undertaken. If not remove and disconnect the items now. See the appropriate Section.

4 Remove the rocker cover and its gasket once the crankcase fume rebreather pipe has been removed. Unscrew the knurled nuts.

5 If the engine is still in the car make absolutely sure at this stage that it is OUT OF GEAR and the handbrake is on. Leaving the valve rocker gear in place undo the 10 cylinder head bolts in the reverse sequence of the tightening order which is shown in Fig.1.5.

10.4 The crankcase (rocker cover) fume breather.

10.9 You can use a bar instead of tubes to hold the cylinder liners.

6 Once all the bolts are out, the head should lift straight off. (Keep the bolts in the correct order for refitting). It is an aluminium head - do not hit it if it is reluctant to lift off. Tap the spark plug side very, very gently in a horizontal plane and it will move. Place the head on a flat, safe surface.

7 Do not turn the crankshaft over to remove the head because you will disturb the removable cylinder liners. Once these are disturbed the pistons have to be removed etc, and if it was only your intention to replace the cylinder head gasket you have created a lot of unnecessary work. When the head is removed the pushrods will be left floating in the tappet chest. Remove these and place them through a piece of cardboard in their correct order for replacement. Be careful that the cam followers do not become dislodged at this stage.

8 Remove the old cylinder head gasket and retain for inspection.

9 Once the head is removed and you do not wish to dismantle the pistons, liners and their seals, place retaining clamps on the liners. These can be made from large washers about 1½ inches in diameter, and some metal tubing, galvanised pipe used on building sites is ideal, about 2 inches long. You will need four of each. Replace the four head bolts which go between cylinders one and two and three and four with the washers flat on the block and the tube over them. Once the bolts are fairly tight the liners will not shift.

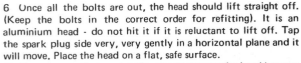

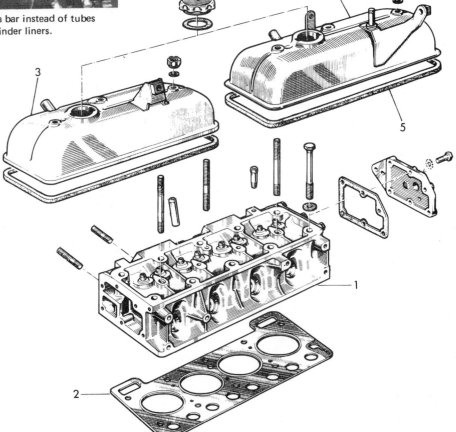

FIG. 1.4. CYLINDER HEAD AND ROCKER COVER

| 1 Cylinder head | 3 R1170, R1171 and | 4 R1177 rocker cover | 5 Rocker cover gasket |
| 2 Gasket | R1330 rocker cover | | |

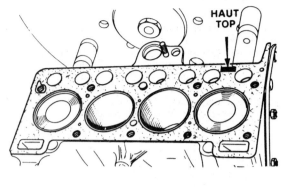

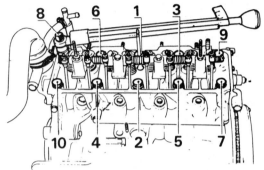

Fig. 1.5. The top illustration shows the correct position for the cylinder head gasket.
The lower shows the cylinder head bolt tightening sequence

11 Valve removal

1   With the valve rocker gear removed and with the water pump taken off, see Chapter 2, the valves are relatively easy to remove with the cylinder head on the bench, with a proprietary spring compressor.

2   Place the cylinder head on the 'spark plug' side and fit the compressor. Work should start at one end and follow on down the head.

3   Tighten the compressor so that the 'foot' is in the centre of the valve being released. The 'claw' should sit on the top of the valve spring cap. Continue to compress the spring until the collets are loose.

4   Release the pressure on the valve cap once the collets are extracted, remove the cap (sometimes known as spring seat), the spring (single springs only are used on all valves but be sure to record those from the inlet valves and those from the exhaust separately - they differ in strength) and the lower washers.

5   Do one combustion chamber at a time before extracting the valves themselves. Repeat the process for each chamber and record the order in which the valves are removed. Place them through a piece of cardboard in order, as you would the push-rods, for further inspection.

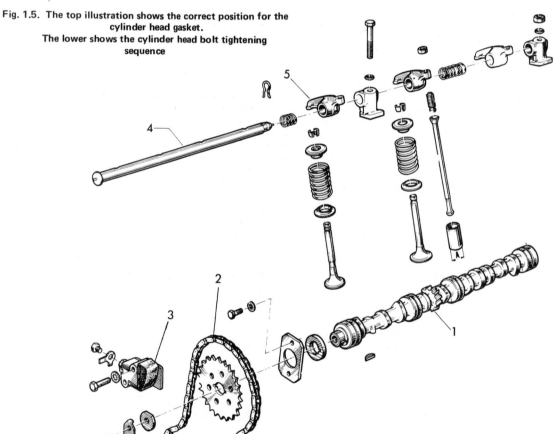

FIG. 1.6. CAMSHAFT AND ROCKER GEAR

1 Camshaft	2 Timing chain	3 Chain tensioner	4 Rocker gear shaft
			5 Rocker

11.3 Catch the collets as they are released.

11.5 Twist the valve as its removed

12 Tappet removal

1   With the cylinder head and the pushrods removed the tappets can be extracted.

2   Each one can be removed by pushing one's index finger right into the tappet, pushing out the oil and then pulling it upwards. A technique will soon be developed to raise them up in this way.

3   Place the tappets in their correct order for inspection and possible correct replacement.

13 Timing cover, gears and chain - removal

1   The timing chain cover is situated at the front of the engine. It is possible to remove the cover and then the timing chain and gear with the engine still in the car but it is much easier with the engine out.

2   With the engine still in the car it is necessary to remove the following components in order to remove the timing cover:
a)   The radiator - the cooling system must be drained
b)   The water pump and fan belt and hence the generator
c)   The sump
d)   The starter dog and crankshaft pulley

3   Once all the surrounding equipment is removed with the engine still in the car, proceed as follows, a description of the removal with the engine out of the car.

4   Using a socket undo and remove the 10 timing cover fixing bolt and retrieve the washers. Now remove the timing cover and pull off the gasket.

5   Obtain a 3 mm hexagonal socket screw (Allen key) and insert it into the timing chain tensioner retaining cylinder and slowly undo it clockwise so that the chain ceases to be under tension.

6   Then undo the locating bolts and remove the chain tensioner.

7   An oil filter made of thin gauze should be left in the cylinder block directly below the chain tensioner body. Leave this in place unless a complete engine overhaul is taking place.

8   Bend back the locking tab washer locking the camshaft sprocket retaining bolt and then undo the bolt.

9   You should be able to lever the camshaft sprocket off the shaft without force with a screwdriver. Leave the chain on the sprocket at this stage.

10   Once the sprocket and chain attached are off the shaft, remove it with the chain from the crankshaft sprocket. The timing gear is now dismantled.

NOTE: If it is wished to remove the crankshaft sprocket a two legged puller must be used. Depending on the type of puller used, there may not be room to do this with the engine in the car. If there is room or the engine is out of the car the sprocket should be pulled off in the normal way. Do not try to drive it off.

14 Camshaft - removal

1   It is not impossible to remove the camshaft with the engine still in the car but the increase in effort does not make it worth it. It is easier to take the engine out.

2   The camshaft runs directly in the cylinder block and there is therefore no need to worry about bearings being removed with the camshaft. However, it is necessary to remove the cylinder head and then the pushrods and tappets so that they do not become dislodged. See Sections 10 and 12.

3   Remove the timing gear as described in the previous Section.

4   With the camshaft sprocket removed, the camshaft retaining flange is visible. Undo the two bolts which fix the flange to the cylinder block and the camshaft should then pull straight out of block.

5   Make sure the camshaft is removed slowly and straight for the bearing surfaces and the lobes could be unnecessarily damaged.

15 Sump - removal

1   The sump may be removed with the engine and gearbox in the car and, of course, with it out, provided the engine has been separated from the gearbox and is lying on its side. With the engine still in the car it is really arm aching work if you are lying on the ground under the car, it is not much better with the car on a ramp or over a pit.

2   Drain the sump of its oil. A 5 pint container is necessary. Replace the sump plug after five minutes.

3   Remove the anti-roll bar mounting brackets and swing the bar back to clear the sump. The side members locate these mountings.

4   Undo all the locating setscrews and retain the locking washers.

5   The sump should now pull away. Retrieve the gaskets which come away in four parts.

Fig. 1.7. Sump and gasket

16 Oil pump - removal

1   The oil pump may be removed from the engine whilst the engine is still in the car. It is necessary first to remove the sump. As the oil pump drive spindle also drives the distributor, care must be taken to ensure that the ignition timing is not lost when the oil pump is removed and eventually replaced. It is, therefore, necessary also to remove the distributor cap and turn the engine until the rotor is in line with the number one plug high tension lead contact. The timing marker on the crankshaft pulley wheel must then also be set against the top dead centre position. For full details of engine timing refer to Chapter 4.

2   Once the crankshaft has been set to the correct position the distributor should be removed. By looking down into the distributor mounting opening it will be possible to see the top of the oil pump spindle and the position of the offset slot. Take a careful note of this position.

3   The pump may be removed by undoing the three setscrews. The inner of the three is difficult to get at with a spanner and much patience should be exercised with this screw. The pump should pull out together with its paper face gasket.

17 Big-end bearings, pistons, connecting rods and liners removal

1   It is possible to remove the big-end bearings, pistons, connecting rods and liners from the engine with engine still in the car, provided that the sump has been removed in all cases and the cylinder head, for the pistons, connecting rods and liners. With the engine removed from the car, the task is much easier and generally cleaner, but, of course, it is understood that if a quick emergency repair job is to be done and speed is of the essence, then it would be in order to do any work with the engine still in the car. The pistons, connecting rods and liners must be removed from the top of the engine once the connecting rod end caps have been removed. Remove the piston/connecting rod and liner as an assembly.

2   With the sump removed and the crankshaft exposed, each of the big-end bearing caps can be detached after removing the two nuts which hold each cap to the connecting rod stud. Rotate the engine to bring each connecting rod cap suitably into position for unscrewing the nuts.

3   With the nuts removed, each big-end bearing cap can be pulled off. It must be noted that the connecting rods and big-end caps are marked with a small punch mark on the end of the connecting rod and cap, which matches up on each one. If the same connecting rods and caps are to be re-used, they must be replaced axactly as they came out. The same applies to the big-end bearing shells which will be released as soon as the connecting rods are detached from the crankshaft. It is inadvisable to re-use these shells anyway, but if they are not renewed they must be put back in exactly the same location from which they came.

4   If any difficulty is experienced in removing the big-end bearing caps from the studs of the connecting rods, it will help if the crankshaft is revolved in order to dislodge them. If this is done, however, care must taken to ensure that nothing gets jammed when the connecting rod comes away from the crankshaft at the top of its stroke.

5   Tap the bottom of the liners from beneath with a hard piece of wood which will not tend to split. If you hit them with steel of any kind they will crack without fail and will be instant scrap.

6   Tap all four loose before you remove one. Lift them upwards, and note where they were fitted and which way round. Provided you have drained the cooling system well, little liquid sediment will be left although there will almost certainly be a lot of rust particles there. If the crankshaft is to remain in the block, cover it as well as you can from below with non-fluffy rag to stop the likelihood of liquid or sediment falling on the journal surfaces - it will not actually do them any harm but it is difficult

to remove when you are ready to reassemble. Only now remove the seals which seal the liners to the block.

7   Once the liners have been removed from the cylinder block the piston/connecting rod can be withdrawn through the bottom of each liner. Make sure that the pistons are kept in such a way that they can be easily identified and replaced in the same liner if necessary.

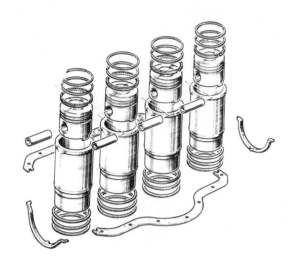

Fig. 1.8. Pistons, cylinder liners, gudgeon pins, rings and sump gasket

18 Gudgeon pins

The gudgeon pins float in the piston and are an interference fit in the connecting rods. This 'interference fit' between gudgeon pin and connecting rod, means that heat is required (230–260°C) before a pin can be satisfactorily replaced in the connecting rod. If it is necessary to replace either the piston or connecting rod, we strongly recommend that the assembly of the two be entrusted to someone with experience. Misapplied heat can ruin one, or all, of the components very easily.

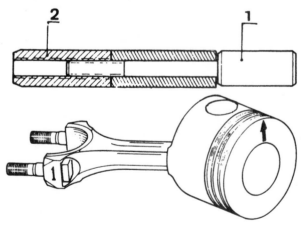

Fig. 1.9. The top illustration shows the proper Renault tool for fitting the gudgeon pin

1   The mandrel   2   Gudgeon pin

The lower shows the correct position of a piston relative to the connecting rod

19 Flywheel - removal

1 The flywheel may be removed with the engine in the car provided that the gearbox and clutch assembly are removed first. Under normal circumstances the engine would be removed rather than the transmission.

2 With the engine out of the car, and firmly supported, the seven flywheel locating bolts should be undone. It may be necessary to lock the flywheel to obtain leverage on the securing bolts. Use a screwdriver on the starter ring and lock it onto the block. It is obvious where to do this. As there are two positions to locate the flywheel on the crankshaft flange it is necessary to mark the exact locating position of the flywheel. Scribe a mark across the flange onto the flywheel to ensure correct relocation. It will be necessary to use a little leverage in order to draw the flywheel off and great care should be taken that it does not come off with a sudden jerk and fall down. One way of preventing this is by putting a stud, another, longer bolt with the head sawn off, into one of the bolt holes so that when the flywheel comes free, the end of the stud will support it.

20 Crankshaft and main bearing removal

1 It is only possible to inspect and replace three of the five main bearing shells with the engine still in the car, at least for all practical purposes. For this reason if you want to be really sure of an adequate inspection and renewal of these bearings, they must only be looked at as a total operation ie: the five main bearings together, and this can only be done with the engine out of the car. Main bearings seldom need renewing by themselves, it is more than likely that further overhaul is necessary and therefore the engine is likely to be out of the car.

2 With the engine removed from the car it is necessary for the sump, oil pump, timing cover and gear (but not crankshaft sprocket) to be removed, together with the flywheel. It is also desirable that the cylinder head should have been removed so that the engine may be stood inverted. If the liners are to be retained the engine should be placed on its side.

3 The connecting rod bearing caps should all have been removed and, of course, this will have been done if the pistons are being removed from the engine as well.

4 Using a good quality socket spanner remove the two bolts from each of the five main bearing caps. Then lift off each of the caps.

5 With the five main bearing caps removed the crankshaft may be carefully lifted out of the block and it should then be placed somewhere safe where it cannot fall or be damaged. The upper half main bearing shells may then be removed from the crankcase, together with the semi-circular thrust washers fitted at the centre main bearing.

NOTE: With flywheel end main bearing cap removed it will be necessary to pull out the circular oil seal. Pull it off the crankshaft before lifting the crankshaft and throw it away. Never refit this old oil seal.

21 Lubrication system - description

The engine has a very basic but effective oil flow system. Oil from the sump is pumped by the submerged oil pump up to the centre main bearing and then up to the main oil gallery under pressure. From there it is distributed through drillings to the other main bearings, the big end bearings, the camshaft bearing surfaces, the rocker shafts and arms, the timing gear and the cylinder bores. A film of oil should be maintained on all these surfaces by this method. There are normally adequate gaskets to keep the oil inside the block at the sump, rocker cover and timing cover and aluminium plugs at each end of the oil gallery. Oil drips back into the sump to be recirculated. There is a removable cartridge oil filter fitted. A gauze filter is also fitted to the oil pump inlet.

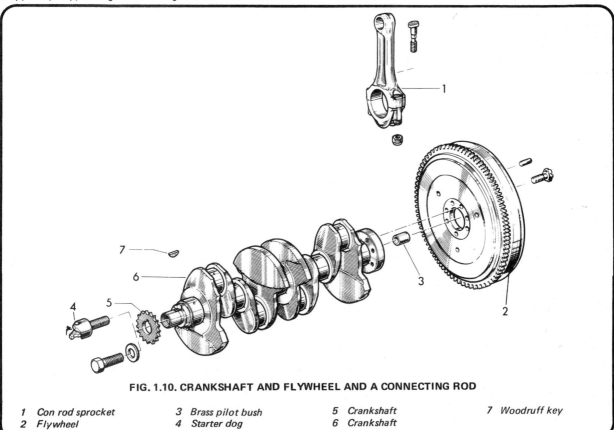

FIG. 1.10. CRANKSHAFT AND FLYWHEEL AND A CONNECTING ROD

1 Con rod sprocket	3 Brass pilot bush	5 Crankshaft	7 Woodruff key
2 Flywheel	4 Starter dog	6 Crankshaft	

22 Engine mountings - removal

1   Removal of the engine mountings is essential for engine removal. See Section 5. They can be removed and replaced without engine removal by following the instructions in Section 5 relevant to their actual removal.

2   Jack the engine up as high as it will go without fouling the fan or the radiator, keep the engine support there, and remove the mountings.

PART 2 – EXAMINATION AND RENOVATION

23 Engine - examination

1   Examination of an engine runs in two phases. The first is a visual and aural examination when it is running and in the car, and the second is when it is out of the car, having decided that something is wrong and needs repairing. It is a matter to decide when to take the car off the road, and do something about putting right whatever faults there may be. In general, if the oil and fuel consumption are perfectly reasonable, the performance is satisfactory, and it is not suffering from overheating, under-heating, or any other fault which causes aggravation and irrit-ation on the road to a large degree, it is best left alone. Provided the regular maintenance requirements are carried out there is no need to take it to pieces.

2   The first indications of an engine becoming worn (if one has not been able to get the exact mileage that the engine has travelled) are an increase in oil consumption and possibly a corresponding increase in fuel consumption. This may also be accompanied by a falling off in performance. On any car it is not always easy to detect a falling off in performance and it is quite a good idea to drive another car of the same type, which is known to be in very good condition, to make a comparison. If the signs are that the engine is performing poorly, using too much petrol and beginning to burn oil, then one of the first things to do is to test the compression in each cylinder with a proper compression testing gauge. This will indicate whether the pistons are leaking in the cylinders or the valves are leaking in the head. Depending on the results, the cylinder head may be removed and further examinations carried out to the bores and head as described in subsequent Sections. Early action at this stage could well restore the engine to a satisfactory condition. Furthermore, such action would not call for a great deal of either money or time. If the condition is left, however, it will get progressively worse until such time as the simple repairs which would have been needed earlier have reached the stage where more major operations are necessary. This will be proportion-ately much more expensive and time consuming.

24 Crankshaft and main bearings - examination and renovation

1   With the crankshaft removed examine all the crankpins and main bearing journals for signs of scoring or scratches. If all the surfaces of the bearing journals are obviously undamaged, check next that all the journals are round. This can be done with a micrometer or caliper gauge, taking readings across the diameter of each journal at six or seven points. If you do not own a micrometer or know how to use one, you should have little difficulty at any garage that has good mechanics to get someone to measure it for you.

2   If the crankshaft has ridges or severe score marks in it, it must be reground. The manufacturers of the Renault go further and say that a crankshaft in this condition should be renewed but as this can be a very expensive procedure, it is felt that regrinding should suffice in all but the most extraordinary situation. If there are no signs of ridging or severe scoring of the journals, it may be that the measurements indicate that the journals are not round. If the amount of ovality does not exceed

0.002 inch it is possible that regrinding may be necessary. Certainly if it is more than this figure it is necessary. Here again it is best to get the advice of someone who is experienced and familiar with crankshafts and regrinding them to give an opinion.

3   The main bearing shells themselves are normally a matt grey in colour all over and should have no signs of pitting or ridging or discolouration as this usually indicates that the surface bearing metal has worn away and the backing material is showing through. It is worthwhile renewing the main bearing shells anyway if you have gone to the trouble of removing the crank-shaft, but they must, of course, be renewed if there is any sign of damage to them or if the crankshaft has been reground. When the crankshaft is reground the diameter is reduced and con-sequently one must obtain the proper undersized bearing shells to fit. These will normally be supplied by the firm which has reground the crankshaft. Regrinding is normally done in multiples of 0.010 inch as necessary and bearing shells are obtainable to suit these standard regrinding sizes. If the crank-shaft is not being reground, yet bearing shells are being renewed, make sure that you check whether or not the crankshaft has been reground once before. This will be indicated by looking at the back of the bearing shell and this will indicate whether or not it is minus 0.010 inch or more. The same type of shell bearing must be used when they are renewed.

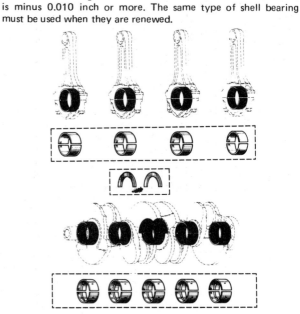

Fig. 1.11. Main bearing and connecting (big-end bearing) shells in profile

25 Big end bearings - examination and renovation

The connecting rod, or big end bearings, are subject to wear at a greater rate than those for the crankshaft. Signs that one or more big end bearings is getting badly worn are a pronounced knocking noise from the engine, accompanied by a significant drop in oil pressure due to the increased clearance between the bearing and the journal permitting oil to flow more freely through the resultantly larger space. If this should happen quite suddenly and action is taken immediately, and by immediately is meant within a few miles, then it is possible that the bearing shell may be replaced without any further work needing to be done. If this happens in an engine which has been neglected and oil changes and oil filter changes (on those models so fitted) have not been carried out as they should have been, it is most likely that the rest of the engine is in a pretty terrible state anyway. If it occurs in an engine which has been recently overhauled, then it is almost certainly due to a piece of grit or swarf which has got into the oil circulation system and finally come to rest in the bearing shell and scored it. It is in these instances where a replacement of the shell alone accompanied by a thorough flush out of the lubrication system may be all that is required.

26 Cylinder liner bores - examination and renovation

1   The liner bores may be examined for wear either in or out of the engine block; the cylinder head must, of course, be removed in each case. If the liners are still in the block and it is hoped that they will not need renovation the liner retainers must be left in place so that relocation does not have to take place. However, if you have got to the stage where the pistons are out it is better to remove the liners for inspection even if they do not require renovation. Relocation itself does not take much time, skill or money. Each bore may be examined in turn with the piston at the bottom of its stroke. A perfect cylinder is, as its name implies, perfectly cylindrical in shape. That is, the sides are parallel and a cross section is perfectly circular.

2   First of all examine the top of the cylinder about a quarter of an inch below the top of the liner and with the finger feel if there is any ridge running round the circumference of the bore. In a worn cylinder bore a ridge will develop at the point where the top ring on the piston comes to the uppermost limit of its stroke. An excessive ridge indicates that the bore below the ridge is worn. If there is no ridge it is reasonable to assume that the cylinder is not badly worn. Measurement of the diameter of the cylinder bore both in line with the piston gudgeon pin and at right angles to it, at the top and bottom of the cylinder, is also another check to be made. A cylinder is expected to wear at the sides where the thrust of the piston presses against it. In time this causes the cylinder to assume an oval shape. Furthermore, the top of the cylinder is likely to wear more than the bottom of the cylinder. It will be necessary to use a proper bore measuring instrument in order to measure the differences in bore diameter across the cylinder and variations between the top and bottom ends of thee cylinder. As a general guide it may be assumed that any variations more than 0.010 inch indicate that the liners need renewing. Provided all variations are less than 0.010 inch it is probable that the fitting of new piston rings will cure the problems of piston to cylinder bore clearances. Once again it is difficult to give a firm ruling on this as so much depends on the amount of time and effort which the individual owner is pre-pared or wishes to spend on the task. Certainly, if the cylinder bores are obviously deeply grooved or scored, they must be renewed regardless of any measurement differences in the cylinder diameter. If the engine has been removed from the car for overhaul anyway, any cylinder bore wear in excess of 0.005 inch certainly qualifies it for a rebore, to do otherwise would be a waste of time and effort. However, one must bear in mind again the fact that a rebore will require the fitment of new pistons and the expense of this once again could affect the owner's decision.

2 7 Connecting rods, pistons and piston rings - examination and renovation

1   Pistons and rings are normally examined in relation to the cylinder bores. With the cylinder head removed it is possible to check the amount of movement between the piston and the wall, both visually and with the aid of a feeler gauge. Liner retainers must be fitted. If the condition of the bores seems to be satis-factory, any excessive clearance between piston and bore (0.010 inch and upwards) could be due to wear of the piston itself. Piston ring wear is almost certain to·have taken place also if this is the case, and will necessitate the removal of the piston/liner assemblies for further examination. First of all, look for signs of damage to the piston ring grooves, and to the sides of the piston where scoring may be apparent. Any deep scoring or any obvious breakage between the piston ring grooves and the top of the

piston will, of course, call for a new piston. If the pistons do not appear worn or damaged, next check the clearance between the piston rings and the piston ring grooves. This can be done with a feeler gauge and if it is in excess of the specified clearance the pistons should be renewed. Excessive clearance between the rings and the grooves allows the rings to chatter and they will break very easily. Unfortunately, the wear usually occurs on the piston rather than on the piston rings, although new rings should be used as a check before condemning the pistons.

2   To check the condition of the rings it will be necessary to remove them from the piston. Only the top ring on each piston need be checked and, in fact, if one of the four piston rings is bad it is reasonable to assume that the others will be similar and the whole lot should be replaced. Remove the top piston ring by spreading the ends apart sufficiently to enable it to be pulled out of the groove and over the top of the piston. Care must be taken not to twist the ring or draw it off unevenly, otherwise it could easily break. The ring should then be placed inside the cylinder bore from which it came and pressed down approximately two inches. It should lie perfectly horizontal across the bore and this can be achieved by using a piston from which all the rings have been removed to press it down square. Then the gap between the ends of the piston rings should be measured with a feeler gauge; if the piston ring gap exceeds that specified then the piston ring is worn out and should be renewed. If the top ring is worn it is reasonable to assume that the other two are worn on the same piston as well. Rings are normally only obtainable in sets anyway so any thoughts of economy by renewing one or two rings on a set of four pistons are really not worthwhile.

3   Provided the engine has not seized up or had some other calamitous damage caused to it, it is most unlikely that the connecting rods are in need of renewal at any time. In cases of seizure one or more could have become bent and to check this they will need setting up on a special jig. This is normally only within the competence of a specialist engineering organisation.

4   See Section 18 of this Chapter for details of the removal and refitting of new pistons, gudgeon pins and small end bushes.

28 Valve rocker gear - examination and renovation

Each rocker should move freely on the rocker shaft without any signs of looseness or slackness. If any slackness is apparent it will be necessary to dismantle the assembly. If either the rocker bushes in the rocker arms and/or pedestals or the rocker shaft are obviously scored and worn at those points where the rockers are pivoting then they should be renewed. The rockers them-selves should also be examined on the faces where they bear onto the top of the valve stems and if signs of wear are excessive they should also be renewed.

29 Cylinder head, valves, valve springs and guides - examination and renovation

1   Once the cylinder head has been removed, it should be placed upon a work bench so that a thorough examination can be carried out.

2   First of all, all the valves should be removed.

3   The valves should be examined for signs of pitting or burning, particularly around their edges and where they seat into the cylinder head. If the valves are very much contaminated with carbon, this should first of all be removed with a wire brush. Very hard spots of carbon may need chipping off with the edge of a very hard blade or tool. Be very careful, it is an aluminium head! Exhaust valves are the ones most likely to suffer from burning and if this is apparently quite severe, then the valves should be discarded. Next replace each valve into its own guide, after thoroughly cleaning the guide and valve stem, and check to see that there is no sideways movement of the valve in the guide. A very small amount of play is permissible but if it is very considerable, then it means that oil and exhaust gases can all make their way past the stem of the valve and this is not conducive to good performance. If the guides are obviously

badly worn, then it will be necessary to have new ones fitted, together with new valves. The fitting of valve guides on this engine is a specialist task as they have to be reamed out to give a very close tolerance after fitting. If it is thought that the wear is on the valve stem rather than in the guide, the best way to check is to obtain a new valve and try it in position.

4 If the valves are apparently in good general condition the next thing to do is to examine the valve seats themselves in the cylinder head. Here again, there should be no signs of pitting or burning. The valve seats should also be checked to make sure there are no cracks. If there are signs of damage to the seat in any way, then the head itself may need fitting with new valve seat inserts. Possibly, the existing valve seats may be recut. Give this job to a specialist. Provided the valves and seats are in good condition, then it is possible to reseat them by grinding in position using a carborundum paste. This grinding-in process should also be carried out when a new valve is being fitted.

5 The carborundum paste used for this job is normally supplied in a double ended tin with coarse paste at one end and fine paste at the other. In addition, a suction tool for holding the valve head so that it may be rotated is also required. To grind in a valve, first smear a trace of the coarse paste onto the seat face and fit the suction grinder to the valve head. Then with a semi-rotary motion grind the valve head into its seat, lifting the valve occasionally to redistribute the grinding paste. When a dull matt continuous line is produced on both the valve seat and the valve then the paste can be wiped off. Apply a little fine paste and finish off the grinding process. If a light spring is placed over the valve stem behind the head this can often be of assistance in raising the valve from time to time against the pressure of the grinding tool so as to redistribute the paste evenly round the job. The width of the line which is produced after grinding should not be more than 1.8 mm. If, after a moderate amount of grinding, it is apparent that the seating line is much wider than this then it means that the seat has already probably been cut back once or more times previously, or else the valve has been ground in several times. Here again, specialist advice is best sought on occasions such as this.

6 After each valve has been ground in, the traces of carborundum paste which will remain in the area of the seat and inlet port must be thoroughly flushed away with paraffin. If possible, a high pressure air line should be used to blow away the final traces. Obviously, particles of carborundum grit are not wanted anywhere inside the engine.

7 Before the valves are finally replaced, all traces of carbon should be cleaned from them and also from the cylinder head itself. A wire cup brush and an electric drill are very useful in doing this work in the head. The face of the cylinder head should also be scraped perfectly clean and free from accumulations of carbon which may be upon it. Do not use any abrasive paper for cleaning but rather a flat bladed scraper. Make sure that no odd particles of gasket or carbon fall into the orifices in the casting. If they should, get them blown out.

8 Examine all the valve springs to make sure that they are of the correct length according to the specifications. It will have been noticed when they were being removed whether any were broken, and if they are then they should be replaced. It is a good idea to replace all the valve springs anyway. If you have reached this stage it is false economy not to do so. They are relatively cheap.

9 It is a good idea to replace the valve spring seating washers which sit directly on the cylinder head. These wear reasonably quickly.

10 Before reassembling the valves and springs to the cylinder head make a final check that everything is thoroughly clean and free from grit and then lightly smear all the valve stems with engine oil prior to reassembly.

30 Timing chain and sprockets - examination and renovation

Examine the teeth of both sprockets for wear. Each tooth on the sprocket is in the shape of an inverted V and if the side of the tooth is concave in shape it is an indication that the tooth is worn badly and the sprocket should, therefore, be replaced. If the sprockets are worn and have to be renewed then the chains should also be renewed. If the sprockets are satisfactory, examine the chain to make sure there is no play between the links and if the chain is held out it should not bend when held horizontal. In view of the relative cheapness of these items it is worthwhile putting on a new chain anyway. Examine the tensioner pivot for signs of excessive wear which could cause rattling and also the tensioner itself. If the chain has gouged a deep groove into the tensioner renew it.

31 Camshaft and tappets - examination and renovation

1 The camshaft lobes should be examined for signs of flats or scoring or any other form of wear and damage. At the same time the tappets should also be examined, particularly on the faces where they bear against the camshaft, for signs of wear. If the case hardened surfaces of the cam lobes or tappet faces have been penetrated it will be quite obvious as there will be a darker, rougher pitted appearance to the surface in question. In such cases, the tappet or the camshaft will need renewal. Where the camshaft or tappet surface is still bright and clean and showing slight signs of wear it is best left alone. Any attempt to reface either will only result in the case hardened surface being reduced in thickness with the possibility of extreme and rapid wear later on.

2 The skew gear in the camshaft which drives the oil pump shaft and indirectly the distributor also should be examined for signs of extreme wear on the teeth. Here again if the skew gear teeth are very badly worn and ridged, it will mean renewal of the complete camshaft. This is quite probable on 'tired' engines. Examine also in conjunction with this the teeth on the driven gear.

3 The camshaft bearing journals should be perfectly smooth and show no signs of pitting or scoring as they are relatively free from stress. If the bearing surfaces are scored or discoloured it would suggest that the camshaft is not 'running true'. This will certainly mean camshaft renewal - if very bad have your local engineering works or Renault agent check the alignment of the block and the camshaft as the camshaft runs directly in the block. Proprietary camshaft replacement bearings are not available. Fortunately, it is rare for the camshaft journals and bearings to wear out at anything like the same rate as the rest of the engine. Having ascertained that the faces of the tappets are satisfactory, check also that the tappets are not a loose fit in their respective bores. It is not likely that they are loosely fitting, but if so they should be renewed.

32 Flywheel - examination and renovation

1 There are two areas in which the flywheel may have been worn or damaged. Firstly, is on the driving face where the clutch friction plate bears against it. Should the clutch plate have been permitted to wear down beyond the level of the rivets, it is possible that the flywheel has been scored. If this scoring is severe it may be necessary to have it refaced or even renewed.

2 The other part to examine is the teeth of the starter ring gear around the periphery of the flywheel. If several of the teeth are broken or missing, or the front edges of all teeth are obviously very badly chewed up, then it would be advisable to fit a new ring gear.

3 The old ring gear can be removed by cutting a slot with a hacksaw down between two of the teeth as far as possible, without cutting into the flywheel itself. Once the cut is made a chisel will split the ring gear which can then be drawn off. To fit a new ring gear requires it to be heated first to a temperature of 220°C, no more. This is best done in a bath of oil or an oven, but not, preferable, with a naked flame. It is much more difficult to spread the heat evenly and control it to the required temperature with a naked flame. Once the ring gear has attained the

correct temperature it can be placed onto the flywheel making sure that it beds down properly onto the register. It should then be allowed to cool down naturally. If by mischance, the ring gear is overheated, it should not be used. The temper will have been lost, therefore softening it, and it will wear out in a very short space of time.

4 Although it is not actually fitted into the flywheel itself, there is a bush in the centre of the crankshaft flange onto which the flywheel fits. Although this bush is more correctly associated with the gearbox or clutch it is mentioned here as well as it would be a pity to ignore it whilst carrying out work on the flywheel. If it shows signs of wear it should be renewed. If suitable extractors are not available to get it out another method is to fill the recess with grease and then drive in a piece of close fitting steel bar. This should force the bush out. A new bush may be pressed in.

33 Oil pump - examination and renovation

1 Only work on the oil pump with it removed from the block.
2 Unscrew the four setscrews which hold the cover face and filter to the main body.
3 Take care with the ball seating boss, the ball bearing and the pressure relief spring which will come away when the cover face is removed.
4 Take out the driven gear and then the drive gear and the shaft.
5 Clean all the parts with petrol or paraffin and check the condition of the splines on the drive shaft. They should be unchewed and straight.

6 Check the condition of the ball bearing and its seating. There should be no irregularity nor ridges in either. The ball should be replaced anyway if you have reached this stage.
7 Check the spring. If possible replace it anyway at this stage. Obtain the correct replacement without fail.
8 Check the clearance between the pump gears and their body. If over 0.20 mm replace the gears. Also check the cover joint face for marks and irregularities. Replace if scored.
9 It may be found that if two or more parts need replacing that it is more economic and quicker to replace the whole pump. There is no exchange scheme.

34 Inlet/exhaust manifold - inspection

Exhaust and inlet manifolds should be examined for signs of cracks or other breakages, particularly on the mounting lugs. The mating faces of both manifolds where they join the cylinder head should be examined to make sure that they are completely flat and free from pitting or burrs of any sort. Use a straight edge to check the faces of the manifold for distortion. If there is any distortion or signs of severe pitting or burning the manifold should be renewed. Provided the manifolds are sound, accumulations of carbon within the ports may be removed with a wire brush or scraper.

35 Decarbonisation

1 Modern engines, together with modern fuels and lubricants, have virtually nullified the need for the engine to have a 'decoke'

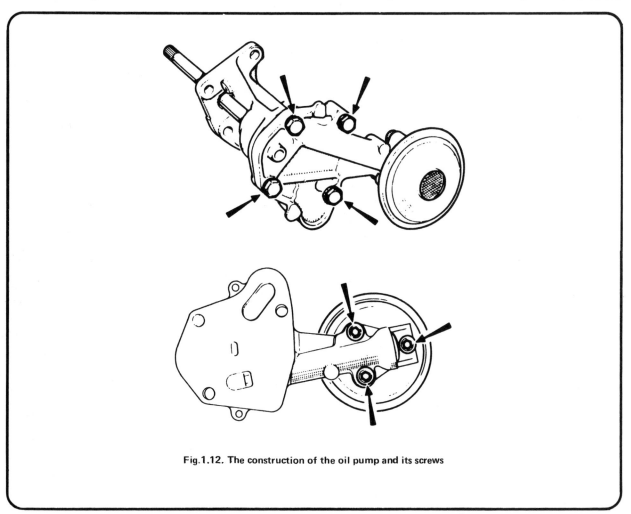

Fig.1.12. The construction of the oil pump and its screws

which was common enough only a few years ago. Carbon deposits are formed mostly on the modern engine only when it has to do a great deal of slow speed, stop/start running, for example, in busy traffic and city traffic conditions. If carbon deposit symptoms are apparent, such as pinking or pre-ignition and running on after the engine has been switched off, then a good high speed run on a motorway or straight stretch of road is usually sufficient to clear these deposits out. It is beneficial to any motor car to give it a good high speed run from time to time.

2 There will always be some carbon deposits, of course, so if the occasion demands the removal of the cylinder head for some reason or another, it is a good idea to remove the carbon deposits when the opportunity presents itself. Carbon deposits in the combustion chambers of the cylinder head can be dealt with as described under the section head 'Cylinder head - inspection and renovation'. The other carbon deposits which have to be dealt with are those on the crowns of the pistons. This work can easily be carried out with the engine in the car, but great care must be taken to ensure that no particles of dislodged carbon fall either into the cylinder bores and down past the piston rings or into the water jacket orifices in the cylinder block. Liner retainers must be fitted.

3 Bring the first piston to be cleaned to the top of its stroke and then using a sheet of strong paper and some self adhesive tape, mask off the other three cylinders and surrounding block to prevent any particles falling into the open orifices in the block. To prevent small particles of dislodged carbon from finding their way down the side of the piston which is actually being decarbonised, press grease into the gap between the piston and the cylinder wall. Carbon deposits should then be scraped away carefully with a flat blade from the top of the crown of the piston and the surrounding top edge of the cylinder. Great care must be taken to ensure that the scraper does not gouge away into the soft aluminium surface of the piston crown.

4 A wire brush, either operated by hand or a power drill, should not be used if decarbonising is being done with the engine still in the car. It is virtually impossible to prevent carbon particles being distributed over a large area and the time saved by this method is very little.

5 After each piston has been attended to clean out the grease and carbon particles from the gap where it has been pressed in. As the engine is revolved to bring the next piston to the top of its stroke for attention, check the bore of the cylinder which has just been decarbonised and make sure that no traces of carbon or grease are adhering to the inside of the bore.

PART 3 – REASSEMBLY AND REPLACEMENT

36 Engine reassembly - general

It is during the process of engine reassembly that the job is either made a success or a failure. From the very word go there are three basic rules which it is folly to ignore, namely:

1 Absolute cleanliness. The working area, the components of the engine and the hands of those working on the engine must be completely free of grime and grit. One small piece of carborundum dust or swarf can ruin a big end in no time, and nullify all the time and effort you have spent. No matter what the pundits say this engine and its other components can be reconditioned and rebuilt very successfully and continue working efficiently. It is necessary to rebuild this engine in operating theatre conditions - warmth, light and space.

2 ALWAYS, no matter what the circumstances may be, use new gaskets, locking tabs, seals, nyloc nuts and any other parts mentioned in the Sections in this Chapter. It is pointless to dismantle an engine, spend considerable money and time on it and then to waste all this for the sake of something as small as a failed oil seal. Delay the rebuilding if necessary.

3 Don't rush it. The most skilled and experienced mechanic can easily make a mistake if he is rushed.

4 Check that all nuts and bolts are clean and in good condition and ideally renew all spring washers, lockwasher and tab washers

as a matter of course. A supply of clean engine oil and clean cloths (to wipe excessive clean oil off your hands only!) and a torque spanner are the only things which should be required in addition to all the tools used in dismantling the engine.

37 Engine block preparation

1 Assuming that the engine has been completely stripped for reconditioning and that the block is now bare, before any reassembly takes place it must be thoroughly cleaned both inside and out.

2 The ideal situation is to dip the block in a garage's cleaning tank usually filled with a mixture of paraffin and cleansing fluid, and then to leave it submerged for an hour or so. Then get to work on it with a wire brush and screwdriver. Clean out all the crevices, do not scratch any machined surfaces, and scrub both the inside and out. The tappet chest is prone to hide sludge. A great deal of sediment often collects around the liner seatings. Chip this away if necessary.

3 Hose down the block with a garden hose and if possible dry it off with an air jet. Dry and thoroughly clean out the block with non-fluffy rag until it is spotless. The water will not make it go rusty provided you dry it off well.

4 Clean out all the oilways with a test tube/bottle brush and finally dry these. You should now not need to worry if you had to eat your lunch from the side of the block!

5 Check the two oil gallery aluminium plugs at each end of the block and the two screw-in camshaft bearing plugs on the top of the block. These should be solidly intact and show no signs of being weepy. If they do, drill a hole in their centre and corkscrew them out. Tap and peen in new ones very gently. These are supplied with the gasket sets necessary for the rest of the overhaul. (If you are reluctant to do this job ask your engineering works to do it for you - it is, however, quite easy).

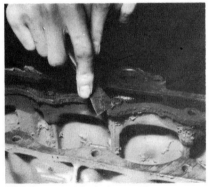

37.2 Clean the block thoroughly

38 Crankshaft and main bearing - reassembly

1 Stand the cylinder block inverted on the bench and gather together the bearing caps, new bearing shells and have the crankshaft without the flywheel fitted alongside lined up in the way in which it will eventually be placed into the cylinder block. Make sure that the oilways in the crankshaft are all quite clear. (photo)

2 Make sure that the bearing housings in the cylinder block are perfectly clean and smooth in preparation for the fitting of the top halves of the main bearing shells. Each bearing shell has an oil hole in it, some have two, and this must line up with the corresponding hole in the cylinder block. Each shell is notched, and this notch also must line up with the corresponding notch in the cylinder block. Carefully fit each shell into its proper position, taking care not to bend, distort or scratch it in any way. When they are in position lubricate the shells with a liberal quantity of clean engine oil. (photo)

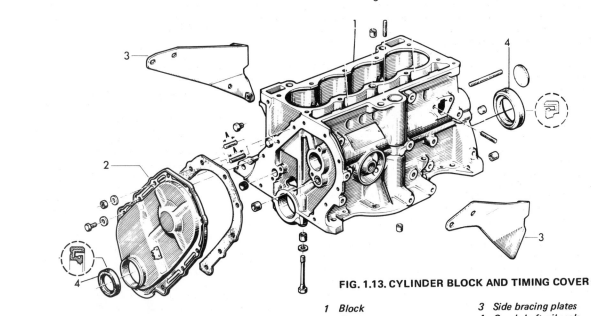

FIG. 1.13. CYLINDER BLOCK AND TIMING COVER

1 Block
2 Timing cover
3 Side bracing plates
4 Crankshaft oil seals

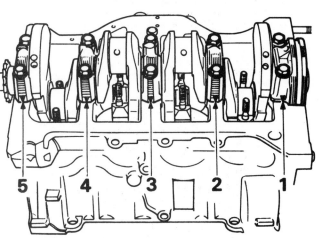

Fig. 1.14. The order of the five main bearings and markings
No.1 at flywheel end.

3 Making sure that the crankshaft is the right way round, next
pick ip up and very carefully lower it square and straight into
position on the shell bearings in the crankcase. (photo)
4 Again, make sure that the bearing caps are perfectly clean
and fit the shells so that the notches in their ends line up and fit
snugly into the grooves in the bearing caps. There are no oilways
in the bearing caps so that the holes in the end bearing shells will
not line up with anything. (photo)
5 The crankshaft end float is controlled by two semi-circular
thrust washers which fit at the sides of the centre main bearing
journal. Place these in position and slide them round into the gap
between the bearing housing and the flange of the crankshaft,
making sure that the white metal/grooved faces abut onto the
crankshaft. Once these are in position the end float can be
checked by pushing the crankshaft as far as it will go in one
direction and measuring the gap between the face of the thrust
washer and the machined surface of the flange with a feeler
blade. End float should be between 0.05 and 0.125 mm. (Adjusting flanges of differing size are available - the correct ones should
have been supplied with the new bearing by your machinists.)
6 Next arrange all the bearing caps complete with their shells so
that you know precisely where each one should go. They are

easily identifiable by their particular shape. As there is the
possibility of a seepage of oil through the end main bearing cap
mating faces it is permissible to put a very thin smear of
non-setting jointing compound onto the outside edge of the
vertical face where the bearing cap locates into the crankcase.
Lubricate the main journals of the crankshaft liberally with clean
engine oil and place all the bearing caps in position and fit the
bolts. The front main bearing cap has a machined front face and
this must line up with the rear surface of the cylinder block.
Make sure that this is done with a straight edge before finally
tightening down the bolts.
7 When all the caps are settled correctly in position, tighten the
bolts down evenly, starting at No. 1, at the flywheel end and
working to No. 5, using a torque spanner, to the correct torque
as given under the specifications. When this has been done
revolve the crankshaft to make sure that there are no inter-
mittent tight spots. Any signs that something is binding whilst
the crankshaft is being revolved indicates that something is
wrong and there may be a high spot on one of the bearings or on
the crankshaft itself. This must be investigated or a damaged
bearing could result.
8 Now fit the front main bearing oil seal. This is a circular oil
seal, which has a very fragile inner lip. Always fit a new one. Oil
it well with engine oil, and press it by hand into the correct
position. Tap it gently fully home with a piece of wooden dowel
until it is fully in. There should be a slight recess between it and
the outer edge of the block/bearing cap.

39 Pistons, gudgeon pins and connecting rods - reassembly

As mentioned in Section 18 the connecting rods and gudgeon
pins are an interference fit requiring heat to enable them to be
correctly assembled. This work should be entrusted to someone
with the necessary experience and equipment. It is important
that the piston and connecting rod are assembled the proper way
round to ensure that the offset of the piston is on the thrust side
of the cylinder.
With the connecting rod lying on the bench have the number
stamped on the 'big end' facing you, the arrow on the piston top
MUST face upwards.

38.2 Swamp the bearing shells with clean oil

38.3 Be careful, squarely and gently

38.4 Locate the lip properly

38.5a Marks on the thrust washer towards the web

38.5b Other half of the thrust washer

38.6 Washers and bolts

38.7 Use a torque wrench (in order)

38.8 You can use your fingers to locate the oil seal

40 Piston rings - replacement on pistons

1   Before fitting new piston rings to the old pistons, make sure the ring grooves in the piston are completely clean and free of carbon deposits. A piece of old, broken piston ring is a useful tool for doing this, but make sure that the sharp edge is not permitted to gouge out any pieces of metal. Check also that the specified gap between the edge of the new piston ring and the groove is correct.

2   All rings must be fitted from the top of the piston. To get the new rings into position involves spreading them sufficiently to clear the diameter of the piston itself and then moving them down over the existing grooves into their appropriate positions. Care must be taken to avoid straining them to a point where they could break. A piece of thin shim steel or an old feeler gauge blade is a very useful means of guiding the ends of the rings over the grooves to prevent them inadvertently dropping in, rather than passing over each groove.

3   Before fitting the rings to the piston it is important to check that the end gap matches the cylinder bore into which they will eventually be fitted. Push the rings down the bores using the piston until they are about 2½ inches below the top surface of the top of the liner. Then measure the gap. If the gap is too large you have either got the wrong piston rings or the cylinder bores are worn more than you had anticipated. If the gap is too small then it will be necessary to remove a piece of material from the end of the ring. The gap may be increased to the correct specification by clamping the end of the ring in a vice so that a very small portion of the end projects above the top of the vice. Then use a fine file to take off the material in very small quantities at a time. Do not clamp the ring so that the end being filed projects too far above the vice jaws or it may easily be snapped off while the filing is being done.

4   When every ring has been checked and the gaps made correct the rings should be assembled to the piston to prevent them being mixed up with other rings which will be fitted to other

bores. Fit the bottom scraper ring first by placing it over the top of the piston and spreading the ends. Move it down the piston a little at a time, taking care to prevent it from snagging in the grooves over which it will pass. The next ring to be fitted is the lower compression ring and this only goes on one way up. The top edge of the ring will be marked 'top' and this, of course, should go uppermost. Don't be misled into thinking that this means that the ring is the top one on the piston. The top compression ring, which is the last one to go on can be fitted either way up on the piston. When all the rings are in position in their grooves, try and arrange the gaps to be equally spaced around the piston. Place the gap of the oil control ring over an undrilled portion of the groove. Obviously, if the gaps of all the rings are in a straight line there will be a much greater tendency for compression loss at that point.

40.4 Ring gaps spaced at 120⁰ will retain compression

41 Liner fitment check

1 If the liners have been removed to be checked, relocated or just to be reseated they should be located after the crankshaft has been fitted - to ease the fitting of the crankshaft, but it in fact matters little. In the majority of cases the crankshaft is in the block and the procedure for fitting is the same whether the engine is in or out of the car.

2 If new liners are purchased with new pistons as a set you must keep that piston with its liner. This means that if you have already fitted the pistons to the rods that you must be careful as to the order in which the liners go into the block, ie. that No. 1 rod with its piston still goes into its respective liner in the No. 1 position.

3 When fitting liners into the block you must first do so without the pistons fitted in the liners, but this is only a trial run. It is in fact a good idea to make this trial run without committing yourself to placing any piston and its liner to any position, place your liner before you fit the piston to any particular connecting rod. Once the liners are placed in their easiest position you can then match the position of the liner to the piston to the connecting rod. All liners are interchangeable in the block.

4 Check that the liners are in good, clean condition without any cracks, even hairline ones, on the outside. Make sure you have a selection of base seals of differing thicknesses. These seals are available in 0.08 mm marked with a blue spot, 0.10 mm marked with a red spot and 0.12 mm marked with a green spot. Buy the latest type. They are usually copper or aluminum coated with a plastic which softens and seals but sometimes paper.

5 Lightly oil the holes in the block into which the liners must fit and hold the block upright on the bench by supporting the sump face of the block on blocks of wood. (It is easier to do this with the block held in position in the car!)

6 Hold a liner on the bench and slide the thinnest of the seals over the end. With the seal fully home place the liner carefully into the block until it sits firmly in. Do not place the seal in the block and then slide in the liner; it does not work!

7 Repeat this with the other three liners using the same thickness of seal. Tap all four liners very gently with a rubber faced hammer to make sure they are fully home.

8 Using a metric feeler gauge measure the projection of the top of each liner in turn above the surface of the block. This is done by placing the blade or blades on the block face and running your finger across (you should have clean hands anyway) from the feeler gauge to the liner top. The projection should be between 0.04 and 0.011 mm. The nearer 0.011 mm the better. If you are some way out remove the liners and then replace them using a different thickness of seal. Go through the permutations until you have it right. Provided you have all four liners with the same projection it matters little that one liner has used one thickness of seal and the others another.

9 Now that you have found out which seals to use, you cannot know without doing this, you should remove the liners, recording their order and the seals used, to fit them with their pistons and connecting rods outside the engine. If the liners have been removed, never attempt to fit the liners to the block and then fit the pistons.

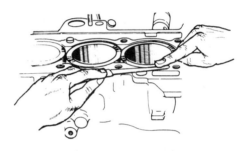

Fig. 1.15. Liner projection check with a feeler blade

42 Pistons, connecting rods and big end bearings - reassembly into liners

1 Do not attempt to fit the pistons to the liners with the liners in the block, whether the engine is in or out of the car. Remove the liners and assemble them on a bench.

2 If new piston rings, on either new pistons or the old pistons, are going into the original cylinder bores it is important that the piston ring gaps should be checked before fitting the piston assemblies. This will mean removing the rings from a new piston in order to check them. In order to assist the bedding in of the new piston rings to the original cylinder bore, it is a good idea to remove the oil glaze which builds up on a bore as an engine becomes more used. This can be done with very fine glass paper, wrapped round a wooden plug of suitable diameter. Careful and thorough cleaning out afterwards will also be necessary, so unless you are perfectly sure that you can do this job safely, it is best not to do it at all.

3 Place the liners in their order of fitment, positioned with their flats mating with each other.

4 Oil the piston. Tap the piston and connecting rod assembly into the top of the liner making sure the arrow on the crown of the piston faces the flywheel and that the number stamped on the big end faces away from the camshaft (once all is assembled in the block). Fit a suitable clamp around all the piston rings to

compress them into the grooves of the piston. It is possible to improvise a ring compressor out of a suitably sized hose clip, but great care should be exercised if this is done as it is not possible to get it to lie dead flat due to the adjusting screw housing projecting beyond the edge of the clip. This can permit the edge of a piston ring to escape its control and then be trapped against the cylinder block face and consequently break. If a strip of sheet metal is cut from an old tin and used in conjunction with a hose clip this is less likely to happen. With the rings suitably clamped, the piston may then be gently tapped into the bore.

5   Fit a new shell bearing into the connecting rod half of the big end, making sure that the notch in the end of the shell lines up with the notch in the connecting rod. (photo)

6   Repeat for each piston and then place the liners and piston assemblies into the block, as has been described in the previous Section.

7   Lubricate the big end journal on the crankshaft with clean engine oil and pull the connecting rod down onto the journal. Fit a new shell bearing into the cap, lining up the notch accordingly. Oil the shell and replace it onto the big end studs. With the big end bearing caps marked there should be no difficulty in making sure that the same cap goes onto the same connecting rod the right way round. Refit the nuts and tighten them down to the correct torque. It is a good idea to purchase a set of new big end nuts each time this job is done. These nuts do sometimes stretch and weaken. Loctite is a good additional safety measure.

8   With the pistons and liners assembled in the block recheck the liner projection with a feeler gauge as previously described. If now outside the tolerances you must disassemble and start again.

9   Do not now turn the engine over until the liner retainers are installed or the cylinder head is replaced.

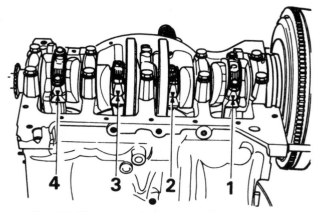

Fig. 1.16. The order of the big end bearings and markings

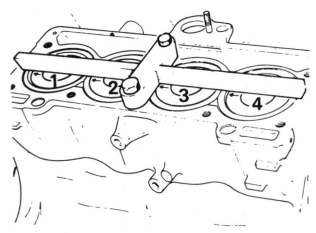

Fig. 1.17 The positions of the arrows on the pistons when installed in the block (1 towards flywheel). The clamp is the proper Renault one

42.4a Always use a piston ring clamp

42.4b Note the direction of the piston arrow

42.5 Grease the liner location

42.6a Push the bearing shells into the rod

42.6b Feed over the liner seal

42.6c Finally check all for cleanliness

42.7 Again oil well

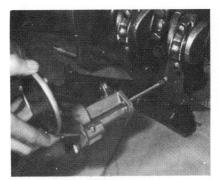

43.1 No gasket is fitted

43.2 A 'small' spanner is needed for the oil pump

44.4a Be as careful with the camshaft as with the crankshaft

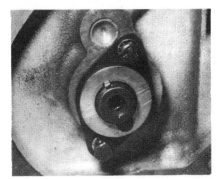

44.4b The camshaft locking flange

43 Oil pump - replacement

1 Wipe clean the mating surfaces of the oil pump and the cylinder block.
2 Offer up the pump and screw up the three holding setscrews. Do not forget their spring washers. No gasket is required. r. Tighten hard, it is not possible to use a torque wrench. You do not have to worry about engine timing at this stage.

44 Camshaft - replacement into cylinder block

1 Refitting the camshaft and tappets is virtually the reversal of their removal. Never refit the tappets before the camshaft. It does not matter however whether the oil pump is fitted. The distributor and the skew gear drive must be removed.
2 Clean the timing cover end of the block.
3 Lubricate the lobes and bearing surfaces of the camshaft.
4 Insert the camshaft into the block straight and gently. You do not want to damage the lobes or bearing surfaces. With no obstructions and once fully home bolt up the flange. (photos)
5 If you have purchased a new camshaft, have your Renault agent press on the flange for you. It must be positioned with the correct amount of end float (0.06 mm to 0.011 mm).

45 Timing gear and cover - replacement

1 Before replacing any of the timing gear check that all the cylinder block oil ducts to the timing gear are free and not covered by any dirt or old type timing cover plates.
2 If the crankshaft has not yet had its sprocket remounted it is not easy once it is off to remount it with the crankshaft out of the engine. Push in the Woodruff key and after heating the sprocket in boiling water push it onto the shaft with the timing punch mark outermost. It should slide on up to its fullest extent. (photo)
3 Place the camshaft sprocket with its arrow punched mark facing outwards just onto the camshaft. Turn the sprocket and camshaft so that the two arrow marks, on the two sprockets, camshaft and crankshaft, are nearest to each other in a straight line with the centres of the two sprockets. See Fig.1.18..
4 Remove the camshaft sprocket without disturbing the camshaft and fit the timing chain onto the sprocket.
5 Achieve the same positioning of the sprockets again but this time with the chain on the crankshaft sprocket as well. Press the camshaft sprocket onto the camshaft. Check the alignment again. (photo)
6 Place the flat washer, locking tab and bolt onto the camshaft sprocket and screw it in. (photo)

7 Hold the camshaft sprocket with a screwdriver through one of its centre drillings and tighten the bolt. (photo)
8 Lock the locking tab with a pair of grips. (photo)
9 Refit the chain tensioner together with its thrust plate. (photo)
10 Insert the 3 mm Allen key into the retaining cylinder and turn in a clockwise direction until the pad carrier presses against the chain, with tension. Do not overtighten, you will wear out the pad. (photo)
11 Tighten the retaining cylinder bolts.
12 The timing cover should be replaced, as a direct reversal of the removal sequence, see Section 13. Inside the cover is an oil seal, similar to the main bearing oil seal on the end of the crankshaft. This should be driven out with a socket and replaced by tapping lightly. Never re-use an old seal.
13 Refitment of the timing/fan pulley is described in the next Chapter.

46 Sump - replacement

1 Replacing the sump gasket is one of the most difficult jobs to do well on this engine with the engine out of the car - with the engine in the car it is worse! With the engine in the car and you underneath everything gets in the way!
2 With the engine on the bench make sure that it is the cylinder head down resting on wooden blocks. The flywheel need not be fitted but the timing cover must. Before replacing the sump make quite sure that all big end bearing cap nuts are tight, all main bearing cap bolts are tight, and that the oil pump has been replaced and securely tightened down. Clean the block and sump mating surfaces until they are quite clean and dry.
3 Fit the two rubber end gaskets first. It is obvious which one fits which end. Place them carefully in the groove at the lower

45.2 Drift on the crankshaft sprocket

45.5 Alignment of the camshaft and crankshaft sprocket

45.6 Washer, locking tab and bolt

45.7 Lock the sprocket with a screwdriver

45.8 Bend over the lock tab

45.9 Use your fingers to pull in the chain when fitting the tensioner

45.10 Do not 'over' adjust. It wears out the adjuster

45.12a Stick the gasket to the block

45.12b Locate the timing cover. Watch the oil seal

end of the timing cover (rear) and the groove in the main bearing cap (front). Their feet must rest on the mating surface of the block.

4   Fit the two pieces of cork gasket, having greased the mating surface - make sure the bolt holes line up, and this will ensure the gasket is correctly fitted. The ends of the cork gasket must sit over the feet of the end rubber gaskets.

5   Refit the sump carefully over and onto the gasket. Place all the bolts and washers into their locations before tightening any.

6   When you are happy that all is correctly positioned tighten all the bolts progressively round the sump. Do not overtighten for threads may strip.

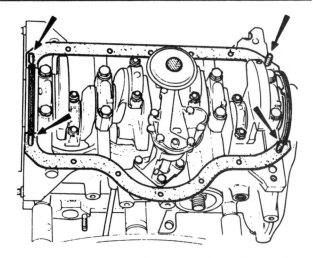

Fig. 1.20. Correct seating of the sump gasket, cork over rubber

46.3a Timing cover end sump gasket

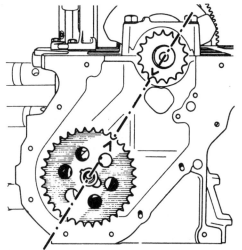

Fig. 1.18. Alignment marks of the camshaft and crankshaft sprockets

46.3b Main bearing cap sump gasket. Note balance drillings in crankshaft

46.4. Cork side gasket over the rubber end gasket

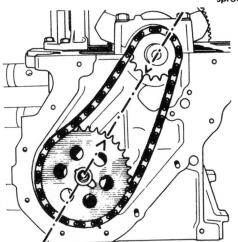

Fig. 1.19. Timing chain is now fitted with the marks still aligned

46.5 Clean out the sump well

47 Flywheel - replacement

1 Before replacing the flywheel to the crankshaft flange, the mating faces must be examined carefully for any signs of dents or burrs and be cleaned up as necessary. All traces of oil and grit must also be removed. Offer up the flywheel to the flange squarely in the previously marked position and locate it carefully into position without damaging the edges of the mating faces. (photo)

2 Once the flywheel is securely mounted the set bolts should be fitted and progressively tightened up to the specified torque. If possible, it is a good idea to check the flywheel run-out at the outer edge of the clutch facing. If this exceeds a total of 0.08 mm then it means that the flywheel is not fitted square with the crankshaft and serious vibration problems could result when the engine is running. A dial gauge will be needed to check this run-out. (photos)

3 Now would be a suitable time to refit the clutch plate and cover. See Chapter 5.

48 Tappet - replacement

Replace the tappets into their respective chambers once well oiled, if you are re-using them. It is always a good idea to replace them if you are in the least bit doubtful as to their condition. Once fitted do not turn the block on its side without the cylinder head in place otherwise they may fall out. (photo)

49 Cylinder head and pushrods - refitting to the cylinder block

1 Again the procedure for refitting the head is similar whether the engine is in or out of the car.

2 Make sure that the new cylinder head gasket is the correct one. Clean the top of the block of all dust and make sure that it and the head surfaces are perfectly flat.

3 Remove the cylinder liner retaining clamps.

4 Fit the gasket in position on the block. HAUT is stamped on the gasket. This should appear uppermost, away from the block. Do not use any gasket cement or grease. (photo)

5 Position the cylinder head on the gasket and fit the bolts and their washers. Make sure that the right length bolts go in the right place - this does matter.

6 Tighten the bolts in the correct sequence progressively. First to 25 lbf ft, then all to 40 lbf ft and then finally to 50 lbf ft. You must , of course, use the correct socket and drive together with a torque spanner, see Section 10 (photo).

7 After the first 3000 miles of running with a new cylinder head gasket wait until the engine is cold then undo the cylinder head bolts ¼ of a turn and retorque them in the correct sequence to 50 lbf ft. Loosen and tighten one bolt at a time.

8 The pushrods will have to be guided in. Refit the pushrods into their respective tappets, cup end up. (photo)

50 Valves and springs - reassembly to cylinder head

1 With the head perfectly clean and having carried out all the necessary renewals and renovations as required, lightly lubricate the valve stem for the first valve to be replaced and fit it in its guide. If the same valves are being used again they should have been kept in order so that they may go back in the same place.

2 Using the same valve spring compressor that was used in disassembly, replace the valves, springs and collets in order. The closer coils of the valve springs go next to the cylinder head.

3 With the spring fully compressed pop the two collet pairs into the top of the spring seat. Remember that not only are the inlet valves and their springs different from the exhaust but so are the collets. The exhaust collets have two round ridges, one at the bottom and one in the middle, and the inlet has one 'square' ridge in its centre.

51 Valve rocker gear - reassembly

1 The rocker shaft is reassembled in a reverse sequence of its disassembly. See Section 9. Do not leave out any springs or clips and make sure the assembly looks like the one shown in Fig. 1.6. .

2 Replacement of the rocker gear onto the cylinder head is again a direct reversal sequence of its removal. Do not forget the washers under the two centre bolts and before tightening these two bolts and the two nuts on the outer studs that all the ball pins are properly seated in the cups on the ends of the pushrods. Then tighten the shaft down progressively. (photo).

47.1a Re-locate the flywheel in its original position to keep balance

52 Valve rocker clearances - checking and adjustment

1 The valve rocker clearances are important as they control the amount a valve opens and when it opens and thus can affect the efficiency of the engine.

2 The clearance should be measured and set by using a feeler blade between the rocker arm and the end of each valve stem. This is done when the valve is closed and the tappet is resting on the lowest point of the cam. Use metric feelers. (photo)

3 To enable each valve to be in the correct position for checking with the minimum amount of engine turning, the procedure and order of checking should follow the sequence given in the following tables. In the table the valves are numbered 1 to 8, starting from the front of the cylinder head. A valve is fully open when the rocker arm has pushed the valve down to its lowest point.

Open Valve	Adjust clearance (cold)
No. 8 (ex)	No. 1 (ex 0.20 mm)
No. 6 (in)	No. 3 (in (0.15 mm)
No. 4 (ex)	No. 5 (ex 0.20 mm)
No. 7 (in)	No. 2 (in 0.15 mm)
No. 1 (ex)	No. 8 (ex 0.20 mm)
No. 3 (in)	No. 6 (in 0.15 mm)
No. 5 (ex)	No. 4 (ex 0.20 mm)
No. 2 (in)	No. 7 (in 0.15 mm)

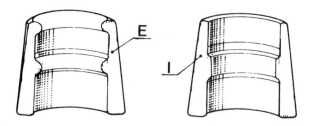

Fig. 1.21. The two types of valve collets: I for inlet, E for exhaust

47.1b This shows the two punch marks made at disassembly

47.2 Use a torque wrench

48.1 Location of the cam followers (tappets)

49.4 You can't put the head gasket upside down

49.5 Carefully locate the head

49.6 Tighten in the correct order to avoid distortion

49.8 Now the pushrods, preferably in their original placing

51.2 Fit the rocker gear on the studs, in the pushrods and on the valve ends

52.2 Use two spanners, not pliers, note the position of the feeler blade

4 Using two spanners, first slacken the locknut on the adjusting screw and then put the feeler of appropriate thickness, between the rocker arm and valve stem of the valve being adjusted. Slacken the adjuster if the gap is too small to accept the blade.

5 Turn the adjusting screw until the feeler blade can be felt to drag lightly when it is drawn out of the gap.

6 Hold the adjuster with a screwdriver and tighten the locknut. Check the gap once more to make sure it has not altered as a result of locking the stud.

7 If the engine is being assembled on the bench, or after the head has been taken off, the gaps should be set 0.2 mm more than specification in the first instance.

53 Engine reassembly - ancillaries - before installation

1 With the engine in the main reassembled the following parts should be replaced now before the engine is replaced in the car.
2 The fuel pump - one stud and one bolt. Do not forget the proper gaskets which should be new ones.
3 The oil pressure sender unit. Do not forget the copper sealing ring.
4 The oil filter, cartridge type, must be fitted, replace it with a new one now. Make sure a new sealing ring is fitted and that the stud and the ring are greased, before fitment. Tighten the oil filter cartridge with hand pressure only even though a strap or chain wrench was probably required to remove the old one.
5 Fit new spark plugs. Clean their orifices with a non-fluffy rag and screw them in by hand. Do not overtighten them with a plug spanner for they may strip the thread in the aluminium head. It is possible to have heli-coil threads fitted if a thread has been ruined.

6 Place the engine with No.1 cylinder at TDC (Top Dead Centre) — see Chapter 4 for details. Insert a 12 mm bolt, about 3 inches long, into the distributor drive pinion and lower it into the distributor locating hole. Place it into engagement with the camshaft skew gear so that the slot in the pinion is at right angles to a line passing longitudinally down the engine, with the largest offset towards the flywheel end of the engine.

7 Lower the distributor into its position on the block. (photo) Make sure that the offset drive mates up with the drive pinion just placed on the block. It will mate up when it rests fully on the block.

8 Fit the distributor clamp claw and tighten. You should now time the engine correctly as described in Chapter 4 (photo).

9 Refit the water pump (if removed) and tighten the bolts. Use a new gasket. See Chapter 2. (photos)

10 Refit the water temperature sender unit at the front end of the cylinder head. Clean the bolt threads first.

11 Refit the generator onto the block. Make sure the spacer is fitted to the lower mounting bolt which should be pushed through from the water pump end. Fit the top pressed steel mounting bracket and leave the bolts loose.

12 Replace the two engine side braces.

13 Refit the coil mounting bracket and then the coil.

14 Pull out the oil rocker cover gasket and carefully fit in the new one. It must fit well in the groove, even if it may mean stretching it slightly to pull it over the lips.

15 Place the rocker cover onto the engine, having made sure that the tappet clearances have been adjusted. See Section 52. It is possible and in fact easier to set these with the engine still out of the car. Do not overtighten the three holding down nuts - just to a point where they start to push in the cover.

16 Finally make sure that the dipstick is in position in the cylinder block and that the plug leads are all connected. Make sure the firing order is correct. See Chapter 4.

17 The engine should now be assembled onto the transmission unit or lifted into the bodyshell if the gearbox is still located in the car.

54 Engine installation onto transmission in car

1 Follow the reverse procedure of the engine removal as described in Section 5 to the letter but read carefully the next paragraph first.

2 If the engine is being refitted with the gearbox in place it is important that no strain is imposed on the gearbox input shaft when centering it into the clutch cover assembly. It may be necessary to wiggle the engine about a little but if the clutch assembly has been correctly assembled (see Chapter 5) there should be little difficulty.

55 Engine and transmission - installation into car

Once again if the exact reverse procedure as described in Section 5 is followed there will be no problems with replacement.

56 Engine now in car - final examination

The following check list should ensure that the engine starts safely and with little or no delay and that the car is ready to move:

a) Fuel pipes to fuel pump and carburettor connected and tight
b) Coolant hoses to radiator and heater connected and tight
c) Radiator and block coolant drain plugs shut and tight
d) Cooling system filled and bled
e) Sump drain plug screwed and tight
f) Oil filter cartridge tight
g) Oil in sump and dipstick replaced
h) Oil in transmission unit and plugs tight
i) LT wires connected to the distributor
j) Spark plugs clean and tight

53.6a Use the 13 mm bolt to hold the skew gear when fitting

53.6b Note the position of the skew gear offset

53.6c The offset pegs of the distributor. Check the location

53.7 There is no washer between the distributor and the block

53.8 The clamp

53.14 Always use a new rocker cover gasket

k) Valve rocker clearances set
l) HT leads all connected and secure
m) Distributor rotor arm fitted
n) Choke and accelerator cable fitted and working through their total range
o) Earthing cable from engine block to battery and battery to inner wing secure
p) Starter motor cable to battery connected and secure
q) Generator leads connected, fan belt on
r) Oil pressure warning and coolant temperature sender unit cables connected
s) Battery charged and secure in position
t) All loose tools removed from the engine compartment
u) Clutch cable refitted and adjusted
v) Gear change linkage replaced
w) Distributor vacuum advance pipe fitted
x) Crankcase fume rebreather pipe fitted
y) Drive shafts refitted to transmission unit and roll pins replaced and greased, and speedometer cable replaced. See Chapter 7.
z) Engine mountings secure.

Leave the bonnet off for the initial start but replace before venturing on to the road!

As soon as the engine starts, run it steadily at a fast tick-over for several minutes and look all round for signs of leaks and loose or unclipped pipes and wires. Watch the instruments and warning lights and stop the engine at the first indications of anything nasty!

DIAGNOSIS AND FAULT-FINDING

1 Scope of diagnosis

1 Though nominally part of the engine Chapter, diagnosis and fault-finding cannot be dissassociated from the problems of components the subject of other Chapters. The matter is therefore covered most fully here, and only narrowly in the other Chapters.
2 The word 'diagnosis' is used to refer to the consideration of symptoms of major mechanical problems, such as noises implying expensive repair or overhaul is needed.
3 'Fault-finding' implies the tracing of a defect preventing some component from functioning.
4 Defects can often be cured by luck. At other times there is no defect, merely a foolish mistake has been made. For example the engine may now start because the rotor arm has been left out, but proper diagnosis or fault finding requires knowledge as to how the thing works, and its construction. Experience helps a lot, for then symptoms can be recognised better. Symptoms must be considered and tests made in an orderly and logical way, step by step, to eliminate possibilities. Beware the dogmatic reputed expert. The true expert is usually non-committal until proved correct by actually finding the faulty component or effecting a cure. You need patience.
5 Many obtuse defects defy diagnosis by garages as they cure themselves temporarily when the car gets there. The owner who cures his own has a great advantage over the garage mechanic as he lives with the symptoms. He knows how everything has been functioning in the past; and may have some item on his conscience, such as plugs overdue for cleaning.
6 The subject is dealt with as follows:
Fault-finding - engine will not run
Fault-finding - engine runs erratically
Diagnosis of knocks and noises.

2 Fault-finding - engine will not run at all

1 Problems in this section will occur under two main circumstances: either when you come to start up the engine initially; or when previously running satisfactorily.

2 Under these circumstances there are many possibilities, so the elimination system in the diagram should be followed.
3 Stoppages on the road have been found from large samples of breakdowns to be most often an ignition defect. The diagnosis therefore at an early stage aims to eliminate the fuel system.
4 Failure to start from cold is usually a combination of damp with dirt, weak spark because of overdue maintenance of the ignition system, and a weak battery.
5 Therefore in deciding to treat the car's temperament as a 'defect' may be misleading. On a cold damp day it is often best to try a push start before going into the fault-finding sequence. The slightest lack of verve in the way the starter spins the engine should therefore be interpreted in the chart as 'starter cranks sluggishly'.
6 The fault-finding chart is adjacent. In it reference is made to various tests. These are listed after the diagnosis tables.

3 Fault-finding - engine runs erratically

1 Erratic running is nearly always a partial fuel blockage. It is therefore best first to eliminate any ignition failures.
2 An ignition fault that gives erratic running will probably be a loose lead. Anything else would give difficult starting. A check should therefore be made of all leads.
3 Having dismissed the ignition system, carefully note the circumstances that provoke the erratic running, and then refer to the fault section of Chapter 3.

4 Knocks and noises - roughness or smoke

1 The car will often give audible warning of mechanical failure in very good time. If these are heeded when faint and diagnosed then, disaster and more expensive repair bills can be avoided.
2 You will need to know how to interpret noises when you are buying a second hand car. If you are inexperienced then you will need help. A run in a similar car but one known to be in good mechanical order can set your standards.
3 Then as you get to know your car you will learn its normal noises and must be alert to the possibility of new ones appearing. Listening to what the car has to say is helped by ruthless tracking down of minor rattles.
4 The overall noise produced is not very loud, but it is characteristic to this engine.
5 The general noise level is fairly continuous, and difficult to locate through. Noises due to defects are heard through this background, are usually not continuous, being provoked by some circumstance.
6 Rough running due to the partial failure of a cylinder is sometimes difficult to detect. A smoky exhaust, or excessive oil consumption are important symptoms. Beware of mistaking tight wisps of vapour of condensation in cold weather as smoke.
7 Two tests can help to keep a check on a car's condition: These are acceleration and compression tests, and are described later.
8 Adjacent are tabled various defects. Each is treated individually. In practise faults or wear may, or probably will occur simultaneously. So neither the symptoms nor the faults would be so clear-cut. Tests referred to in the diagnosis tables are described with the fault-finding tests on later pages.
9 If the diagnosis tells you something serious is amiss it would be wise to get a second opinion. If you decide to get a reconditioned engine it is sufficient to learn that the old engine is badly worn. If you are going to overhaul the engine yourself, then a more exact diagnosis could help you decide whether the work really is within what you think you can cope with, and that it is not bad enough to warrant a reconditioned one. It would also let you order up the spares in advance. If the engine is in good enough order to continue to run without damaging itself and making the subsequent repair much more expensive, then there is opportunity to prolong the observation of the symptoms, so assess them better. Finally, the ultimate most accurate and thorough diagnosis is to take it apart and look inside.

5 Details of fault-finding tests

The systematic fault finding chart calls for various tests to be done. These are given below.

1   Tests of the ignition system:

Test 1.1.
Check ignition HT at a plug.
a) Switch on
b) Take lead off a plug
c) Hold metal contact of the fitting on the end of the lead 1/8th inch from a bright metal "earth" such as the cylinder head. If the plug lead fitting has a shroud to cover the plug stick a ¼ inch bolt into the contact as a probe.
d) Operate the starter (by an assistant, or direct to the switch on the starter with your other hand).
e) There should be an easily noticeable spark.

Test 1.2.
Ignition HT at source.
a) If possible take the HT lead from the distributor and hold the end 1/8 inch from earth and then check as for Test 1.
b) If HT lead is not readily detachable from the distributor cap, remove it from the coil, and rig up a temporary lead.

Test 1.3.
Check ignition LT at contact breaker.
a) Remove distributor cap
b) Ignition switch on
c) Open points with a thin screwdriver, or if points already open on the cam, short them with the screwdriver.
d) There should be a small but definite spark.

Test 1.4.
Check the rotor arm.
a) This test is to see if there is a short through the rotor arm's body to the spindle underneath.
b) Rig up the HT lead or a substitute as for Test 2
c) But hold the lead near the centre of the contact arm on the rotor
d) Operate the starter
e) There should be only the one small spark as the metallic mass of the rotor arm is electrically charged, and then no further sparks.
f) Continued sparks mean there is current flow to somewhere; thus a faulty rotor arm.

2   Tests of the fuel system:

Test P.1.
Check fuel flow into the carburettor.
a) Remove the union for the pipe into the carburettor
b) Operate the starter
c) Fuel should flood from the pipe.

Test P.2.
Check fuel flow into the pump.
a) This is a difficult check unless the car is facing steeply downhill
b) In this case removal of the pipe into the pump from the tank should allow fuel flow by syphoning
c) If syphoning does not occur, try blowing back down the pipe. This should be an easy blow, and an assistant should be able to hear the air bubbling out in the tank

d) The blow could even have unwittingly cleared a stoppage, and it is worth trying to start after it
e) Also, with the pipe off the pump inlet, and the engine turning on the starter, a finger over the inlet union should feel suction.

3   Test of engine acceleration:

It is very difficult to judge properly if the engine is giving its correct power. An objective test is needed.
a) Choose a long straight hill up which the car can just accelerate in the speed range 35 to 45 mph.
b) Choose prominant landmarks at beginning and end of the test stretch
c) If possible time the car over the test stretch with a stop watch. Anyway, note the speedometer reading at the beginning and end
d) Always enter the test stretch at the same speed. Only do tests in conditions of light winds
e) Do the test a number of times when you know the car is going well. Also try and do it with another similar car, known to be in good order. Record these results so that when you are suspicious of the car's performance a test can straight away give useful information.

4   Test of engine compression:

Useful information in defect diagnosis is the amount of pressure that can be achieved in the cylinders. This will indicate the state of the pistons in relation to the bores, as they must build up the pressure, and also it shows whether the valves are sealing the cylinders properly.
a) An engine compression test gauge is needed. This is the sort of equipment the most enthusiastic owner-mechanic gets, but probably the Renault 12 owner will have to get a garage to do this test.
b) Warm up the engine. Remove the spark plugs
c) Hold the rubber seal of the gauge tightly over the spark plug hole in the cylinder head
d) Get an assistant to operate the starter whilst holding the throttle open wide. The starter will need to work for about 3 seconds, to allow a reading to stabilise on the gauge.
e) Note down the reading.
f) Release the pressure from the gauge, and then do the test on the other cylinder. After that do both cylinders for the second time. If the second reading is more than 2% different from the first for that cylinder, do a third test to get an average.
g) The readings for the two cylinders should be within 5% of each other. The reading should be about 100-107 lbs in^2 (7 - 7.5 kg cm^2). But more important, it is the difference between the two that gives the indication of poor compression.

5   Stethoscope for engine noises:

A simple stethoscope can be made to listen to odd engine noises.
a) Get a piece of plastic petrol pipe about 3 ft long
b) In one end put a probe of thin metal pipe about 4 inches long
c) Put the end of the plastic tube in an ear, and search for noises with the metal end
d) The stethoscope will probably not help in locating major knocks deep in the engine, such as big ends, but it is good for locating strange noises in such things as the dynamo.

Chapter 2 Cooling system and heater/ventilation

Contents

Specifications

Type of system	Sealed circuit with expansion chamber. Pressurised with centrifugal circulation pump, fan and thermostat
Coolant capacity with heater	8.75 Imp pints (5 litres/10.5 US pints)
Thermostat - opening temperature	84°C (186°F)
- by-pass port closes at	95°C (203°F)
Radiator type...	3 row gilled tube
Water pump	Centrifugal, driven by belt from crankshaft pulley
Expansion chamber	Glass bottle
Coolant liquid	Equal part solution of glycol antifreeze and distilled water
Heater motor	SEV 08090000 or Ducellier 49241 or Sofica and Faessa
Heater matrix	Twin tube type
Fan belt tension	6.5 to 7.5 mm (0.256 to 0.296 in)

1 General description

The engine cooling system is of conventional design. It is of the sealed type. The radiator is affixed in the centre of a panel which is placed in a parallel position approximately 8 inches from the front of the engine. There is an expansion chamber; a glass bottle under the bonnet near the battery. The expansion chamber is fitted with a pressurised escape valve while the radiator has a fixed screw top. A crankshaft driven fan belt drives the water pump/cooling fan (and the generator). The coolant also heats the inlet manifold of the carburettor (see Chapter 3) and passes through hoses to a special heater matrix on the front bulkhead of the car (see Chapter 11).

The coolant fluid which should be an equal mixture of distilled water and glycol based antifreeze surrounds the cylinder liners in the block and cylinder head in specially constructed water jackets, and is connected to the radiator at its top and bottom by two hoses. When the engine is started and warms up,

the coolant obviously warms up with it and circulates within the water jackets by the action of the fan belt driven water pump. When the water is of sufficient temperature for a cooling action to take place rather than a warming up process, a thermostat adjacent to the water pump gradually opens and allows the hot water to be pumped past it and into the 'cooling' system of the radiator. Cooler fluid then passes out of the radiator back into the water jackets and is recircularised. As the total coolant becomes hotter and expands, the then excess fluid, flows into the expansion chamber. When the system cools again it will flow out of the expansion chamber into the radiator.

2 Special maintenance

It is important that the cooling system is kept in first class condition at all times (see this section in Chapter 1). While it is a totally adequate system it does need regular maintenance.

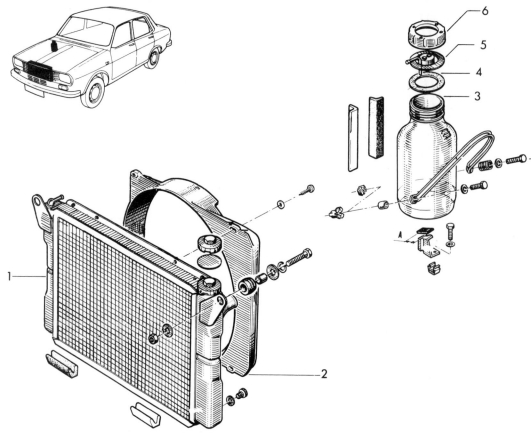

FIG. 2.1. RADIATOR AND EXPANSION BOTTLE

1 Radiator matrix	2 Fan shield (R1177 only)	3 Expansion bottle 4 Sealing ring	5 Valve 6 Cap

3 Cooling system - draining

1 Stand the car on level ground and if hot allow to cool for 15 minutes. It helps to open the bonnet. Remove the expansion chamber safety valve cap (use a piece of cloth wrapped round the cap and a pair of grips).

2 Make sure that the heater is in the 'HOT' position. Undo the radiator drain plug which is situated at the bottom right hand side, with a spanner, not grips. To save the coolant is pointless because most of it drains under the car at many points and collecting it is a hit and miss affair. Nevertheless, lay newspaper under the car to soak as much as possible and leave one receptacle underneath which may collect some. Wait until the coolant begins to gush from this draining point before removing the cap from the radiator. This will make sure that the expansion chamber is empty.

3 Now open the 2 heater bleed screws but do not remove. See Fig. 2.2.

4 Using this method you will have drained out most of the coolant except for a little still left in the cylinder block. The block drain plug is located deep inside the engine compartment, at the end of the block. (photo)

5 You will only need to undo this drain plug if you wish to remove the engine or work on the internals of the engine - it is not necessary just for the removal of the radiator or to change a hose. It is quite difficult to undo.

6 After another five minutes, having allowed the rest of the coolant to drain out, poke the drain holes with a piece of wire to unblock any sediment which may have restricted draining.

7 Although it functions as a sealed system the cooling system is quite conventional in terms of repair. Individual hoses or the thermostat can be replaced without worry in the normal way provided all is sealed in the end and the system is properly bled.

3.4 Block drain plug

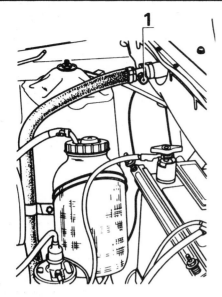

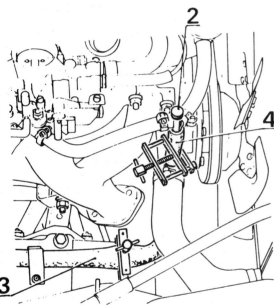

FIG. 2.2. BLEEDING THE COOLING SYSTEM

1 Bleed screw   3 Inlet pipe clamp
2 Bleed screw   4 Water pump clamp

4 Cooling system - flushing

1 In theory the cooling system should never need flushing for if the correct solution of coolant has always been used no sediment will have any opportunity to build up nor any corrosion have taken place. The correct solution, that of equal measures of distilled water and glycol antifreeze is as chemically inert as possible. However most systems will have been subjected to an amount of abuse possibly being topped up with non-distilled water or being run with a slight leak allowing oxidisation to take place. This does not affect coolant efficiency but can lead to clogging eventually.

2 If any clogging has taken place or the coolant is very dirty in colour it makes good sense to flush the system out. To check the need for flushing open the radiator drain tap and if the liquid coming out is obviously very dirty, although it can be a deep colour, and full of solid particles let it run out. If it clears as more runs out and the outflow is in no way restricted then there

is no great problem. If, however, constant poking with a piece of wire is needed and the liquid continues very dirty then obviously a flush is needed.

3 To flush out, simply leave the radiator and block drain taps open and after removing the radiator cap, run a hose through the system for about 15 minutes (ordinary water is quite safe). If the taps show signs of blockage keep poking them out. If the blocking is persistent remove the tap completely so that a larger orifice may permit the obstruction to clear itself. In some bad cases a reverse flush may help and this is easily done by removing the radiator and running the hose into the bottom tank so that it flows out of the filler neck.

4 If the radiator flow is restricted by something other than loose sediment then no amount of flushing will shift it and it is then that a proprietary chemical cleaner, suitable for aluminium heads, is needed. Use this according to the directions and make sure that the residue is fully flushed out afterwards. If leaks develop after using a chemical cleaner, a proprietary radiator sealer may cure them but the signs are that the radiator has suffered considerable chemical corrosion and that the metal is obviously getting very thin in places.

5 Cooling system - refilling and bleeding

1 Always flush out before refilling if the old coolant was particularly dirty. (Clean out the glass expansion chamber too.)
2 Screw up both block and radiator drain plugs. Make sure that a copper washer is fitted to the radiator plug. Make sure all the hose clips are tight and that the hoses are in good condition.
3 Mix 50 per cent distilled water and 50 per cent antifreeze in two clean gallon cans. Mix a further pint of the coolant in addition to the specified capacity. It is essential to use a glycol based antifreeze, such as Castrol Antifreeze, so that it cannot damage the cylinder head. Ideally distilled water should be used to ensure long life of the system as it is by definition very pure, however it is possible to use clean soft water, if distilled water is not available.
4 Fill the glass bottle with coolant 1 3/16 inches above the 'maximum' mark. Refit the valve and sealing ring.
5 Open the two heating/cooling bleed screws. (photos)
6 Fill the radiator with coolant. When it is full clamp the two hoses (3 and 4 in Fig. 2.2) as close to the water pump as possible.
7 Start the engine and run at a very fast idle (1500 rpm) and continue to fill the radiator.
8 When the coolant runs continuously out of the two bleed screws (no air spurts must be seen) screw them up tight. Remove the clamps and leave the bleed screws alone.
9 Top up the radiator, fit its cap and stop the engine. (photo)
10 When all is cool again check the level in the expansion chamber on the side of the glass.
11 Recheck the system for leaks.

6 Radiator - removal, inspection, cleaning and replacement

1 Disconnect the battery earth terminal.
2 Drain the cooling system (see Section 3).
3 Remove the radiator hoses at the radiator and the water pump, and expansion chamber hose at the radiator. (photos)
4 Remove the two radiator securing screws and lift the radiator out. Detach the rubber buffers. Only the R1177 has a radiator/fan cowling made of plastic fixed by some sheet metal screws.
5 Thoroughly clean the exterior of the radiator. It has presumably been removed in order to repair a leak or for further examination of a suspected blockage.
6 Some radiators are made of steel and brass, some of all brass. If the steel has rusted through, little short of replacement can take place but all brass parts can be repaired with solder where exterior leaks are accessible. The technique of soldering is not discussed here but suffice it to say that the surfaces to be joined must be thoroughly cleaned, then tinned and the solder able to

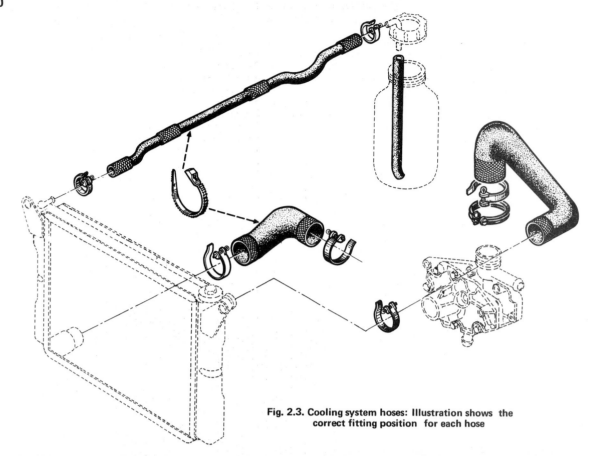

Fig. 2.3. Cooling system hoses: Illustration shows the correct fitting position for each hose

5.5a The inlet manifold water heating pipe

5.5b Use a new gasket for the water pump

5.9 Use a spanner not grips on the radiator cap

6.3a Throw these 'sardine tin' hose clips away.....

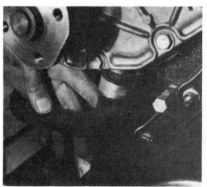

6.3b .....replace with proper worm drive clips

8.3 The thermostat sits inside the hose and is located by the second hose clip

'run' in the repair. It is fruitless merely depositing blobs of solder about the place. It would be better to use a resin filler paste which in fact can be used for such repairs in limited application. Care must also be taken when soldering to localise any heat used. Otherwise the radiator may start to disintegrate where you least want it to. A leak in the internal parts of the honeycomb, if not severe, can be cured with one of the specialist sealers added to the cooling liquid. If severe, professional attention will be needed. Another way for emergencies only, is to block the whole of the honeycomb in the suspect area with resin filler paste. Old fashioned remedies such as mustard, egg whites and porridge oates added to the water, are not recommended as they have been known to have sinister effects on water pumps and thermostats. There is much less liquid in modern systems and these foodstuffs cannot be digested so readily!

7 Replacement of the radiator and its hoses is straightforward. Always use worm drive hose clips and bleed the cooling system fully once installed.

7 Expansion bottle - removal and replacement

1 The expansion bottle located near the battery is fixed by a 'sprung' wire clip and is obviously and easily replaced. It can be cleaned with hot water and detergent. Never replace without using the proper seal.

2 Should the cooling system get so hot as to cause the safety valve on the top of the expansion chamber to 'blow', the valve should not remain in service. Replace it when the cause of the overheating has been resolved.

8 Thermostat

1 If the engine gets too hot or stays too cool, or the heater is inefficient, then the thermostat is probably to blame.

2 Drain out sufficient coolant to lower the level about 4 inches (say a quart) so that no more will be lost when the top radiator hose is next detached from the thermostat housing.

3 Remove the top radiator hose totally. In the largest diameter ends should be the thermostat. It does sometimes fall into its housing if the bottom hose clip is fully undone. Pull the thermostat out. (photo)

4 To test the thermostat, suspend it on a piece of cotton in a pan of water and see how it behaves at the necessary opening temperatures. The valve should start to open within 3°C of the normal operating temperature. Then, after another 2 to 3 minutes, it should open 6.5 mm (¼ inch) to the 'by-pass port closed' position. After being once more placed in cooler water it should close within 15 to 20 seconds.

5 If a thermostat does not operate correctly it should be renewed. If one is not immediately available leave the old one out to avoid damage by possible overheating of the engine.

6 Refit the thermostat by placing it in its housing and push the radiator hose over it (it is obvious which end of the hose fits) making sure that it is not necessary, when fitting the other end of the hose to the radiator, to twist it. Secure the hose clips, refill the radiator with coolant and check for leaks.

NOTE: it has been known for the thermostat itself to travel up the hose about ¾ inch when the coolant is hot. To stop excess flow of coolant, malfunctioning thermostat and hose stretch, lightly tighten a hose clip around the hose over the thermostat body located in the hose in its correct place.

9 Water pump - removal and replacement

1 If the water pump leaks or the bearing is obviously worn it will need to be removed and renewed; there is no facility for repair, the parts not being supplied. An indication of whether the pump is unreliable is for the bearing to be very noisy, particularly at tick-over, for the fan belt to be out of alignment and for the pump to spray the engine compartment with a slimy brown liquid. Its renewal can be undertaken with the engine and the radiator still in the car.

2 Drain the cooling system and then undo the hoses which are connected to the pump.

3 Slacken the generator mounting points and remove the fan belt.

4 Disconnect the battery.

5 Remove the radiator.

6 Remove the fan by undoing with a ring spanner the four fixing bolts in its centre. Remove carefully. With it will come the fan belt pulley.

7 Now remove the eleven bolts which fix the water pump to the cylinder head. Recover the washers. Remove the bolts before trying to prise the outer body from the pump.

8 If you just wish to replace the water pump it is possible to replace the outer/impellor body only. If this is the case leave the inner body attached to the face of the cylinder head and just remove the outer body and its gasket. If the complete pump is to be removed then undo the remaining bolts and prise that off. Be careful pulling the pump bodies off because both they and the cylinder head are easily damaged by sharp objects.

9 There is no point in attempting any repair to the water pump for no parts are available, and exchange units are relatively cheap.

10 Before replacing the pump to the cylinder head all the mating faces must be perfectly clean and free of traces of old gaskets. Fit new gaskets using jointing compound, on both sides and tighten the bolts evenly to ensure a watertight joint.

11 Refit the fan and pulley, replace the fan belt and adjust the tension and connect the water hoses. Refix the radiator. Refill the system with coolant. Examine for leaks when cold and at normal running temperature. Make sure that pulleys all run true to each other.

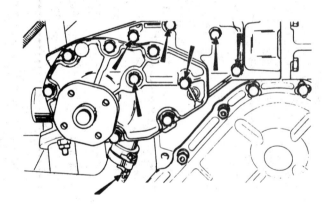

Fig. 2.4. Water pump fixing screw locations

10 Inlet manifold heating hoses

1 Models are fitted with some sort of inlet/carburettor base water heating system. This is basically a simple hose system feeding hot water from the cooling system. It is essential for its proper working to be leak-free and connected correctly.

2 If in any doubt check that the hoses are in good condition and that the hose clips have not eaten through them. If necessary remove and replace both the clips and the hoses with new ones. Remove them in the normal way. Do not worry about any loss of coolant for the amount which will be lost is minute and will quickly be replenished from the excess in the expansion chamber.

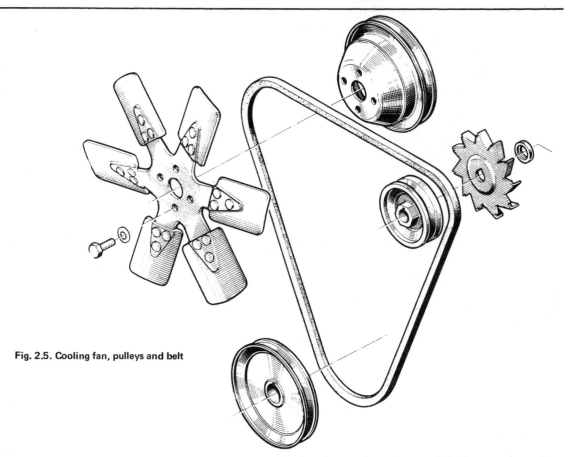

Fig. 2.5. Cooling fan, pulleys and belt

11 Fan belt - removal, replacement and adjustment

1   One fan belt is fitted to drive the generator and water pump. Pulleys are fitted to both these components and are driven by a V belt from a pulley on the end of the crankshaft. Adjustment of the belt is made by moving the generator either away or towards the engine block pivoting on a long bolt.

2   It is fairly easy to replace the belt without removing anything from the engine or its ancillaries but only by loosening sufficiently the generator. Be careful if the engine is hot!

3   If the fan belt is obviously worn or stretched so far that it is still too slack at maximum adjustment, it should be replaced. In case of breakages it is wise to carry a spare.

4   To change the fan belt, loosen the fixing bolts at either end of the rod which holds the bottom of the generator to the water pump. Slacken off the nut at the end of the dynamo pivot bolt on its top side.

5   Remove the old fan belt if not broken, and carefully thread over the new belt, over the blades of the fan first. Be caredul that the fine edges of the fan, radiator cowl or generator do not foul and cut it. 'Peel' the belt over the generator pulley and tighten up the generator, making sure that the belt has the correct tightness. Do not overtighten; deflection should be about ¼ inch on its longest run.

6   After a new belt has run for a few hundred miles check the tension again as the initial stretch may require re-adjustment. There are no definite rules as regards frequency of checking but it only takes a second every time the oil level is checked.

12 Water temperature sender unit

1   The water temperature sender unit is located on the end of the cylinder head just above the flywheel. It is bolted straight down.

2   Whilst operating in the same way in the majority of its

applications its actual warning can differ from car to car. Most cars are fitted with a red warning light on the facia panel which is lit by the sender unit when the car is overheating. The temperatures at which it operates vary from application to application.

3   To replace it, if you are certain it has ceased to operate properly, just disconnect the electrical feed and unbolt. Replace with a new unit.

13 Heater

1   The heater and its controls consist of three components: the water fan, the radiator (matrix) and the control panel. The control panel controls the flow of the engine cooling system's hot water through the heater matrix located under the windscreen. The fan blows through the matrix when the motion of the car is not sufficient to take air through external grilles, when activated. The control panel houses the heater open - close valve and the ventilation flaps. A separate switch activates the electric heater fan.

2   For both efficient engine cooling and heater heating the cooling system must be bled. See Section 5.

3   The heater components should only be touched if there has been serious body damage or there is malfunction. The heater matrix may leak and the heater motor could fail. The usual stiff action of the controls may require repair. Before starting any dismantling make sure FIRST that the cooling system is bled properly.

4   To remove either the heater radiator or the open - close valve first remove the scuttle grille panel under the bonnet and disconnect the appropriate inlet and outlet heater hoses. Always renew the hose clips.

5   The radiator is retained by hooked wire. To remove it, cut the wire and lift up the three hooks.

6   You will now have to remove the open - close valve (ignore paragraph 5 if the valve only is faulty). Unscrew the bolt which retains the valve control under the fascia. Remove the heater

valve securing nut and pull it out. This will now enable the heater radiator to be lifted out, forwards first.

7   Replacement of both components is a reversal of their removal procedure. Note: Check correct operation before fitting the scuttle grille panel and then make sure the panel is properly sealed against the weather. You will see the proper sealing upon removal.

8   The heater motor and fan is located under the fascia behind the glove compartment 'cardboard', on the right. To remove, pull back the cardboard and disconnect the feed wire. Ignore the three centre screws but remove the ones round the edge. The complete housing should then come away.

9   Replacement is a simple reverse process. Make sure the housing is properly sealed.

10 To overhaul the heater motor it is necessary to remove its fan and the housing. Now unscrew the three centre screws previously mentioned. Hold the fan and unscrew the centre shaft bolt with a ring spanner. It may have to be 'shocked' off.

11 Overhaul of the motor, apart from renewing the brushes is not practical. To remove the brushes, unhook the long spring holding them (the conventional method) and then free the brushes themselves. Unsolder the old, and solder in new brushes and replace. Clean the armature with a little methylated spirit. If anything more serious is amiss with the motor, exchange it.

12 Replacement is an exact reverse process to its removal.

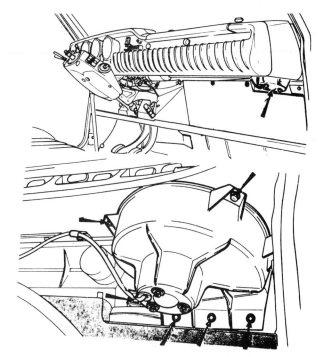

Fig. 2.6. Heater fan location and fixing screws

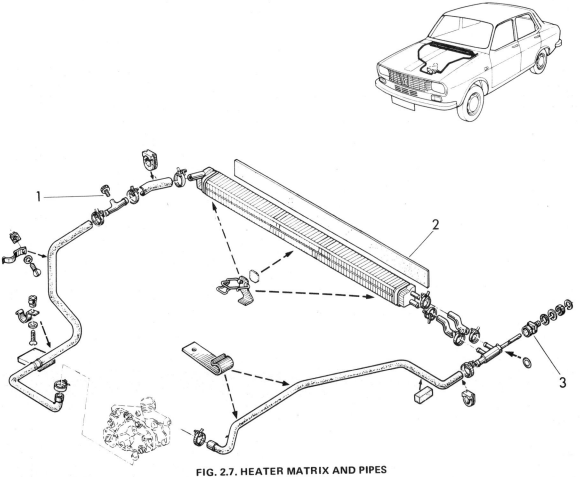

FIG. 2.7. HEATER MATRIX AND PIPES

| 1   Bleed screw | 2   Matrix | 3   Hot water valve (heater on-off) |

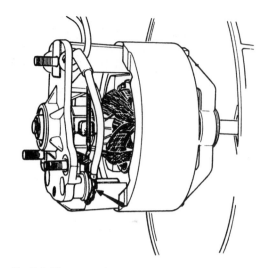

Fig. 2.9. The arrow shows heater motor brush location

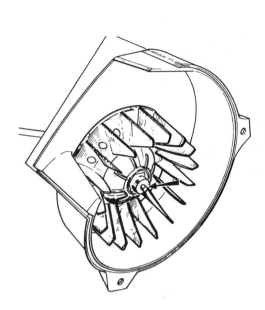

Fig. 2.8. Fan blade fixing

14 Ventilation and heater controls

1   Both ventilation and the heater controls are dealt with in the same section because their systems are closely interelated.

2   The ventilation/heater controls apart from the open - close valve control dealt with in Section 13 paragraph 6. The control panel is located under the facia. First remove the ashtray, set one lever to the far left, the other to the right and then unscrew the fixing screws through the ashtray aperture. The control panel assembly will now be free to drop down.

3   Detach the wiring terminals and note their position to aid quick replacement. Disconnect the cable attachment and remove the panel complete.

4   Before the ventilation air flap assembly cable can be removed in a case of failure, the air flaps have to be removed. Do not remove the fascia.

5   However, remove the windscreen wiper mechanism, see Chapter 9. Unscrew the bottom glove compartment tray securing screws and then the flaps assembly securing screws. Both will now come away with some careful juggling.

6   Open the cable inner bend at the flap under the bonnet and pull the complete inner and outer cable away.

7   Refitment is an obvious reverse procedure. Note, however, before assembling further than the installation of the control cable, check that it can operate through its full travel to correspond exactly with the movement of the control lever. Grease, lightly, the inner cable.

15 Heater box

1   The heater box is part of the heater/ventilating system and is situated under the grille panel below the windscreen. It is of no significant repair or overhaul importance, simply being an air collecting box for the system. It does, however, collect water as well, through the grille.

2   It is fitted with three special one way drain valves to allow this water out but no dust or engine fumes in. They consist of rubber bulb flaps. They should be inspected periodically and replaced if perished or damaged. Otherwise they are best left alone. Their operation is simple: as the bulb fills with water and its weight becomes sufficient, it forces open some internal rubber lips and drains away. These lips automatically close when lightened.

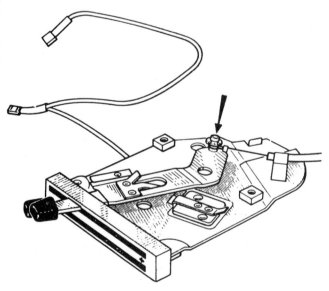

Fig. 2.10. Heater/ventilator control cable connection

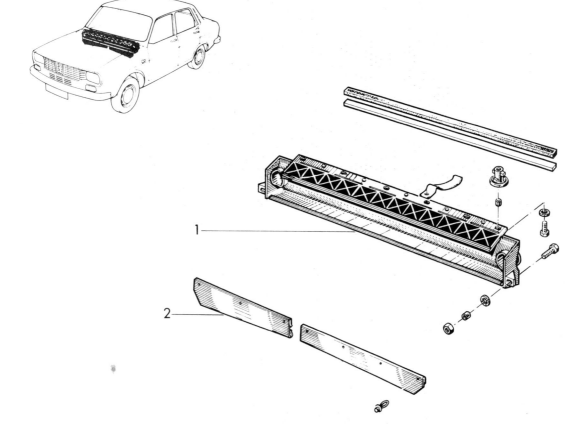

FIG. 2.11. VENTILATOR FLAPS COMPONENTS

1   Ventilator   2   Ventilator flaps

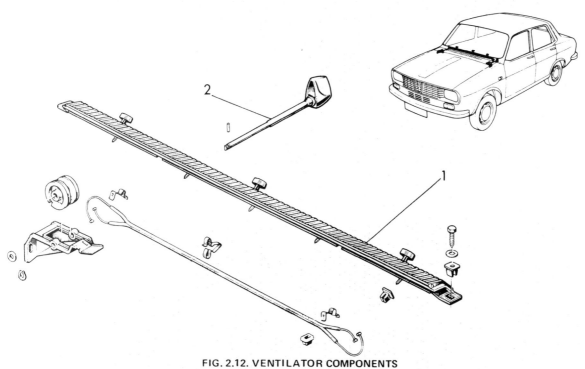

FIG. 2.12. VENTILATOR COMPONENTS

1   Interior ventilator grille   2   Heater on - off lever

16 Cooling system - fault diagnosis

Symptom	Reason/s	Remedy
Loss of coolant but no overheating provided coolant level is kept topped up	Expansion bottle empty Small leaks in system	Half fill expansion bottle Examine all hoses and connections for signs of cracks and leaks when engine is both cold and hot, stationary and running. If no signs, use proprietary sealer in coolant to stop any invisible leaks.
Overheating and loss of coolant only when overheated	Faulty thermostat Fan belt slipping Engine out of tune due to ignition and/or fuel system settings being incorrect Blockage or restriction in circulation of cooling water Radiator cooling fins clogged up Blown cylinder head gasket or cracked cylinder head Sheared water pump impeller shaft Cracked cylinder body New engine still tight	Check and renew if faulty. Check and adjust. Check ignition and fuel systems and adjust as required. Check that no hoses have collapsed. Drain, flush out and refill cooling system. Use chemical flushing compound if necessary Remove radiator and clean exterior as needed. Remove cylinder head for examination. Remove pump and check. Remove engine and examine and repair (if possible). Adjust engine speeds to suit until run in.
Engine runs too cool and heater inefficient	Thermostat missing or stuck open	Remove housing cover and inspect.

Chapter 3 Fuel system and exhaust

Contents

Specifications

Fuel pump ... ... AC, SEV or Guiot. Mechanical
  Pressure (min) ... ... 2.6 psi
  (max) ... ... 4.0 psi

Carburettor
Makes and types fitted: Solex 32 EISA—2 mark 473 or 501 or
519 ... ... Manual choke and water heated manifold
Weber ... ... (R1177 only) - manual choke and water heated manifold

The type and mark number are stamped on a plate fastened to the float chamber.

Solex 32 EISA—2
  Choke tube 24
  Spring loaded needle valve ... ... 7.5 mm
  Accelerator pump jet 35
  Initial throttle opening ... ... 0.65 mm — 0.75 mm
  Idle speed ... ... 750 to 800 rpm
  Main jet 145
  Air compensator jet 155
  Idling jet 42.5
  Enricher 35
  Throttle opening at accelerator pump end of travel ... ... 1.4 mm

Weber 32 DIR 21

	1st barrel	2nd barrel
Choke tube	23	24
Main jet	125	125
Air compensator jet	160	150
Idle speed jet	50	60
Needle valve	1.75 mm	
Float	11 gr	
Float level	7 mm	
Initial throttle opening	0.85 mm	
Idle speed	650 — 675 rpm	

Fuel tank capacity
  R1170, R1171/R1330 ... ... 11 gallons
  R1177 ... ... 10 gallons

1 General description

The Renault 12 fuel system is conventional in principle. The fuel tank is mounted at the rear of the car and is fed from the rear of the saloon and the side of the estate. Access to the tank is gained from inside the rear of the car. A mechanically driven diaphragm pump feeds fuel to the carburettor.

All models except the Renault 12 TS are equipped with a Solex single choke fixed jet carburettor. The Renault 12 TS is equipped with a twin choke Weber carburettor.

2 Air filter - removal and replacement

1 See the Routine Maintenance Section for details of the frequency of air filter element renewal.
2 To renew just the filter element it is not necessary to undo anything more than the filter end covering.
3 Unscrew the end wing nut and lift off the cover together with the old element.
4 Clean out the interior of the filter housing. If the same element is to be refitted tap it on a flat surface to remove any loose accumulations of dust. Do NOT try and wash it, brush it - or blow it with compressed air.
5 When fitting the element, it should seat snugly in the locating ridges in the housing.
6 The casing of the air filter is fitted by two brackets and bolts to the inner wing. The filter has a moulded feed pipe from the casing to the top of the carburettor. The fixed parts, the casing and the moulding are easily removed from the car. Always check the condition of the moulding and fixing clips (which are a special fitment) and replace if split or perished.
7 Never drive without a filter element fitted and always reconnect the air feed tube - it feeds in cold, clean air.

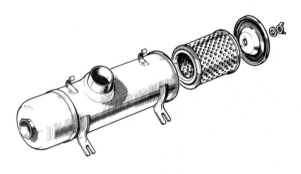

Fig. 3.1. Saloon/estate carburettor air cleaner components

3 Solex carburettor - description

The carburettor is basically a tube through which air is drawn into the engine by the action of the pistons and en route fuel is introduced into the air stream in the tube due to the fact that the air pressure is lowered when drawn through the 'tube'. A scent spray works on the same principle.

The main fuel discharge point is situated in the 'tube' - choke is the proper name for the tube to be used from now on - between two flaps which can block off the tube. One of these is the throttle flap - operated by the accelerator pedal and positioned at the engine end of the choke tube. The other is the strangler - which is operated by a manual device.

When the engine is warm and running normally the strangler is wide open and the throttle open partially or fully - the amount of fuel/air mixture being controlled according to the required speed.

When cold the strangler is closed - partially or fully and the suction therefore draws more fuel or less air, ie: a richer mixture to aid starting a cold engine.

At idling speeds the throttle flap is shut so that no air and fuel can get to the engine in the regular way. For this there are separate routes leading to small holes in the side of the choke tube, on the engine side of the throttle flap. These 'bleed' the requisite amounts of fuel and air to the engine for slow speeds only.

The fuel is held in a separate chamber alongside the choke tube and its level is governed by a float so that it is not too high or low. If too high it would pass into the choke tube without suction. If too low it would only be drawn in at a higher suction than required for proper operation.

The main jet, which is simply an orifice of a particular size through which the fuel passes, is designed to let so much fuel flow at particular conditions of suction (properly called depression) in the choke tube. At idling speed the depression draws fuel from orifices below the throttle which has passed through the main jet and after that a pilot jet to reduce the quantity further.

Both main and pilot or idling jets have air bleed jets also which let in air to assist emulsification of the eventual fuel/air mixture.

The strangler flap (more commonly known as the 'choke' flap) is controlled by the choke cable. Thus the driver will control its use as the engine is cold, and will not use it when it is warm. There is a choke flap stop screw which will leave it partially open so that the engine will not flood (for no air would get through!).

Finally there is another device - an accelerator pump. This is another diaphragm operated pump which is directly linked to the accelerator controls. When sudden acceleration is required the pump is operated and delivers neat fuel into the choke tube. This overcomes the time lag that would otherwise occur in waiting for the fuel to be drawn from the main jet. The fuel in the float chamber is regulated at the correct height by a float which operates a needle valve. When the level drops the needle is lowered away from the entry orifice and fuel under pressure from the fuel pump enters. When the level rises the flow is shut off. The pump delivery potential is always greater than the maximum requirement from the carburettor.

4 Solex carburettor - removal, dismantling and replacement

1 The carburettor should not be dismantled without reason. Such reasons would be for cleaning or renewal of the float and needle valve assembly and, in rare circumstances, the jets. Partial dismantling would also be necessary for checking and setting the float chamber fuel level.
2 Disconnect the battery positive cable. (The earth, at the battery, is not sufficient).
3 Remove the air filter body completely.
4 Pull off the vacuum advance pipe which leads from the distributor.
5 Pull off the fuel pipe which leads from the fuel pump.
6 Disconnect the rocker cover oil fume rebreathing pipe.
7 Disconnect the throttle return spring, then pull off, it is a plastic snap fitting, the throttle link arm from the spindle arm. The rest of this fitting should remain on a plate which is part of the carburettor-to-manifold gasket. Disconnect the choke cable.
8 Unscrew all the hose clips which tighten the manifold heating hoses to the carburettor, at the carburettor and pull the hoses off at that end. There is little point in clamping the hoses to avoid loss of coolant - little escapes.
9 Remove the two base fixing nuts of the carburettor and lift it away. The exterior of the carburettor should be clinically clean before dismantling proceeds.
10 The first stage of dismantling should be to remove the screws holding the top to the base. Separate the two halves carefully and remove the paper gasket taking care to keep it from being damaged. It can be re-used.

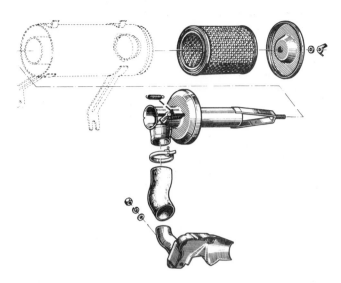

Fig. 3.2. R1177 (R12TS) carburettor air cleaner components

11 To clean out the float chamber, invert the carburettor body; the float complete with pivot pin will fall out. If it needs a little help to get it out do not under any circumstances strain it in such a way that the pin or bracket are bent. When the float is removed the bowl may be flushed out and sediment removed with a small brush.

12 The needle valve is screwed into the top cover and when taking it out note the washer mounted underneath it. The simplest way to check this for leaks is to try blowing through it. It should not be possible to do so when the plunger is lightly pushed in. If in doubt, then renew the assembly, as a leaking valve will result in an over-rich mixture with consequent loss of performance and increased fuel consumption.

13 The accelerator pump diaphragm may be examined when the four cover securing screws, cover and spring have been removed. Be careful not to damage the diaphragm. Renew it if there are signs of holes or cracks which may reduce its efficiency.

14 The main jet is situated behind a hexagonal headed plug in the base of the float chamber. This can of course be removed without taking the carburettor off the car. Remove the plug and then unscrew the jet from behind it with a screwdriver. The pilot jet is fixed similarly in the body but alongside the accelerator pump housing, except that it is on the opposite side. When cleaning these jets do not use anything other than air pressure. Any poking with wire could damage the fine tolerance bores and upset the fuel mixtures.

15 The air correction jet and emulsion tube is mounted vertically in the body of the carburettor by the side of the choke tube. This too may be unscrewed for cleaning. Blow through the passageway in the carburettor also when it is removed.

16 Before reassembly check that the float is undamaged and unpunctured. It can be checked by immersion in hot water.

17 The accelerator pump inspection tube may be inadvertently moved so check that the outlet points down in such a way that the jet of fuel cannot impinge on any part of the carburettor or open throttle on its way down to the inlet manifold.

18 If the throttle flap spindle should be very loose in its bearings in the main body of the carburettor then air may leak past and affect the air to fuel ratio of the mixture. In such cases the easiest remedy is a new carburettor. An alternative is to drill and fit bushes to suit but this needs some expertise and time.

19 Reassembly is a reversal of the dismantling procedure but the following points should be watched carefully. Do not forget the washer when replacing the needle valve. Make sure that the gasket between body and cover is correctly positioned. When refitting the accelerator pump cover, the screws should be tightened with the diaphragm centre pushed in. This means holding the operating lever out whilst the screws are tightened. Do not bend or distort the float arm when replacing it into the float chamber.

20 For the air and fuel screw see the next section. Never dismantle further than described here.

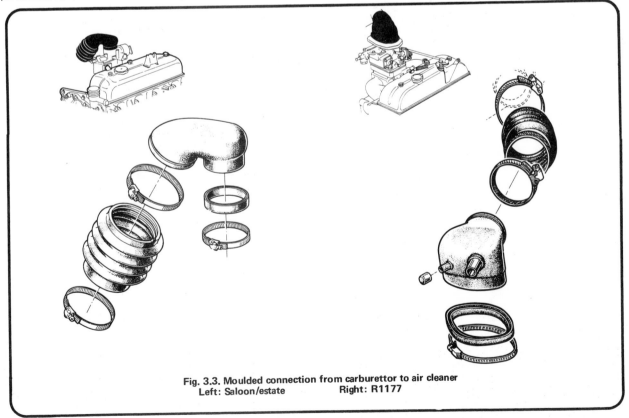

Fig. 3.3. Moulded connection from carburettor to air cleaner
Left: Saloon/estate   Right: R1177

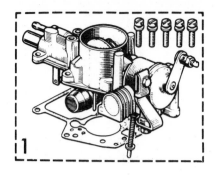

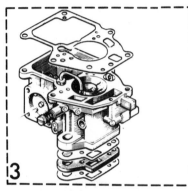

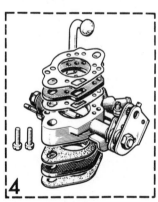

FIG. 3.4. SOLEX CARBURETTOR COMPONENTS SHOWN IN GROUPS WHICH ARE NORMALLY SUPPLIED AS 'COMPLETE' COMPONENTS

1 Body cover	4 Base and gaskets
2 Throttle lever	5 Accelerator diaphragm
3 Body	

FIG. 3.5. SOLEX CARBURETTOR ADJUSTMENTS AND LOCATIONS

1 & 2   Throttle stop screws: NOT TO BE ALTERED
a   Air compensator jet
k   Choke tube
l   Accelerator pump
Gg   Main jet
g   Idling jet

A   Air screw
B   Fuel screw

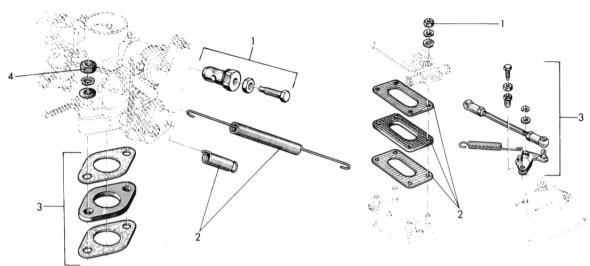

FIG. 3.6. GASKETS AND THROTTLE MECHANISM

Left: Saloon/estate
        1 Throttle cable clamp
        2 Return springs
        3 Gaskets
        4 Fixing nuts

Right: R1177
        1 Fixing nuts
        2 Gaskets
        3 Return spring and mechanism for throttle

5 Solex carburettor - adjustments

1   The less that is done with these carburettors, the better. If the car is running well, don't fiddle. On all accounts do NOT touch the throttle bleed screw nor the throttle butterfly adjustment screw. These are pre-set at the factory. DO NOT TOUCH THEM or the carburettor will never function properly.

2   The only adjustment readily available is that of idling speed. This carburettor is not fitted with an idling speed adjusting screw acting on the butterfly opening to obtain the desired airflow. It is replaced by an air screw (A) acting directly on the airflow by means of internal passages. It also has a fuel screw (B) acting on the air/fuel mixture.

3   To set the tickover turn the air screw (A) until the engine runs at a speed of 750 to 800 rpm. Then turn the fuel screw (B) until the engine runs at as high a speed as possible. Now turn the air screw (A) to bring the engine speed within 750 to 800 rpm.

4   Turn the fuel screw (B) until the engine runs at as high a speed as possible. Repeat the last 2 operations until the highest possible speed of the engine, when turning the fuel screw (B), is between 750 to 800 rpm.

5   Do not try to set the idling speed too low - particularly if the engine is not in the first flush of youth. You will waste hours trying to achieve the impossible.

6   The setting of the accelerator cable into the throttle operating arm is important if full throttle opening is to be possible and also if excessive strain is to be avoided. Obviously one wants to have the throttle flap fully open when the accelerator pedal is fully depressed. At the same time one does not want to have the throttle fully open and up to the stop before the pedal has been fully depressed, otherwise the pedal pressure will stretch the cable and put considerable strain on the bracket and spindle. With the accelerator cable end in position but unclamped, move the throttle lever round to the fully open position, up to the stop. Then let it come back so that there is a gap of 1 mm between the

stop and the lever. At the same time someone else should depress the accelerator pedal right to the floor. In this position the cable end may be tightened into position. Check the accelerator pedal movement to see that the gap is maintained when the pedal is pressed to the floor.

6 Weber carburettor (R1177)

1   The Weber 32 DIR21 fitted to the Renault 12TS is a twin progressive choke downdraught carburettor which has the same operating principle as the Solex variety. It is basically two single choke carburettors in one body, one choke of which is open at tick-over whilst the other only begins to open at heavier throttle loadings, activated by the first choke as it itself is nearing a fully open state. This facility allows for comparative economy at low speeds (operating on one choke) and extra performance when needed (both chokes operating). It has a manual operated cold starting strangler (choke) by a cable. This carburettor has a water heated manifold.

2   This carburettor is an expensive component. Consequently it is advised that under no circumstances should the carburettor be dismantled further than the removal of the float chamber/choke flaps cover, and this only to clean the float chamber and to check the level of the float. If you are certain that the carburettor is at fault, and not simply an adjustment or ignition fault then the carburettor must be removed from the car and taken to a good experienced Renault agency or a Weber agency. DO NOT attempt any home renovation - it will only make matters worse. (photos).

3   Removal of this carburettor is undertaken in exactly the same way as for the Solex. The carburettor is bolted down with four nuts instead of two.

4   The top cover of the carburettor is located by five screws. These should all be undone and then the cover lifted off. Make sure a new paper gasket is available. The float level and jet removal (only if absolutely necessary) should be undertaken in

the same way as for the Solex. Make sure you understand what you are doing first. Read that section thoroughly.

5   Carburettor adjustment is undertaken in exactly the same way as for the Solex using the appropriate adjusting screws. Read Section 5. (photo)

7   Fuel pump - removal and replacement

1   The fuel pump will need removing if it is to be dismantled for overhaul, the filter can be cleaned in situ. Disconnect the fuel lines on the inlet and outlet sides by pulling off the connector pipes on both sides.

2   Undo the two nuts, one is a nut on a stud the other is a setscrew, holding the pump flange to the crankcase, and take the pump off. Keep the spacer and gaskets together and do not discard them. If necessary blank off the fuel line from the tank to prevent loss of fuel.

3   Replacement is a reversal of the removal procedure. Make sure that the total thickness of gaskets and spacer is the same as came off. Check that the fuel line connections are not leaking after starting the engine.

4   It may be necessary to prime the carburettor if a fuel pump has been removed, or if you run out of petrol.

8   Fuel pump - dismantling, inspection and reassembly

1   First clean the pump exterior thoroughly and mark the edges of the two halves of the body. (photo)

2   Unscrew the top dome retaining screw and remove the dome, sealing ring and filter gauze. (photos)

3   It should be noted that some pumps cannot be dismantled further and will have to be renewed. Others, indicated by eight screws being visible around their diaphragm can be. Proceed as follows. Remove the eight screws and washers holding the two halves of the pump together and the top half may then be lifted off.

4   The diaphragm and pushrod should be removed next but you will have to remove the pump lever and its spindle to release it. This is done by releasing one of the spindle's circlips. This can prove to be very fiddly but with patience and a strong blunt penknife blade the circlip can be 'peeled' off. Push the spindle through and pull out the lever. Retrieve the lever spring. Lift out the diaphragm and its rod carefully. This spindle is usually known as the rocker arm pivot pin.

5   If there are signs of wear in the rocker arm pivot pin, and rocker arm and link bushes then they should be renewed.

6   The valve assemblies should only be removed from the upper body if renewal is necessary. They are staked into the body and are destroyed when levered out.

6.2a The two chokes of the Weber carburettor with the top cover removed

6.2b The float chamber fuel filter (Weber)

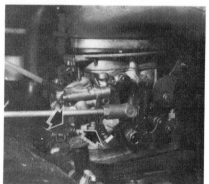
6.5 The left arrow shows the volume control screw. The right arrow shows the speed control screw

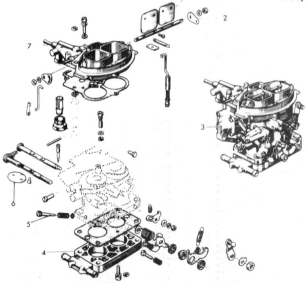

FIG. 3.7. WEBER CARBURETTOR COMPONENTS (R1177)

1 Top butterflies	3 Complete carburettor showing accelerator pump diaphragm	4 Carburettor base
2 Spindle		5 Fuel screw

6   Lower butterflies
7   Carburettor cover

7 Examine the diaphragm for signs of cracking or perforation and renew if necessary.

8 Overhaul kits are available for these pumps and are supplied with a new diaphragm, valves and sealing rings. Check the manufacture of the pump first.

9 When fitting new valve assemblies to the body, first fit the seating washers and then place the valves, making sure that they are the correct way up according to inlet and outlet. The body will have to be restaked at six (different) places round the edge so that the assemblies are firmly held in their positions. If this is not done properly and leakage occurs between the valve assembly and the seating ring the pump will not operate efficiently.

10 To replace the diaphragm and lever arm it will be necessary to place the diaphragm spring in the body of the pump. Then the diaphragm and its rod. Press the diaphragm spring down and fit the spring, push in the lever (the right way up) and connect over the top of the machined stop on the rod. Push in the rocker arm pivot pin and push through the lever. Replace the circlip on the pivot pin. Always use a new circlip.

11 Fit the upper half of the pump body and line up the mating marks. In order to assemble the two halves and the diaphragm properly push the rocker arm upwards so that the diaphragm is drawn level. Then place the six or eight screws in position lightly. It is best if the base of the pump is held in a vice whilst the rocker arm is pushed right up to bring the diaphragm to the bottom of its stroke. A short piece of tube over the rocker arm will provide easy leverage. In this position the screws should be tightened evenly and alternately.

12 Refit the individual pump top halves - filters, covers and sealing rings - fit new where possible.

13 When the pump is reassembled the suction and delivery pressure can be felt at the inlet and outlet ports when the rocker arm is operated. Be careful not to block the inlet port completely when testing suction. If the rocker arm were to be operated strongly and the inlet side was blocked the diaphragm could be damaged.

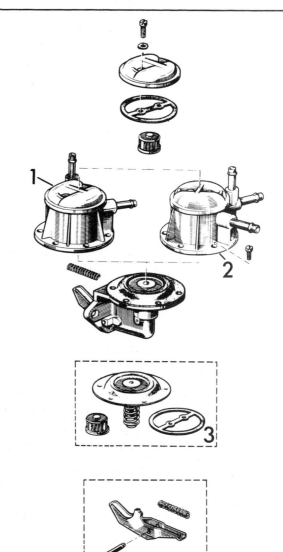

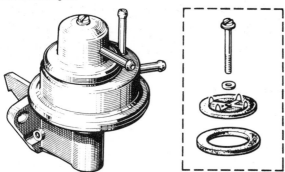

FIG.3.8. NON REPAIRABLE R1177 FUEL PUMP

FIG. 3.9. SALOON/ESTATE FUEL PUMP COMPONENTS

1   Early type cover (inlet/outlet)
2   Later type cover (inlet/outlet/recirculator)
3   Diaphragm kit
4   Lever arm kit

8.1 The fuel pump has a gasket

8.2a Clean the mating faces

8.2b Wash out the gauze filter

9 Fuel tank and fuel gauge sender unit

1   The fuel tank of all models is located in the rear of the car and must be removed upwards through the boot (saloons) or floor deck (estate). If damage has taken place or the tank leaks, try to run it empty before removal; do not try to unscrew the drain plug - it won't!

2   Remove the floor covering. Unscrew the fixing screws and remove. Remove the filler cap. On the estate disconnect the breather pipe and loosen the hose clips on the filler pipe. Loosen them all and then pull the lower hose off the inlet pipe. Disconnect the sender unit feed line.

3   Lift the front edge of the tank, prop it, and pull off the two petrol pipes. Now wriggle the tank away from the inlet hose and lift away.

4   If the tank is persistently contaminating the fuel because of deterioration of the interior, flush it out as best as possible with fuel and give consideration to fitting a line filter in the flexible pipe just before the petrol pump. It is much cheaper than a new tank and is easily fitted and readily available from accessory shops.

5   The fuel gauge sender unit is a twist fit to the top of the tank and can, of course, be removed separately with the tank installed. It cannot be repaired, but must be renewed. Failure at the fuel gauge is usually a sender unit fault.

6   If the fuel gauge fails to give a reading with the ignition on or reads 'FULL' all the time, then a check must be made to see if the fault is in the gauge, sender unit, or wire in between.

7   Turn the ignition on and disconnect the wire from the fuel tank sender unit. Check that the fuel gauge needle is on the empty mark. To check if the fuel gauge is in order now earth the fuel tank sender unit wire. This should send the needle to the full mark.

8   If the fuel gauge is in order check the wiring for leaks or loose connections. If none can be found, then the sender unit will be at fault and must be renewed.

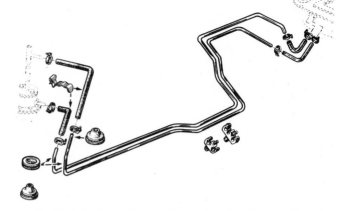

Fig. 3.11. Fuel pipes from tank to carburettor showing return flow recirculating pipe on later models

10 Inlet/exhaust manifold

1   The removal and replacement of the inlet/exhaust manifold has been described in Chapter 1, during engine removal.

2   Several types of inlet/exhaust manifold have been used, depending on the engine. The R1177 fitment carries a different fitting of carburettor but is otherwise very similar to that of other models. (photo)

3   The UK standard models are fitted with a cast iron integral inlet/exhaust manifold whilst the R1177 has an aluminium inlet manifold bolted to a cast iron exhaust manifold. A starter motor heat shield is fitted on two studs cast into the exhaust manifold.

4   No special checks or instructions are applicable, simply look for cracks and fractures.

5   Always obtain the proper gasket and make sure the manifold mounting studs are fitted the correct way round - short thread inwards. (photo)

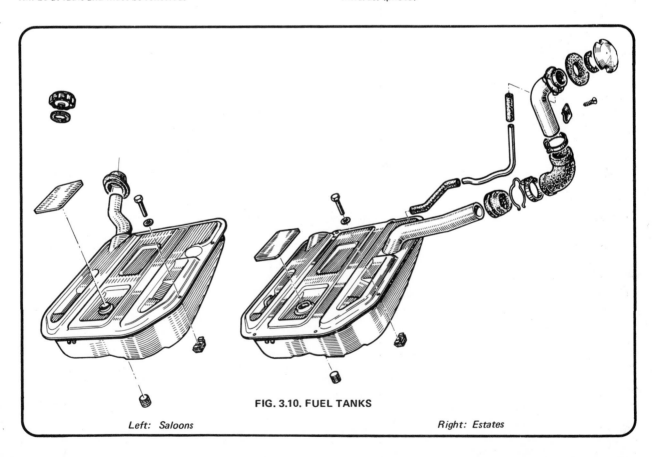

FIG. 3.10. FUEL TANKS

Left: Saloons   *Right: Estates*

10.2 The screwdriver shows both heater pipes on the inlet manifold

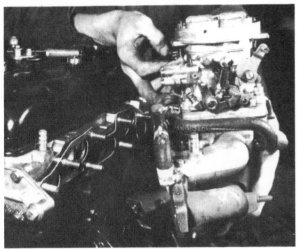

10.5 The inlet/exhaust manifold gasket exposed

11 Exhaust system

1   The exhaust system is conventional. It is wise only to use original type exhaust clamps and proprietary made systems.

2   When any one section of the exhaust system needs renewal it indicates that the rest of the system is suspect. Check this, but never 'patch' any section. Renew if in doubt.

3   It is most important when fitting exhausts that the twists and contours are carefully followed and that each connecting joint overlaps the correct distance. Any stresses or strain imparted, in order to force the system to fit the hanger brackets, will result in early fractures and failures.

4   When fitting a new part or a complete system it is well worth removing ALL the system from the car and cleaning up all the joints so that they fit together easily. The time spent struggling with obstinate joints whilst flat on your back under the car is eliminated and the likelihood of distorting or even breaking a section is greatly reduced. Do not waste a lot of time trying to undo rusted and corroded clamps and bolts. Cut them off. New ones will be required anyway if they are that bad.

5   The critical point is the lip sealing joint of exhaust manifold-to-silencer top pipe. Only finally tighten this clamp when the silencer and tail pipe are bracketed up to a point which is very nearly tight. Tighten this clamp hard and run the engine to check for leaking. If all is well tighten the two other points finally. (photos)

6   Do not try to fit different brackets - this system is well mounted and normally trouble-free.

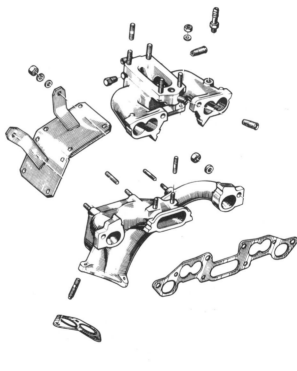

Fig. 3.13. R1177 Heat shield and separate inlet and exhaust manifold

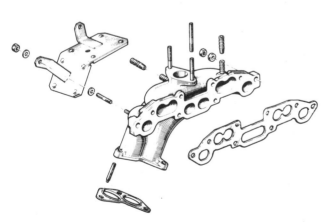

Fig. 3.12. Saloon/estate heat shield and inlet/exhaust manifold

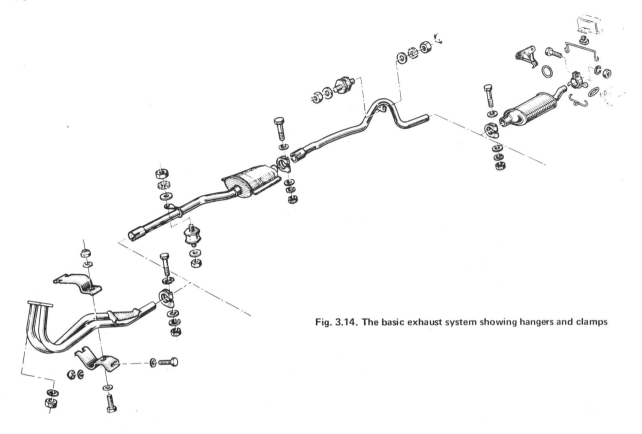

Fig. 3.14. The basic exhaust system showing hangers and clamps

11.5a Below the heat shield

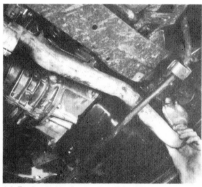

11.5b Loosen the anti-roll bar to remove the down pipe

11.5c The first clamp.....

11.5d ..... the second clamp .....

11.5e ..... and the final bends and silencer

12   Throttle pedal, cable and choke cable

1   The throttle pedal pivots in its centre - as it is pressed down by the foot it pulls on the throttle cable and activates the carburettor. The pedal is fixed to a 'captive' plate on the bulkhead by two screws set diagonally across the rectangular pivot plate. It pivots on two small bushes. If wear takes place, enough to make very sloppy action, the whole pedal and plate will have to be renewed.

2   Disconnect the throttle cable at the top of the pedal by removing the split pin and pushing out the fulcrum pin. Unscrew the pivot plate and remove the pedal. Locate the 'captive' plate and retain for refitting.

3   With the cable disconnected at the pedal, locate the bulkhead end of the throttle cable under the bonnet and remove the circlip from the outer cable boot at the bulkhead. Loosen the adjustment at the carburettor (rocker cover on R1177) and disconnect the inner cable, then the outer cable, from their connections. Pull the cable through to the inside of the car.

4   Only complete inner/outer cables are available as a spare part. Obtain the correct cable. Refitment of the throttle cable and the pedal are an exact reverse procedure. Check, when fitted, that the cable operates through its full travel, smoothly and lightly.

5   The choke cable is an integral component with the choke knob. The choke is held into the facia with a large spring wire clip. Once this is removed from below and the cable is disconnected from the carburettor in a similar fashion to the throttle cable, the whole assembly can be pulled through into the car interior.

6   To replace, simply feed it back through. Make sure there are no severe kinks and that it operates through its full travel.

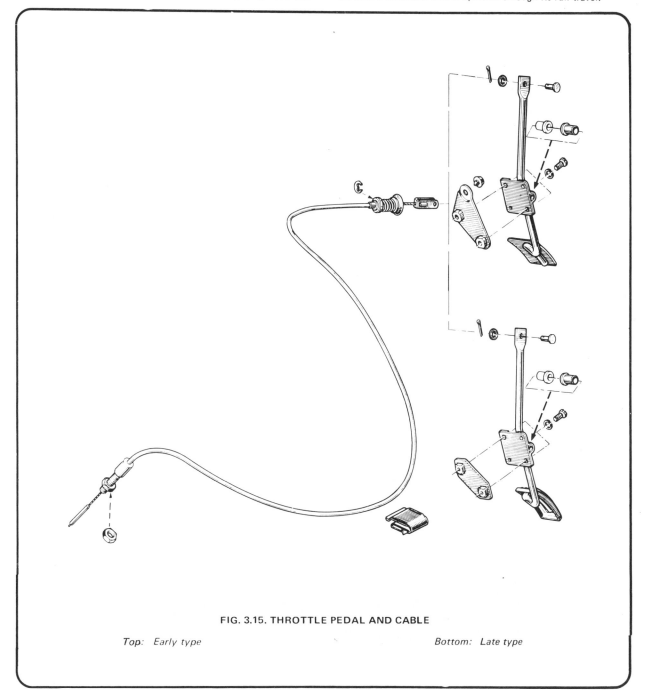

FIG. 3.15. THROTTLE PEDAL AND CABLE

Top: Early type   *Bottom: Late type*

13 Fault diagnosis

Unsatisfactory engine performance and excessive fuel consumption are not necessarily the fault of the fuel system or carburettor. In fact they more commonly occur as a result of ignition faults. Before acting on the fuel system it is necessary to check the ignition system first. Even though a fault may lie in the fuel system it will be difficult to trace unless the ignition is correct.

The table below, therefore, assumes that the ignition system is in order.

Symptom	Reason/s	Remedy
Smell of petrol when engine is stopped	Leaking fuel lines or unions	Repair or renew as necessary.
	Leaking fuel tank	Fill fuel tank to capacity and examine carefully at seams, unions and filler pipe connections. Repair as necessary.
Smell of petrol when engine is idling	Leaking fuel line unions between pump and carburettor	Check line and unions and tighten or repair
	Overflow of fuel from float chamber due to wrong level setting or ineffective needle valve or punctured float	Check fuel level setting and condition of float and needle valve and renew if necessary.
Excessive fuel consumption for reasons not covered by leaks or float chamber	Worn jets	Renew jets
	Choke stuck	Check and free mechanism.
Difficult starting, uneven running, lack of power, cutting out	One or more jets blocked or restricted	Dismantle and clean out float chamber and jets.
	Float chamber fuel level too low or needle valve sticking	Dismantle and check fuel level and needle valve.
	Fuel pump not delivering sufficient fuel	Check pump delivery and clean or repair as required.
	Intake manifold gasket leaking, or manifold fractured	Check tightness of mounting nuts and inspect manifold.

Chapter 4 Ignition system

Contents

Specifications

Spark plugs

AC type (810-02 and 810-97 engines)	43F
AC type (810-05 and 810-06 engines)	42 FS
Champion (all engines) ,..	L87Y
Eyquem-Renault (810-02 and 810-97 engines)	705S
Electrode gap (all)	0.6 mm (0.024 in)

Coil ... ... Ducellier 3920 (with Ducellier distributor)

Distributors

	Dwell angle	Static timing	Static timing (pulley)*	Static timing (flywheel)*
Ducellier 4223-R251	54 to 60°	0 ± 1°	0 ± 1 mm	0 ± 2 mm
Ducellier 4387-R280	54 to 60°	0 ± 1°	–	0 ± 2 mm
Ducellier 4388-R280	54 to 60°	0 ± 1°	–	0 ± 2 mm
Femsa R251	54 to 60°	0 ± 1°	0 ± 1 mm	0 ± 2 mm
Ducellier 4352-A96	54 to 60°	5 to 7° BTDC	6 to 8 mm	10 to 14 mm
Femsa R268	54 to 60°	5 to 7° BTDC	6 to 8 mm	10 to 14 mm
Ducellier 4476-R280	57 to 60°	12 to 13° BTDC	13 to 15 mm	–
Ducellier 4477-R280 ... ...·	57 to 60°	12 to 13° BTDC	13 to 15 mm	–

* These dimensions round the periphery of the pulley or flywheel will normally have been marked in production.

Firing order	1 3 4 2 (No. 1 at flywheel end)
Contact points gap	0.4 mm to 0.5 mm (0.015 in to 0.020 in)
Condenser capacity	25 mfd
Timing mark location	Notch on crankshaft pulley or pointer on block or flywheel mark

For valve timing - see Specifications in Chapter 1

General note:

Development and changes were continuous and often unpublished in this area. With the advent of anti-pollution engines this development intensified - if in any doubt contact a franchised Renault agent who will be able to advise on correct specification.

1 General description

Ignition of the fuel/air mixture in the Renault engine is conventional in that one spark plug per cylinder is used and the high voltage required to produce the spark across the plug electrodes is supplied from a coil (transformer) which converts the volts from the supply battery to the several thousand necessary to produce a spark that will jump a gap under the conditions of heat and pressure that obtain in the cylinder.

In order that the spark will occur at each plug in the correct order and at precisely the correct moment the low voltage current is built up (into the condenser) and abruptly discharged through the coil when the circuit is broken by the interrupter switch (contact points). This break in the low voltage circuit, and the simultaneous high voltage impulse generated from the coil, is directed through the selector switch (rotor arm) to one of four leads which connect to the spark plugs. The condenser contact points and rotor arm are all contained in and operated at the distributor.

Due to different spark timing requirements under certain engine conditions (of varying speed or load) the distributor also has an automatic advance device (advancing the spark means that it comes earlier in relation to the piston position). In the Renault engine this device is operated by vacuum from the induction manifold. When the vacuum is low, for example when the throttle is almost closed at low engine speeds, the ignition is retarded. It advances when the throttle opens and vacuum is high. The low tension (battery) voltage of all cars is 12 volts.

2 Special maintenance

There is nothing of pecularity to the Renault 12 in the way of special maintenance for the ignition system. Normal maintenance and safety measures will ensure the efficiency of the system. Perhaps however it is important that all wiring and contacts are always in good condition. Always have the proper wiring clips in use and take no short cuts. Finding the relevant failed wiring in the system can take a long time.

3 Distributor - contact points - adjustment

1 Remove the distributor cap by unclipping the two leaf springs, one each side of the distributor.
2 Pull off the rotor arm from the cam spindle. (photo)
3 First examine the points by carefully levering them apart with a small screwdriver or something similar. If the faces of the circular contacts are pitted or rough then they cannot be properly set and should be removed for renewal or cleaning up.
4 If the faces are clean then turn the engine so that the moving arm of the breaker rests with the follower on one of the four high points on the cam. The engine can be turned by engaging a gear and moving the car, or by using the starting handle.
5 Select a feeler blade (0.4 mm or 0.5 mm [0.015 to 0.020 in]) and place it between the points. If the gap is too great, slacken the fixed point locking screw and move the plate to alter the gap. If the gap is too small the feeler blade may still fit between the points as the spring loaded arm can simply move back. When setting them, therefore, the feeler gauge blade should only be a very light touch on each contact face. (photos)
6 Lock the fixed plate screw and recheck the gap. Replace the rotor arm making sure that the lug in the rotor recess is fully engaged in the slot on the cam spindle.

Check the inside of the distributor cap before replacing it and verify that the four contacts are clean and the centre carbon brush is intact and moves freely.

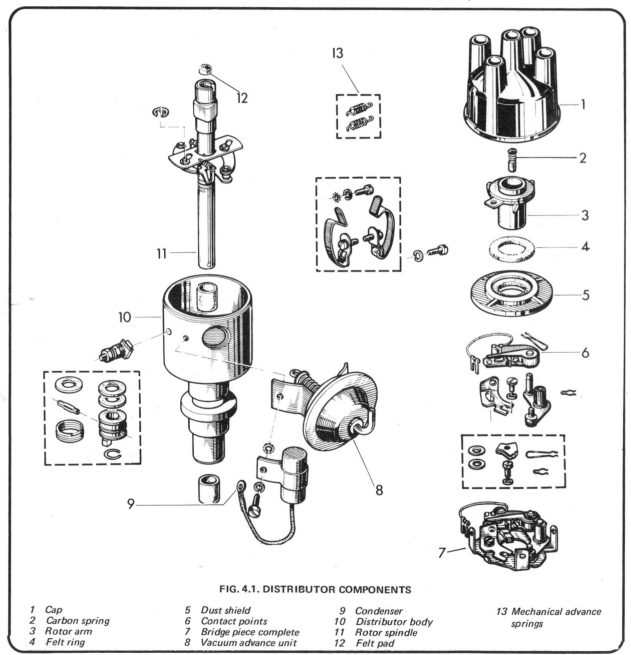

FIG. 4.1. DISTRIBUTOR COMPONENTS

1 Cap	5 Dust shield	9 Condenser
2 Carbon spring	6 Contact points	10 Distributor body
3 Rotor arm	7 Bridge piece complete	11 Rotor spindle
4 Felt ring	8 Vacuum advance unit	12 Felt pad

13 Mechanical advance springs

4 Distributor - contact points - removal and replacement

1 The contact points will need removal if the surfaces are bad enough to require renewal or refacing. Generally it is best to renew the contacts completely.

2 Remove the distributor cap, rotor arm as described in the previous Section and remove the fixed plate locking screw.

3 Remove the small circlip on the terminal post which also secures the end of the spring and lift off the washer. Undo until loose the small nut which secures the lead to the condenser and the spring of the contact breaker arm. Lift upwards the spring contact from the pivot post. Now remove the fixed contact locking screw and lift out this contact. It is wise even for changing contact points to have a set of metric distributor spanners to avoid the use of pliers. (photos)

4 Replacement is the EXACT reversal of the removal sequence. Do not get anything muddled and take your time.

5 Distributor - condenser - testing, removal and replacement

1 A faulty condenser causes interruptions in the ignition circuit or total failure. Elaborate testing methods are pointless as the item is cheap to renew.

2 If the contact points become pitted after a relatively small mileage (under 1000) and if starting is difficult then it is a good idea to renew the condenser when replacing the points. Another way to check is to remove the distributor cap, rotor arm and dust shield and turn the engine so that the points are closed. Then switch on the ignition and open the points using an insulated screwdriver. There should be a small blue spark visible but if the condenser is faulty there will be a fat blue spark.

3 The condenser is external to the workings of the distributor fitted to this engine. Using the correct spanner undo the lead from the condenser to the fixing post on the side of the distributor. Remove the body of the condenser from the other fixing post which also holds one of the distributor cap clips. Fit a new one in reverse order.

6 Distributor - removal and replacement

1 The distributor will need removal if there are indications that the drive spindle is a sloppy fit in the bushes (causing contact gap setting difficulties) or if it is to be dismantled and thoroughly cleaned and checked. It should be also removed before the oil pump is taken out.

2 Before removing the distributor it is helpful to prevent future confusion if the engine is positioned with No. 1 piston at TDC on the firing stroke. This can be done by noting the position of the No. 1 plug lead in the cap and then turning the engine to TDC so that the rotor is adjacent to the No. 1 plug position in the cap. (The cap, of course, will be removed to do this). For details see Section 8 - 'Ignition timing'.

3 Detach the plug leads from the spark plugs and the coil HT lead from the distributor cap or coil. Remove the cap by unclipping the retaining spring clips at each side.

4 Undo the LT lead at the coil - this could be a screw or push-on connector.

5 Before undoing the vertical bolt through the clamping baseplate note the position of its edge nearest to the centre of the distributor and its opposite end on the cylinder block. Use a scriber to make both. This helps to replace the distributor in its 'correct' place. Obviously if a new distributor is going to be fitted it does not matter, but wait until the distributor is away from the engine.

6 Lift the distributor up and out, the locating flange and sealing ring should come with it. Before proceeding any further, note the position of the eccentric slot in the end of the drive shaft inside the distributor mounting recess in the block. This will give a firm timing reference if the oil pump is to be removed.

7 Replacement is a reversal of the removal procedure. Check that the rubber sealing ring between the flange and block is in good condition. Line up the eccentric tongue on the distributor shaft with the slot in the drive shaft and when the sleeve of the body is being pushed down be prepared to rotate the shaft either way a little so as to engage the drive.

8 Upon camshaft removal and replacement this slotted drive gear exactly the same position from which it was removed. See also Chapter 1, Section 53.

7 Distributor - dismantling, inspection and reassembly

1 If the distributor is causing trouble with the ignition system it is often a good idea to fit a completely new unit. Without the proper test equipment it is difficult to diagnose whether or not the centrifugal advance mechanism is performing as it should. However, play in the shaft bushes can be detected by removing the rotor arm and gripping the end and trying to move it sideways. If there is any movement then it means that the cam cannot accurately control the contact points gap. This must receive attention.

2 With the distributor removed take off the rotor, condenser and contact points as described in Section 4. Release the vacuum advance pipe - it is a push-on rubber tube.

3 Remove the felt oil-soak washer from the top of the cam.

4 Remove the contact point baseplate by removing totally the two distributor cap clip fixing setscrews through the side of the distributor body and the condenser/contact spring fixing point. At the same time the vacuum advance mechanism side fixings will be released. Now remove the little circlip above the baseplate from the vacuum advance arm and unhook the inner end of the vacuum advance mechanism. Be gentle so as not to damage the vacuum advance spring.

5 Pull upwards the contact points baseplate and remove.

6 Remove the shaft circlip and washers at the bottom end of the distributor by 'peeling' it off with a penknife.

7 Pull up through the body of the distributor the shaft with the automatic advance mechanism still intact.

8 Remove the centrifugal advance mechanism springs gently. Do not twist or distort them.

9 It is possible to go further still in the dismantling of the shaft and the advance mechanism by driving out the very small through-pin which holds the cam onto the shaft and extracting the circlips which hold the advance weights onto this shaft. This is not worth doing under any circumstances for if you have reached this stage of replacement, it is only worth replacing the whole distributor. These individual parts may well not be available.

10 To renew the bush first press or drive out the old one from inside the distributor body. Before fitting a new bush it should be soaked in engine oil for at least 24 hours - or hot oil for 2 hours - before fitting. It is made of sintered copper/iron and retains its lubricant due to porosity. The new bush should be pushed in from the lower end. When the shoulder part reaches the body the bush should be pressed in with a shouldered mandrel in a press or vice. Any attempt to drive it in - even using blocks of wood - will almost certainly cause it to break up. The bottom and top of the bush should be flush with the distributor body. When fitted the bush should be drilled through in line with the shaft oil drain hole in the body. Make sure there are no burrs or loose metal particles anywhere in the bush. Refit the shaft, lubricate with engine oil. If it is tight it will need 'running in' by hand until there are no traces of binding. The bush must not be reamed as this will impair its self-lubricating properties. Do not forget the distance collar on the shaft under the action plate.

11 Reassembly of the distributor is a reversal of the dismantling process. Do not stretch the centrifugal springs. Smear the contact breaker baseplate with a thin film of oil or grease between it and the moving plate.

3.2 The rotor pulls straight off

3.5a The feeler blade sits between the contact points

3.5b The fixed point locating screw

4.3a The felt pad is shown in the centre of the shaft. Note the spring clip

4.3b Lift the moving contact off its pedestal

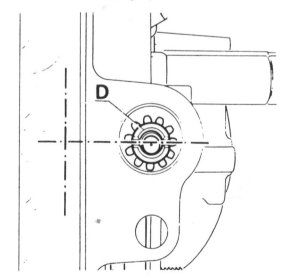
Fig. 4.2. Distributor drive pinion position (No. 1 cylinder at firing position, slot at right angles to centre line of engine, largest offset (D) towards the clutch)

8 Ignition timing

1 It is necessary to time the ignition when it has been upset due to overhauling or dismantling which may have altered the relationship between the position of the pistons and the moment at which the distributor delivers the spark. Also, if mal-adjustments have affected the engine performance it is very desirable, although not always essential, to reset the timing starting from scratch. In the following procedures it is assumed that the intention is to obtain standard performance from the standard engine which is in reasonable condition. It is also assumed that the recommended fuel octane rating is used. It is possible today to have an engine checked on special equipment designed to indicate where different faults may be. These instruments are excellent for indicating what may be wrong with your engine in a variety of areas. They do not, however, compute the full combination of settings needed to get the best possible performance from your particular engine as it is. The final check for ignition timing depends solely on the performance of the car on the road in all the variety of conditions that it meets.

2 The static or datum timing is getting the spark to arrive at a particular position on the crankshaft. (See Section 1). Most manufacturers stick to the convention of using No. 1 cylinder for this adjustment and the Renault is no exception. No. 1 cylinder is at the flywheel end of the engine. The timing marks are either on the crankshaft pulley where there is a notch which aligns with a plate on the timing cover, or on the flywheel which aligns with a mark on the clutch housing. If the engine is turned clockwise, with the starting handle, TDC on No. 1 piston will be achieved when the pointer is the correct distance from the mark on the crankshaft pulley. Do this and then look at the distributor cap and see at which position the HT lead from No. 1 spark plug connects. Then remove the cap and see whether the top of the rotor arm is facing the No. 1 plug contact. If it is, good! If not then the engine must be turned another complete revolution to the TDC mark again. The rotor arm should then be in the correct position. Should the rotor arm still be way out, check whether the distributor body can be rotated enough to compensate by slackening the clamp and trying it. It may be possible, with alterations to plug lead lengths.

3 Now the engine should be set at the correct static advance position.

4 As discussed in the opening section, the spark is produced when the contact points in the LT circuit open. It is now necessary to slacken the distributor clamping screw so that the body of the distributor may be turned (whilst the rotor spindle stays still). The distributor should now be turned slightly, one way or the other, so that the contact points are just about to open. The contact gap MUST be set correctly. As it is difficult to see exactly when the points are just opening, a means of doing this electrically is necessary. Use a continuity tester or a 12 volt bulb and a jumper lead. If the latter is used, put one lead to the terminal where the coil LT lead joins the distributor and the other to a good earth on the engine block. With the ignition switched on the bulb will now light. Turn the body of the distributor anticlockwise until the light just goes out. Then, lightly holding the rotor arm with clockwise pressure, turn the body clockwise again until the light just comes on again. Then tighten the clamping screw. If desired the correctness of the setting can be checked with a stroboscopic timing light but such a device is not essential for accurate setting of the static timing.

5 The performance of the engine should now be checked by road testing. Make any adjustments by loosening the clamp screw and moving the distributor body very slightly to the right to advance it. Lock it again and retest. If the performance is worse repeat the procedure but turn to the left to retard. After a little time going one way or the other, in very small progressions, the 'optimum' timing will result.

6 Should the owner wish, he may check the centrifugal advance of the distributor. For this he will need to employ an accurate tachometer and a stroboscopic timing light. If the distributor

was seriously wrong then the performance of the car would be noticeably affected. Should the distributor be suspected of malfunction in this respect it would be best to get it tested on the specialised equipment available at some garages, or simply fit a new one. Often the cost of thorough checking (which involves removing the distributor if it is to be done very precisely) is not far short of the cost of a new unit.

7 It is possible to make a quick check of the vacuum advance but apart from this, the same points from paragraph 6 of this Section apply. To check, replace the vacuum advance pipe from the carburettor and suck the tube - with the distributor cap released. You should be able to see movement of the vacuum spring. If no movement occurs then it is malfunctioning and should be checked further.

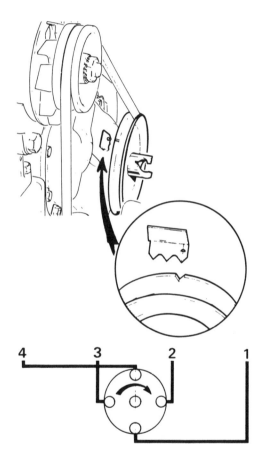

Fig. 4.3. Location of timing pointer on cylinder block and cut in pulley. Rotation of distributor and positions of spark plug fixing relative to the distributor

9 Spark plugs and HT leads

1 The spark plugs should be cleaned and their gaps reset every 3,000 miles (4,500 km).

2 The plugs can be cleaned and regapped once, and the next time it is due they will have to be renewed. It is suggested that two sets of plugs are used, so the new second set can be fitted, and then the old ones cleaned and reset at leisure.

3 The plugs should be cleaned by sand blasting. Then the remnants of sand should be knocked out of the plugs with a clean air blast, whilst the plugs are gently tapped with a hammer on the side of the body. Finally the threads should be wiped clean.

4 The gaps should be set to a clearance 0.024 inch (0.06 mm). It is difficult to get a normal feeler into the gap, so ideally a wire feeler should be used. The gaps are set by bending the side electrodes. Under no circumstances must any pressure be put on the central electrode, lest the porcelain insulator nose be cracked, and later drop a chip into the engine.

5 The HT leads and their connections at both ends should always be clean and dry and, as far as possible, neatly arranged away from each other and nearby metallic parts which could cause premature shorting in weak insulation. The metal connections at the ends should be a firm and secure fit and free from any signs of corrosive deposits. If any lead shows signs of cracking or chafing of the insulation it should be renewed. Remember that radio interference suppression is required when renewing any leads.

NOTE: It is advisable when removing spark plugs from this engine to use a fully cranked 'short' spark plug remover. Be especially careful when refitting plugs to do so without force and screw them up as far as possible by hand first. Do not overtighten. The aluminium head does not take kindly to thread crossing and extra force. The proprietary non-cranked plug caps should always be used to ease fitting and to ensure against HT lead shorting.

10 Coil

1 The coil needs an equal amount of attention to the rest of the ignition system. Testing the coil is dealt with in Section 12.

2 The coil is easily removed by loosening the right hand mounting stud nut, then the left hand one. It can then be swung in a clockwise direction on the right hand stud and lifted upwards. Its actual mounting plate can remain on the cylinder block. Make sure all the leads are removed.

3 To replace with a new unit, unscrew the old coil clamp tightening bolt and remove and place it on it approximately the same position on the new coil and refit to the block. Make sure you have a replacement coil of the correct voltage and connector type.

11 Ignition/starter switch

1 All vehicles are fitted with a switch which is incorporated in the steering column lock. The switch can be replaced without removing the locking device.

2 Disconnect the battery. Remove the steering wheel and then the two lighting switch covers.

3 Disconnect the terminal wires recording their position.

4 Turn the key to the 'Garage' position. Withdraw it.

5 Unscrew the fixing screw, press down the retaining clip with a small screwdriver and push the switch up and out. The switch can be withdrawn from the body by removing the two fixing screws.

6 Replacement is a reversal of the removal procedure but make sure everything is located properly.

12 Ignition faults - symptoms, reasons and remedies

Engine troubles normally associated with, and usually caused by, faults in the ignition system are:
a) Failure to start when the engine is turned
b) Uneven running due to misfiring or mistiming
c) Smooth running at low engine revolutions but misfiring when under load or accelerating or at high constant revolutions
d) Smooth running at higher revolutions and misfiring or cutting-out at low speeds.

a) First check that all wiring is properly connected and dry. If the engine fails to catch when the starter is operated do not continue for more than 5 or 6 short burst attempts or the battery will start to get tired and the problem made worse. Remove the spark plug lead from a plug and turn the engine again holding the lead (by the insulation!) about ¼ inch from the side of the engine block. A spark should jump the gap audibly and visibly. If it does then the plugs are at fault or the static timing is very seriously adrift. If both are good, however, then there must be a fuel supply fault, so go on to that.

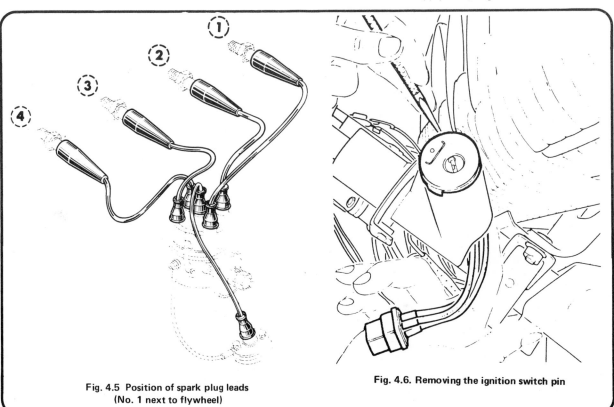

Fig. 4.5 Position of spark plug leads (No. 1 next to flywheel)

Fig. 4.6. Removing the ignition switch pin

Measuring plug gap. A feeler gauge of the correct size (see ignition system specifications) should have a slight 'drag' when slid between the electrodes. Adjust gap if necessary

Adjusting plug gap. The plug gap is adjusted by bending the earth electrode inwards, or outwards, as necessary until the correct clearance is obtained. Note the use of the correct tool

Normal. Grey-brown deposits lightly coated core nose. Gap increasing by around 0.001 in (0.025 mm) per 1000 miles (1600 km). Plugs ideally suited to engine and engine in good condition

Carbon fouling. Dry, black, sooty deposits. Will cause weak spark and eventually misfire. Fault: over-rich fuel mixture. Check: carburettor mixture settings, float level and jet sizes; choke operation and cleanliness of air filter. Plugs can be re-used after cleaning

Oil fouling. Wet, oily deposits. Will cause weak spark and eventually misfire. Fault: worn bores/piston rings or valve guides; sometimes occurs (temporarily) during running-in period. Plugs can be re-used after thorough cleaning

Overheating. Electrodes have glazed appearance, core nose very white - few deposits. Fault: plug overheating. Check: plug value, ignition timing, fuel octane rating (too low) and fuel mixture (too weak). Discard plugs and cure fault immediately

Electrode damage. Electrodes burned away; core nose has burned, glazed appearance. Fault: initial pre-ignition. Check: as for 'Overheating' but may be more severe. Discard plugs and remedy fault before piston or valve damage occurs

Split core nose (may appear initially as a crack). Damage is self-evident, but cracks will only show after cleaning. Fault: pre-ignition or wrong gap-setting technique. Check: ignition timing, cooling system, fuel octane rating (too low) and fuel mixture (too weak). Discard plugs, rectify fault immediately

If no spark is obtained at the end of a plug lead detach the coil HT lead from the centre of the distributor cap and hold that near the block to try and find a spark. If you now get one, then there is something wrong between the centre terminal of the distributor cap and the end of the plug lead. Check the cap itself for damage or damp, the 4 terminal lugs for signs of corrosion, the centre carbon brush in the top (is it jammed?) and the rotor arm.

If no spark comes from the coil HT lead check nect that the contact breaker points are clean and that the gap is correct. A quick check can be made by turning the engine so that the points are closed. Then switch on the ignition and open the points with an insulated screwdriver. There should be a small visible spark and, once again, if the coil HT lead is held near the block at the same time a proper HT spark should occur. If there is a big fat spark at the points but none at the HT lead then the condenser is done for and should be renewed.

If neither of these things happen then the next step in this tale of woe is to see if there is any current (12 volts) reaching the coil (+ terminal). (One could check this at the distributor, but by going back to the input side of the coil a longer length of possible fault line is bracketed and could save time).

With a 12 volt bulb and piece of wire suitably connected (or of course a voltmeter if you have one handy) connect between the + or SW terminal of the coil and earth and switch on the ignition. No light means no volts so the fault is between the battery and the coil via the ignition switch. This is moving out of the realms of just ignition problems - the electrical system is becoming involved in general. So to get home to bed get a piece of wire and connect the + terminal of the coil to the + terminal on the battery and see if sparks occur at the HT leads once more.

If there is current reaching the coil then the coil itself or the wire from its - terminal to the distributor is at fault. Check the — or CB terminal with a bulb with the ignition switched on. If it fails to light then the coil is faulty in its LT windings and needs renewal.

b) Uneven running and misfiring should first be checked by seeing that all leads, particularly HT, are dry and connected properly. See that they are not shorting to earth through broken or cracked insulation. If they are, you should be able to see and hear it. If not, then check the plugs, contact points and condenser just as you would in a case of total failure to start.

c) If misfiring occurs at high speed check the points gap, which may be too small, and the plugs in that order. Check also that the spring tension on the points is not too light, this causing them to bounce. This requires a special pull balance so if in doubt it will be cheaper to buy a new set of contacts rather than go to a garage and get them to check it. If the trouble is still not cured then the fault lies in the carburation or engine itself.

d) If misfiring or stalling occurs only at low speeds the points gap is possibly too big. If not, then the slow running adjustment on the carburettor needs attention.

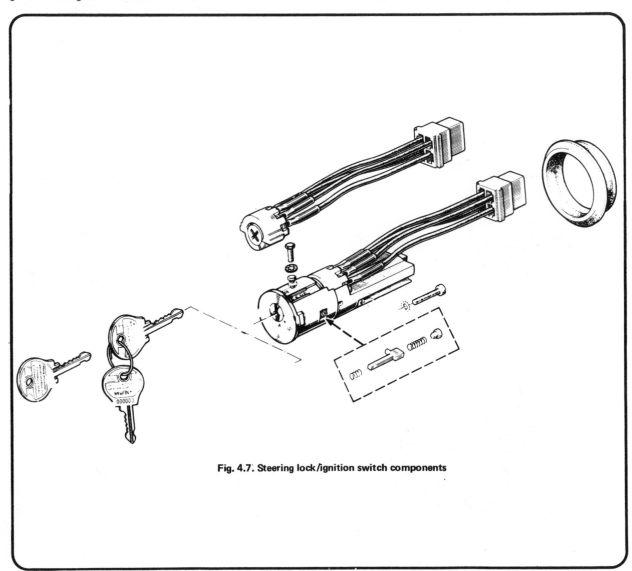

Fig. 4.7. Steering lock/ignition switch components

Chapter 5 Clutch

Contents

Specification

Type ... ... 170DB 275 (20 spline plate, 208 mm diameter)	Single plate disc, diaphragm spring, Renault
Disc thickness	7.4 mm (0.292 in)
Operation	Mechanical, by cable
Clutch release lever play	2.5 to 3.5 mm (3/32 in to 9/64 in)

Clutch release bearing

Type	Guided ball

Torque wrench settings

Clutch cover to flywheel bolts	18 lbf ft (2.5 kgf m)

1 General description

The clutch is a cable operated single dry plate diaphragm type.

The clutch pedal pivots on the same shaft as the brake pedal (see Chapter 9) and operates a cable to the clutch release arm. The release arm activates a thrust bearing (clutch release bearing) which bears on the diaphragm spring of the pressure plate. The diaphragm then releases or engages the clutch driven plate which is splined onto the gearbox primary shaft. The clutch driven plate (disc) spins in between the clutch cover and the flywheel face when it is released, and is held there when engaged, to connect the drive from the engine to the transmission unit.

As wear takes place on the driven plate the clearance between the clutch release bearing and the diaphragm increases. This wear is compensated for, up to the point where the driven plate is worn out, by altering the length of the clutch cable. This adjustment takes place next to the release arm with an adjuster nut on the cable.

2 Clutch cable - removal, adjustment and replacement

1 The clutch cable travels directly from the end of the clutch pedal to the clutch operating lever. It is very easy to replace.
2 To replace a cable first slacken off the clutch release lever completely. It will be necessary to withdraw the cable connection to the lever altogether.
3 Depress the clutch pedal inside the car by hand and release that end of the cable. It will be attached to a U piece to the pedal. A screwdriver to prise open the lip is all that is needed.

4 From under the bonnet, release the other end of the cable from the rod mechanism by unlocking the adjusting nuts and remove them both. The threaded end of the cable will then release. (photo)
5 Pull out the outer cable from its fixing in the bulkhead, the other side of the end of the clutch pedal. It is a push-in fit using a special alloy collar to locate the outer cable.
6 Replacement is an exact reversal of its removal. Adjust the release bearing clearance as described in Section 3.
7 There should be 2.5 to 3.5 mm clearance at the outer end of the clutch release lever.
8 To effect this adjustment unscrew the locknut on the cable at the lever and then screw or unscrew the second holding nut until this clearance is achieved between the holding nut and the release lever.
9 Relock the locknut on the cable.
10 The clutch pedal is dealt with in Chapter 8.

3 Clutch - removal, inspection and replacement

1 If it is necessary to renew the friction plate or examine the clutch in any way it will first of all be necessary to remove the gearbox (see Chapter 6) in order to get at it. If the engine has been removed then the clutch is, of course, accessible. Once the gearbox is removed or the engine taken out the succeeding operations are the same, although work is easier with the engine out when no pit or ramp is available. If the engine and gearbox have been removed from the car together they will have to be separated of course.
2 Before removing the clutch cover bolts mark the position of the cover in relation to the flywheel so that it may be put back

the same way.

3   Slacken off the cover retaining bolts ½ a turn at a time in a diagonal fashion evenly so as to relieve the diaphragm spring pressure without distorting it.

4   When the bolts are removed the friction plate inside will be released. The cover will then come away easily. The friction plate will fall down from the flywheel face.

5   The clutch driven plate should be inspected for wear and for contamination by oil. Wear is gauged by the depth of the rivet heads below the surface of the friction material. If this is less than 0.025 inch (0.6 mm) the linings are worn enough to justify renewal.

Examine the friction faces of the flywheel and clutch pressure plate. These should be bright and smooth. If the linings have worn too much it is possible that the metal surfaces may have been scored by the rivet heads. Dust and grit can have the same effect. If the scoring is very severe it could mean that even with a new clutch driven plate, slip and juddering and other malfunctions will recur. Deep scoring on the flywheel face is serious because the flywheel will have to be removed and machined by a specialist, or renewed. This can be costly. The same applies to the pressure plate in the cover although this is a less costly affair. If the friction linings seem unworn yet are blackened and shiny then the cause is almost certainly due to oil. Such a condition also requires renewal of the plate. The source of oil must be traced also. It will be due to a leaking seal on the transmission input shaft (Chapter 6 gives details of renewal) or on the rear of the engine crankshaft (see Chapter 1 for details of renewal).

6   If the reason for removal of the clutch has been because of slip and the slip has been allowed to go on for any length of time it is possible that the heat generated will have adversely affected the pressure springs in the cover. Some or all may have been affected with the result that the pressure is now uneven and/or insufficient to prevent slip, even with a new friction plate. It is recommended that under such circumstances a new assembly is fitted.

7   Although it is possible to dismantle the clutch cover assembly and, in theory, renew the various springs and levers the economics do not justify it. Clutch cover assemblies are available on an exchange basis. It will probably be necessary to order an assembly in advance as most agencies other than the large distributors carry stocks only sufficient to meet their own requirements. However, it is possible to get assemblies from reputable manufacturers other than Renault; Borg and Beck for instance. Be absolutely sure as to what you are ordering for many types of clutch have been fitted.

8   When replacing the clutch, hold the cover and support the friction disc on one finger through the centre. Make sure the friction disc has the hub offset facing the flywheel. (photo)

9   Replace the six securing bolts and screw them up evenly just enough to grip the friction plate but not enough to prevent it being moved. It is important to line up the central splined hub with the pilot bush in the centre of the camshaft mounting flange. If this is not done it will be impossible to refit the engine to the transmission. It is possible to centralise them by eye but a simple surer way is to select a suitable piece of bar or wooden dowel which will fit snugly into the pilot bush. Some adhesive tape can be wound round to equal the inside diameter of the friction plate boss. By inserting this the friction plate can be moved and centralised with sufficient accuracy. (photo)

10 Finally tighten up the six cover securing bolts evenly and diagonally a little each at a time to a final torque of 18 lb ft.

11 Before refitting the engine after a clutch overhaul check the transmission input shaft oil seal (Chapter 6) and the clutch release operating mechanism (see Section 4).

12 Before finally offering up the engine dust the splines of the gearbox input shaft (which should, of course, be clean and in good condition) with a little graphite or molybdenum powder. Also put a little molybdenum paste (not oil or grease) on the face of the release bearing and clutch release ring.

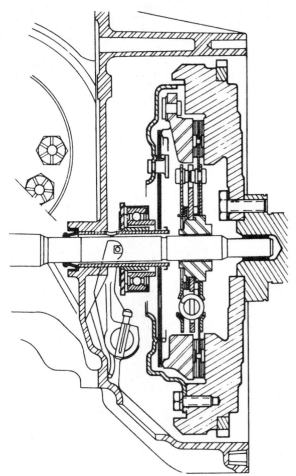

Fig. 5.1. Cross sectioned view of diaphragm clutch

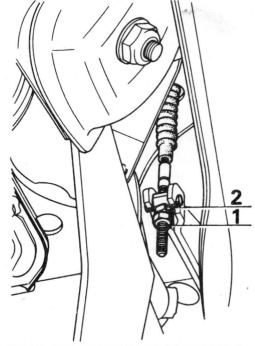

FIG. 5.2. CLUTCH CABLE ADJUSTMENT POINT

1   Lock nut (outer)   *2   Adjusting nut (inner)*

2.4 The bellhousing end of the clutch cable

3.8 Flywheel, clutch plate and clutch cover. Clutch plate flatter side to flywheel

3.9 Centring the clutch plate

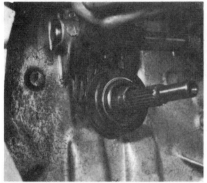

4.3a Release the release bearing spring clips

4.3b Once unclipped the bearing pulls straight off

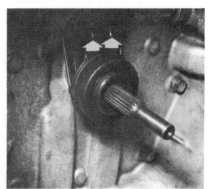

4.5 Note the protrusion of the fork retaining pins

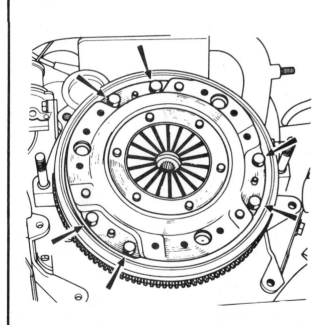

Fig. 5.3 Screws fixing clutch cover to flywheel

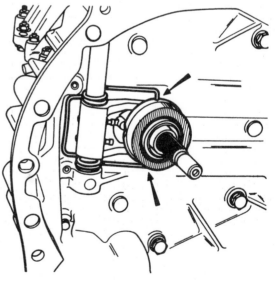

Fig. 5.4. Thrust race locating clip positions

4 Clutch release operating mechanism - inspection and repair

1 Clutch operation can be adversely affected if the release thrust bearing and retaining springs are worn or damaged. Squeals, juddering, slipping or snatching could be caused partly or even wholly by this mechanism.

2 Full examination is only possible when the gearbox is removed and is normally undertaken when the clutch is in need of repair. The mechanism is carried in and attached to the transmission casing/bell housing. Check the bearing itself. The guided ball type should be shiny, and smooth running without any looseness in its revolutions. The retaining spring clips at each side must be a tight fit so that the bearing does not rattle about on its mounting.

3 To inspect the lever fork it is necessary to remove the release bearing by unclipping the holding spring clips and sliding the bearing off the input shaft. Little should go wrong with the lever fork. Renault require a special tool (Emb. 384-01) to withdraw the fork retaining pins, however it should be possible to use a tubular extractor to pull them out. (photos)

4 Do not clean any parts with any cleaning fluid for it will spoil the release bearing. If in doubt renew the bearing; it is safer and less trouble in the long run.

5 Replacement is a straight reversal of its removal of all components here. To lubricate the lever bearing surfaces and the release bearing faces use a little molybdenum paste - never grease or oil.

   Replacing the fork retaining pins is critical. Always use a new rubber seal and then tap the new pins into place. See Fig. 5.5, and leave the shanks protruding 1 mm. (photo)

6 Re-adjust the pedal free play once the gearbox is re-installed.

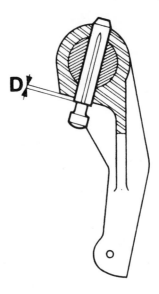

FIG. 5.5. CLUTCH FORK PIN POSITIONS

D = 1 mm (1/32 in.)

---

5 Fault diagnosis and remedies

Symptom	Reason/s	Remedy
Judder when taking up drive	Loose engine/gearbox mountings or over-flexible mountings	Check and tighten all mounting bolts and replace any 'soft' or broken mountings.
	Badly worn friction surfaces or friction plate contaminated with oil/carbon deposit	Remove engine and replace clutch parts as required. Rectify any oil leakage points which may have caused contamination.
	Worn splines in the friction plate hub or on the gearbox input shaft	Renew friction plate and/or input shaft.
Clutch spin (or failure to disengage) so that gears cannot be meshed	Clutch actuating cable clearance too great	Adjust clearance
	Clutch friction disc sticking because of rust on splines (usually apparent after standing idle for some length of time)	As temporary remedy engage top gear, apply handbrake, depress clutch and start engine. (If very badly stuck engine will not turn). When running rev up engine and slip clutch until dis-engagement is normally possible. Renew friction plate at earliest opportunity.
	Damaged or misaligned pressure plate assembly	Replace pressure plate assembly.
	Incorrect release bearing fitted	Replace with correct part.
Clutch slip - (increase in engine speed does not result in increase in car speed-especially on hills)	Clutch actuating cable clearance from fork too small resulting in partially disengaged clutch at all times	Adjust clearance.
	Clutch friction surfaces worn out (beyond further adjustment of operating cable) or clutch surfaces oil soaked	Replace friction plate and remedy source of oil leakage.

Chapter 6 Transmission

Contents

Specifications

BV type 352 pressure die-cast split two piece aluminium casing, 4 forward speeds

1st and 2nd	Renault synchromesh
3rd and 4th	Borg-Warner synchromesh
Primary shaft	5 gears integral
Secondary shaft	4 gears turning free
	2 synchronisers
	3rd and 4th speed sliding gear acting as reverse gear wheel
Reverse shaft	1 gear turning free

Gear ratios

1st	3.61 : 1
2nd	2.26 : 1
3rd	1.48 : 1
4th	1.03 : 1
Reverse	3.08:1

Final drive ratio

	Index No.			Speedometer drive ratio
R1170	352.00	3.875 to 1	(8 x 31)	(6 x 13)
R1170/R1171	352.01	4.375 to 1	(8 x 35)	(7 x 17)
R1170/R1171	352.02	3.777 to 1	(9 x 34)	(6 x 13)
R1170/R1171	352.03	4.125 to 1	(8 x 33)	(6 x 14)
R1170/R1171/R1330	352.06	3.777 to 1	(9 x 34)	(6 x 13)
R1177	352.12	3.777 to 1	(9 x 34)	(6 x 13)

Oil capacity ... ... 3 Imp pints (1.6 litres)

Torque wrench settings

	lbf ft	Nm
Casing bolts (7 mm)	15	20
(8 mm)	20	27
Rear cover bolts	10	14
Clutch bellhousing bolts (8 mm)	15	20
(10 mm)	30	41
Crownwheel bolts	80	109
Speedometer worm gear	85	116
Reverse gear selector	20	27

1 General description

The Renault 12 gearbox is a split casing integral gearbox/final drive of four forward speeds, all of which have synchromesh. Whilst appearing unconventional they are in fact very simple, and conventional to a typical front engined car.

The drive comes from the flywheel/clutch through a split primary shaft over the top of the crownwheel of the final drive and into the main gear casing. The 'gearbox' is in fact in front of the final drive which is obviously between it and the engine. The primary shaft transmits motion via four forward gears to the secondary or pinion shaft, on which is the main gear cluster and synchromesh. The reverse gear is on a third shaft fixed to the gear casing. Motion is then transmitted, when a gear is engaged, by the pinion gear on the end of the pinion shaft to the crownwheel and then to the drive shafts. Gear selector forks are mounted in the side of the casing and are operated by a

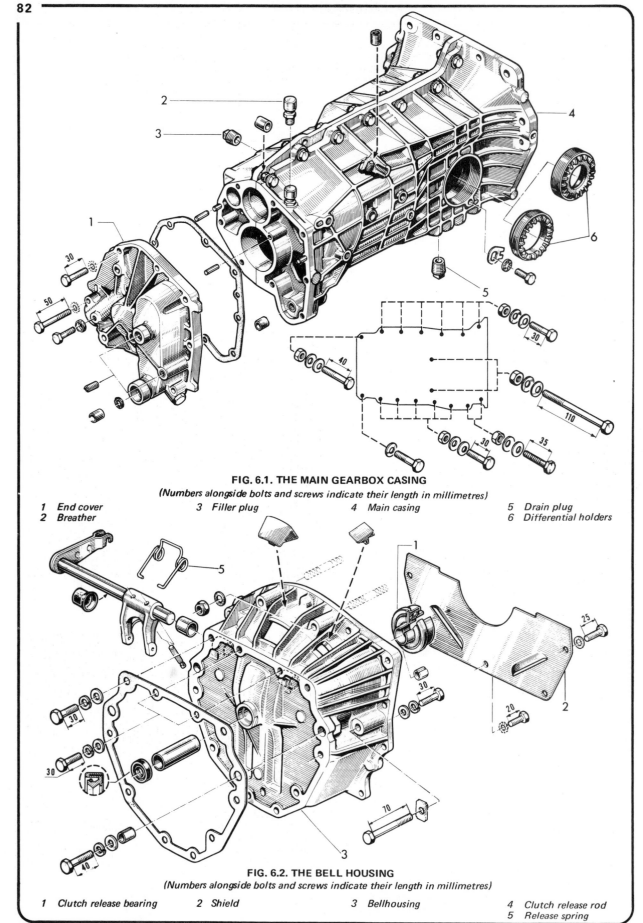

FIG. 6.1. THE MAIN GEARBOX CASING
(Numbers alongside bolts and screws indicate their length in millimetres)

1 *End cover*	3 *Filler plug*	4 *Main casing*	5 *Drain plug*
2 *Breather*			6 *Differential holders*

FIG. 6.2. THE BELL HOUSING
(Numbers alongside bolts and screws indicate their length in millimetres)

1 *Clutch release bearing*	2 *Shield*	3 *Bellhousing*	4 *Clutch release rod*
			5 *Release spring*

to-and-fro and sideways motion of a selector rod/shift mechanism from the front of the casing. These forks select gears on the primary shaft which then mesh with the appropriate gear on the pinion shaft.

Various final drive ratios have been used (see Specifications). The speedometer is gearbox driven. Although already described as a relatively simple transmission unit there are nevertheless a few words of warning which must be stated before any potential dismantlers start work to let them know what they are letting themselves in for.

First of all decide whether the fault you wish to repair is worth all the time and effort involved. Secondly, if the transmission unit is in a very bad state then the cost of the necessary component parts may well exceed the cost of an exchange factory unit. Thirdly, be absolutely sure that you understand how the transmission unit works.

Returning to the second point just mentioned it is possible to dismantle the unit with tools from a normal tool kit but only so far. Fortunately it is at this point where further dismantling once decided to be necessary would suggest that an exchange unit would be a cheaper method of repair. Renault cannot supply individual component parts, rather parts assembled into units, past this point.

Check very carefully the availability and cost of transmission unit parts before dismantling.

2 Transmission - removal and refitting

1 This section describes the removal procedure for the manual gearbox only. To remove the engine and gearbox as a unit refer to Chapter 1, Section 5, paragraph 30.

2 Position suitable spacer legs (T. AV. 509 if available from your Renault dealer) between the shock absorber lower mounting pins and the lower suspension arm pivot pins, then raise the front of the vehicle so that the front wheels are clear of the ground. Support the chassis with stands and check that the spacer legs have remained in position. Disconnect the battery and drain the gearbox oil.

3 Remove the carburettor air filter (Chapter 3) and the accelerator control return spring.

4 Remove the starter motor heat shield, disconnect the two electrical connections and remove the starter motor securing bolts. The inboard one is best taken from below.

5 Remove the two bolts securing the clutch cable sleeve stop, on the bell housing below the fuel pump and then free the clutch cable end from the control cable (see Chapter 5).

6 Remove the top three bell housing to engine bolts easily accessible below the windscreen. Tie back the earthing cable.

7 Disconnect the speedometer cable from the side of the gearbox casing. Once the little lock screw is loosened it should pull out.

8 Remove the gearshift control arm bolt adjacent to the speedo cable fixture. (photo)

9 Undo and loosen the exhaust pipe clamp on the gearbox rear crossmember.

10 Place a trolley jack or overhead sling support on the engine and just take its weight, but only just. Take good care of the fan blades on the radiator matrix from now on.

11 Undo the centre clamps and swing the front suspension anti-roll bar away and then undo the two fixing bolts of the crossmember and place it to one side.

12 Access is now available to undo the exhaust clamp between the manifold and down pipe. Now replace the front crossmember which you removed in paragraph 11.

13 Remove the gearbox rear mounting very carefully by first removing the three bolts which secure the gearbox to the mounting and then the two nuts securing the crossmember to the bodyshell side mounting pads. Now gently lower the trolley jack or hoist so that the engine (and therefore the gearbox) rests on the engine crossmember (just replaced).

14 Punch out the two drive shaft roll pins and then very carefully lever the gearbox from side to side to release the drive

shafts from the splines on the gearbox. Once each one is released, carefully place the drive shaft to one side to avoid it jamming in the gearbox.

15 Now jack (hoist) up the engine slightly and again remove the engine crossmember.

16 Support the gearbox on wooden blocks. Remove the five clutch shield and two bottom bolts securing the engine to the gearbox. The gearbox is now loose. Still on its wooden blocks wriggle the gearbox rearwards, taking good care not to put pressure on the primary shaft which enters the clutch. Have an assistant help you finally support the gearbox and its removal from the car. (photo)

17 Replacement is a reverse procedure but remember to take care of the primary shaft (it is ruined if bent on the flywheel/clutch) and read the appropriate sections on drive shafts, the clutch etc. Select 4th gear to tighten the shift rod.

18 Refill the gearbox with the correct oil!

2.8 Lever the bolt out with a screwdriver if necessary

2.16 The gearbox is long but not very heavy

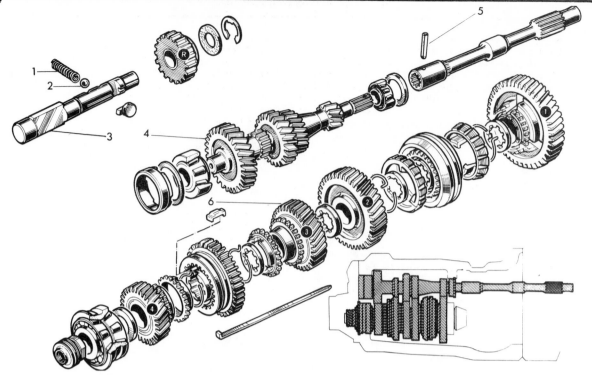

FIG. 6.3. THE PINION AND PRIMARY SHAFT GEAR CLUSTERS (THE SPEED NUMBERS ARE MARKED ON THE COGS)

1 Detent spring	3 Reverse idler shaft	5 Roll pin
2 Detent ball	4 Primary shaft (split)	6 Pinion shaft

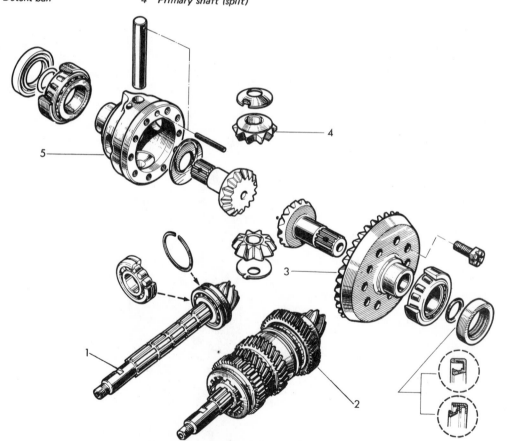

FIG. 6.4. THE DIFFERENTIAL AND PINION SHAFT

1 Pinion shaft	3 Crown wheel	5 Crownwheel differential
2 Pinion shaft with clusters mounted	4 Sun wheels	

3 Dismantling

1 Always work with the gearbox on a good strong table or bench, covered in clean newspaper, having washed the outside casing in a petrol/paraffin mix or water-soluble solvent. Never undertake this work lightly. Estimate the gearbox fault if you can before beginning and try to work out a cost/efficiency base. It may still be cheaper to exchange it!

2 Remove the bell housing bolts, six from 'inside' and six from the rear of the gearbox. Lift it away. (photo)

3 Remove the seven setscrews at the other end of the gearbox. Carefully lift the end cover and gasket away. Now recover the primary shaft bearing adjusting shims and the distance washer. (photos)

4 Mark the exact position of the lock washers on the differential adjusting nuts and remove the set screw and star washer. (photo)

5 Mark the exact position with a punch or scriber of the differential adjusting units and then carefully tap them round with a centre punch and hammer. Note the exact number of turns. This is essential for exact replacement.

6 Place the gearbox on the bench with its right side facing down - the bellhousing to your left. Undo and remove the 7 top casing bolts, the 2 centre through bolts and the 8 bottom casing bolts. Lift off the left casing half. This should now expose the gear clusters on the primary and pinion shafts and the crownwheel. (photo)

7 Lift out the differential from the casing half. (photo)

8 Now lift out the primary split shaft and gear clusters from below the reverse shaft idle lever. This should leave the gear selector mechanism exposed. (photos)

9 Lift out the pinion shaft assembly from the casing once you have removed (pulled out with pliers) the double taper roller bearing outer track stop peg at the speedometer drive cover end. It may, in fact, fall out if you tilt the casing, holding the gear clusters, on its end. (photos)

10 Punch out the roll pin on the top, 3rd/4th fork. Remove the shaft and its end fitting, followed by the fork itself, the locking ball and spring. Remove the locking disc between this shaft and the one below it.

11 Pull out the reverse selector shaft as far as it will go out of the casing - the reverse shaft idle lever top should practically touch and rib in the casing. Punch out the roll pin in the 1st/2nd fork and remove this fork with the shaft.

12 Unscrew the reverse shaft idle lever pin and remove the lever arm.

13 Pull out the reverse selector shaft.

14 To remove the reverse gear from the outer casing half prise out the gear retaining circlip and pull out the shaft retaining the gearwheel, friction washer and guide as well as the locking ball and spring.

15 The two casing halves can now have their differential bearing track rings punched out with a suitable drift if the differential and/or bearings are being renewed. See Section 4.

16 The gearbox is now disassembled into its main components; the primary shaft, pinion shaft and differential. The primary shaft cannot be dismantled further except for the splitting of the 'clutch' shaft from it and the removal of the bearing races, the latter requiring a bearing puller. The pinion shaft can only be dismantled so far, up to the 3rd/4th speed synchro hub without the use of a special hub puller/splitter tool. If the 3rd/4th synchro hub is removed, you again have to stop at the pinion end bearing inner track ring which is bonded to the shaft and cannot be removed. If you have reached the stage of disassembly of the casing and damage or/and wear is visible you are strongly advised to seek the further advice of a Renault agency who will tell you what permutations are available to you; an exchange transmission at this stage or new synchro hubs if they pull the hubs off for you. Do not attempt any 'ham fisted' dismantling now.

17 The primary shaft is split by punching the roll pin out, which fixes the two halves together. This is visible in the centre ferrule. The two end bearing races are pulled off using a special tubular screw extractor. Hold the shaft in a soft jawed vice.

18 The pinion shaft should be placed in a soft jawed vice, gripping the 1st speed gearwheel. Lock the shaft, as if it were engaged in 1st gear. Then unscrew the speedometer worm nut using a pair of adjustables.

19 Lift off the double taper roller bearing followed by the pinion protrusion adjusting washer.

20 Then lift off the 4th speed gearwheel and its synchro ring. Mark the 3rd/4th speed sliding gear and its relative position to the synchro hub and then pull both the sliding gear and keys away from the shaft.

21 Now split and extract, using a special hub puller or press, 3rd/4th speed synchro hub.

22 Lift off the retaining key for the gear stop washers, followed by the 3rd speed gear stop washer and the 3rd speed gearwheel and synchro ring.

23 Follow this with the 2nd speed gear stop washer and the 2nd speed gearwheel and synchro ring. Their removal will expose the 1st/2nd gear synchro sliding gear stop washer. Mark this in relation to the synchro hub and remove.

24 All that will be left is the 1st/2nd gear synchro hub and 1st gear. The 1st/2nd gear synchro hub must be extracted in a similar fashion to the 3rd/4th speed synchro hub. See paragraph 21.

25 Lift off the 1st speed synchro ring, the 1st speed gear stop washer and 1st speed gearwheel.

26 The dismantling of the rear cover/gearshift mechanism is described in Section 6.

3.2 Note the dowel location of the bellhousing

3.3a Always retain the identification disc when removing the end cover

3.3b Pull off the old gasket when the cover is away

3.3c Use your finger to pull out the spacer and shims

3.4 Scribe the position of the lock fork and the number of turns

3.6 Don't lever the cases apart

3.7 Lift out the crown wheel and pinion/differential

3.8a Lift out the locating spacer

3.8b The split primary shaft

3.9a The little lock pin

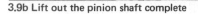

3.9b Lift out the pinion shaft complete

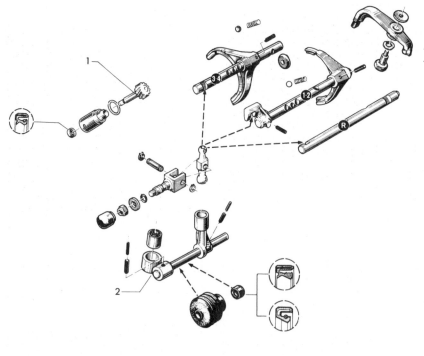

FIG. 6.5. THE SELECTOR MECHANISM (THE RODS ARE MARKED FOR THE GEARS WHICH THEY SELECT)

1   Speedometer cable drive   2   External shaft rod

4 Inspection for wear of transmission components

Once decided that the transmission unit will have to be stripped down because of some minor irritant or major fault it is still not necessary to strip the unit completely. For example there is no need to remove the reverse gear cluster shaft if the synchromesh is being renewed on an otherwise properly functioning gearbox. Consequently you should go slowly once the three major components are removed from the unit because you may be doing unnecessary work. You may also have to face the fact that even when once dismantled that you will do better to reassemble the box there and then (do it properly though) and exchange it for a replacement unit from Renault. The economics of replacing large components is not always on when compared to a complete exchange unit. Remember also that exchange units are likely to be more readily available than individual component parts and that they will carry a guarantee.

Once dismantled into its three major components, the primary shaft, pinion or secondary shaft and final drive, inspection should be detailed. Clean the inside of the unit thoroughly first with a mixture of petrol and paraffin and wipe dry.

1 Check the casting for cracks or damage, particularly near the bearing housings and on the mating surfaces. Casings are only available in matched pairs so both will have to be replaced.

2 Check all the gears for chips and possible cracks and replace where necessary. You should be able to tell whether this should be so from the initial diagnosis before dismantling.

3 Check all the shafts and splines for wear and flat spots and replace if necessary. The gears through which the shafts pass should be a good slide fit and not rock about.

4 Check the synchromesh rings and assembly. All models are prone to early synchromesh failure which should really be replaced as a matter of course as it is cheap enough to do so. The springs should also be renewed.

5 Check the bearings: Primary shaft bearings are generally speaking very reliable and long lived and these are the only bearings apart from the double taper roller bearing on the pinion shaft which can be easily and economically replaced. Check them for scoring and 'wobble'. Pinion shaft bearings: The double taper roller bearing at the opposite end from the final drive is easily renewed although generally long lived. Renew it if in any doubt. The pinion bearing next to the pinion wheel is another matter. If this bearing is worn or faulty the pinion shaft will have to be renewed at a cost of approximately one third of an exchange unit. If this has 'gone' and there are other necessary replacements within the transmission unit, then reassemble (properly) the gearbox and exchange the whole unit for a replacement transmission. It is not economic to do otherwise. The two outer differential bearings should be inspected in the same way. These may be replaced by the home mechanic but he may have difficulty in setting up the final drive in the casing afterwards. Again these bearings are usually reliable.

6 Any failure within the final drive unit will mean replacement of the whole unit, crownwheel assembly in total. Under certain circumstances it will mean changing the bearing and speedo drive gear. See the Specifications at the start of the Chapter. We did not dismantle the crownwheel and pinion because it is not a task which can be undertaken, at least at the reassembly stage, by the home mechanic. The cost of purchasing a new crownwheel without a new pinion, madness anyway, is again approximately half that of a new exchange transmission unit. Purchasing the two together, crownwheel assembly and pinion assembly, to enable them to mesh and set-up correctly is approximately the cost of the exchange transmission and you will not get the guarantee.

7 Check that the nylon speedometer drive gearwheel is in good condition and running easily in its bush.

8 Check the selector forks for wear. Measure them with a pair of calipers and compare their ends with the thickest point; if in doubt renew. They should be only fractionally worn.

9 Check the gear shift mechanism. The tongue which slots into the top of the selectors wears quite rapidly often resulting in non-selected gears and sloppy action. Be absolutely sure the correct replacement lever is supplied. Modifications have been made and parts are NOT interchangeable.

Special Note: Such is the construction of these transmission units that they are generally speaking very reliable but often noisy. They all whine from new to some degree and this should not frighten owners. Obviously it is not possible to detect any increase in whine over a period of time only to suddenly think that it is doing it more than perhaps it should. However this is not good reason in itself to remove and disassemble the unit. The usual reason for discontent is the gradual failure of the synchromesh, particularly on first and second gears. This again is not really good reason for disassembly until it is completely non-functioning and the whine is excessive, from a mechanical point of view. Provided the unit still selects its gears, keeps them there and functions smoothly there is no mechanical reason for worry. Only at a point where it becomes unbearable for the individual owner should this action be taken. See the Fault diagnosis at the end of this Chapter before jumping to conclusions.

5 Transmission - reassembly

Spend time in preparing plenty of clean, clear space and if your work bench is rough cover it with hardboard or paper for a good non-gritty surface. Do not start until you have all the necessary parts and gaskets assembled and make sure that all the ones you have obtained are going to fit. Gasket sets often contain items covering other models so you will not need them all - this is why it helps to keep the old gaskets you take off until the job is eventually finished.

1 Remember that the gear clusters are assembled before they are replaced into the casing halves. It is the reassembly of the clusters which take the most time and require patience and accuracy.

2 Secondary or pinion shaft assembly: If new 1st/2nd speed synchro is to be fitted, first dismantle it after marking the chamfer side of the sliding gear in relation to the synchro hub. Then clean it in a petrol/paraffin mixture. In addition if the 3rd/4th speed synchro is to be renewed mark in the same way and dismantle the new part, then clean it in a petrol/paraffin mixture and reassemble as follows: Fit into the hub the three keys and then the two springs fitting the end of each spring into the same key with the ends crossed over. Then fit the sliding gear on the hub according to the previously made marks.

3 Fit the synchro spring onto the 1st speed gear wheel so that the three notches are totally covered (the spring ends abut on the lip).

4 Make sure the pinion end bearing is already fitted and then push on the following onto the pinion shaft. Start with the 1st speed gear wheel and its synchro ring, synchro ring away from the pinion. Then place on the 1st gear stop washer having soaked it well in oil. It must now be locked in place, so that it holds the 1st gear wheel on the pinion shaft, by making a small lipped key from a flat of steel and inserting it into a spline with an oil hole. Leave the 'dummy' key in place. Place the pinion shaft in a soft jawed vice and hold, supported, by the 1st gear wheel.

5 Heat the 1st/2nd speed synchro hub in an oven (electric) up to 250°C (482°F) - a domestic oven should do this, if left on and pre-heated. Once hot, using oven gloves, fit it onto the pinion shaft with one of the unsplined sections opposite the 'dummy' key, with the previously marked face, facing the 1st gear wheel (chamfer on the splines facing the 1st gear wheel). Press the synchro hub down the shaft, driving it with a soft tubular drift, until it abuts the stop washer. Hold the synchro ring central, with the lugs below the level of the stop washer. When cool release the 'dummy' key.

NOTE: This is quite a difficult yet delicate procedure. If in any doubt as to your ability to undertake this successfully, leave it to a competent Renault agency or specialist engineer.

6 Now fit the 1st/2nd speed synchro hub, matching the previously made marks (chamfer on the 2nd speed gear wheel side). Then fit the stop washer turning it to line up its splines opposite those of the final drive pinion.

7 Read paragraph 3 and then fit the 2nd speed gear synchroniser spring in the same way. Follow it with the 2nd speed gear and its synchroniser spring and then fit the stop washer, as described in the previous paragraph.

8 Fit the 3rd speed gearwheel and its synchro ring, and then fit the stop washer as described in paragraph 6.

9 Fit the same 'dummy' key for the gear stop washers, as previously fitted and then removed, in one of the splines having an oil hole.

10 Using the drift or press having again heated the hub, press on the 3rd/4th gear synchro hub until it touches the 3rd speed stop washer, with the mating marks in line. Make sure that the three notches on the synchro ring are in line with those of the keyways. Remove the 'dummy' key.
Photos: The four photographs show the fitting of the 3rd speed and 3rd/4th synchro hub separately. Photo (A) shows the hub already fitted and the outer retaining spring being fitted, (B) shows the lining up of the keyways, (C) the inserting of the keys and (D) the fitting of the 4th gear wheel and synchro ring holding the keys in place in the 3rd/4th speed synchro hub. This assembly sequence assumes that both are fitted together. See paragraph 2.

11 Fit the 4th speed gear wheel, lining up the synchro rings below it. (photo)

12 Replace the pinion protrusion adjusting washer. (photo)

13 Follow this with the double taper roller bearing and its components. (photo)

14 Replace the speedometer drive gear and holding the shaft firmly gripped in the 1st gear wheel in a soft jawed vice tighten it all up to 85 lb f ft torque. Lock the speedometer drive gear (photos) after reading the next paragraph.

15 Before locking the speedometer gear wheel check that the 3rd speed synchro ring is hard up against the gear cone and that gear wheel presses against the hub. Do this for the 4th speed synchro ring as well. There should be no play, although the clearance between the synchro ring and hub rim should be not less than .2 mm (0.008 inch).

16 Primary shaft assembly: If the end bearings have been removed press or drift new inner races onto each end of the primary shaft, hard up against the gear wheels.

17 Then reconnect the 'clutch' shaft to the main primary shaft using a new roll pin through the ferrule. (photo)

18 Reverse gear shaft reassembly: Place the locking spring and ball into the right hand casing half. (photo)

19 Slide in the reverse shaft and fit the gear wheel with the gear wheel hub facing the differential end. (photo)

20 Next fit the friction washer with its 'drilled' side facing the gear wheel. (photo)

21 Fit the little guide (like a Woodruff key) from inside the bore through which the shaft will pass and then push the shaft into the bore. Fit the drilled cap and 'nick' it in with a small screwdriver. (photo)

22 Push on the gear retaining circlip. (photo)

23 Gear selector mechanism: Insert the reverse gear selector shaft and then fit the fork with its hub towards the differential end of the casing. Punch a new roll pin in, to hold it onto the shaft.

24 Fit the reverse gear selector idle lever and engage the end into the slot in the reverse gear selector shaft. Tighten the lever to 20 lb f ft torque.

25 Fit the 1st/2nd speed selector shaft locking spring and ball and engage them into the 1st/2nd speed selector shaft once fitted. Hold them in place with a small screwdriver when pushing in the shaft.

26 At the outer end of the casing fit the reverse gear selector shaft end fitting and punch a new roll pin in place to lock it. Fit the 1st/2nd selector fork onto its shaft, hub facing away from the differential and punch a new roll pin in place to lock it.

27 Fit the locking disc in between the two selector shafts in its centre position.

28 Now fit the 3rd/4th speed selector shaft locking spring and ball and then insert the shaft. Fit the 3rd/4th speed selector fork onto the shaft and punch a roll pin into it to lock it. Make sure the hub of the fork faces the differential.

29 Final reassembly: Make sure that the two casing halves, with the reverse gear shaft and the selector shafts fitted, are spotlessly clean (photos).

30 Do the same thing with the primary and pinion shafts, and differential. Check now that all is well. (photo)

31 Place the left hand housing on a clean sheet of paper and place the primary shaft with the outer bearing tracks into the casing. Hold the bearing tracks in place with grease and place the stop washer in place at the inner bearing. (photos)

32 Place the pinion shaft into the casing meshing the gears correctly. (photo) Note the outer circlip.

33 Fit new outer rubber O rings to the differential bearings and place the differential into the same casing half. (photos)

34 Place a smear of grease around the mating surface of the same casing half and then place the other casing half onto it. Make sure that the reverse idle lever engages into the slot on the reverse gear wheel shaft when the two halves mate. (photos)

35 Bolt the casing halves together using flat washers on the casing flats and tighten the 8 mm bolts to 20 lb f ft torque and the 7 mm bolts to 15 lb f ft torque progressively and in the order shown in Fig.6.6. Check that the bolts face the correct way.

36 Refit the breather valve if it has been removed. If not, remove it now, and clean it thoroughly in a petrol/paraffin mixture. Replace.

37 Check the movement of the selectors once all is tightened by pressing in the 1st/2nd selector shaft and watching for movement in the reverse gear shaft.

38 Tap the primary shaft outer bearing fully home using a parallel pin punch.

39 Fit on a new gasket to the end face smearing the mating surfaces with gasket cement. Place in the shims which were removed from the end of the primary shaft orifice end and the spacer, and replace the end cover.

40 Replace the two casing half outer differential adjusting nuts and tap them round to the exactly original position marked by your original scribe marks. Replace the locking tabs. (It is, of course, assumed that a new differential has not been fitted nor rear outer track bearings. If they have been renewed you must have their final backlash setting set at a Renault agency. Then finally tighten the locking tab.

41 The bell housing is fitted with a special oil seal. Always punch out the old and refit with a new but be very careful not to damage it. The 'open' face must be innermost towards the gearbox. Use a new gasket, cement and a socket spanner to refit the bell housing. Grease the primary shaft so not to damage the oil seal.

42 Do not forget to refill with oil. Run-in a new gearbox as you would an engine.

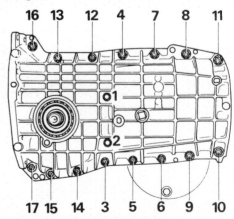

Fig. 6.6. The loosening and tightening sequence for the casing bolts

5.10a Outer retaining spring fitment

5.10b Lining up the keyways

5.10c Inserting the keys

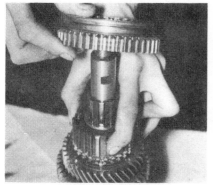

5.10d 4th gear wheel fitment

5.11 4th gear wheel pins synchro rings below

5.12 Pinion protrusion adjusting shim

5.13 Double taper roller bearing

5.14a Wooden jaws are essential

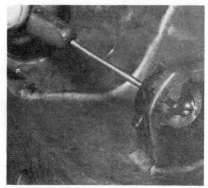

5.14b Use a special torque wrench head

5.14c Bang over the tab

5.17 Roll pin location for the primary shaft

5.18 Reverse shaft locking ball

5.19 Reverse gear wheel.....

5.20.....friction washer.....

5.21.....Now peen over the drilling guide cap

5.22 Retaining circlip

5.29a Hub towards the differential

5.29b Reverse gear selector idle shaft

5.29c Again a torque wrench

5.29d 1st/2nd speed selector shaft locking spring.....

5.29e.....and the ball

5.29f 1st/2nd selector fork and then.....

5.29g .....punch in a new roll pin

5.29h Drop in the locking disc between the selector shafts

5.29j The 3rd/4th selector shaft locking spring.....

5.29k .....and ball

5.29L Fit selector shaft holding in the ball and spring

5.29m Fit the selector shaft

5.29n Punch in a new roll pin to lock it

5.30 The gear shaft layout

5.31a Primary shaft under the reverse idler arm

5.31b Outer bearing track stop washer

5.32 The larger outer circlip next

5.33a Always fit a new 'O' ring

5.33b Primary shaft, pinion shaft and then the differential

5.34a Grease not gasket cement (no gasket)

5.34b Totally clean mating surfaces

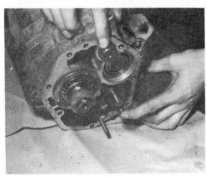

5.34c Note the reverse lever idler arm and its groove in the reverse gear shaft

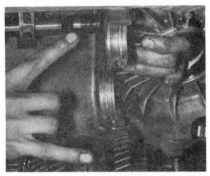

5.37 Check the selecting mechanism now

5.38 Primary shaft bearing track

6 Gear shift mechanism

1 The gear shift mechanism can be divided into three parts: the gearbox end cover, the external shift rod and the gear lever inside the car.

2 Removal and replacement of the end cover has been described in Sections 3 and 5. Once removed, it too can be dismantled.

3 Take off the speedometer drive gear sleeve, its 'O' ring and the speedometer gear. Remove the rubber cap protecting the swing lever shaft and then its nut and washer. Punch out the roll pin and remove the swing lever shaft complete.

4 The swing lever is the part which wears. To remove it from its shaft remove the circlip.

5 Reassembly is straightforward. Always renew the 'O' ring, circlip, roll-pin etc.

6 To remove the external shift rod disconnect it at the gearbox, unhook the lever return spring. It must be removed with the gear lever and then removed.

7 Free the lower bellows from the floor under the car.

8 Undo the gear lever bellows four embellisher ring screws and then the two screws through the front of the front seat runners and lift the cover moulding and embellisher over the gear lever.

9 Pull the bellows up the gear lever. Pull up the protective housing and release the three lever housing setscrews. The gear lever, bellows, protective housing, lever and housing, mechanism and external shift rod should lift up from the floor.

10 Further dismantling is shown in Fig. 6.8. The gear lever knob is glued.

11 Replacement is a straightforward reverse process. Grease all the pivot points prior to reassembly. Select fourth gear to finally tighten the shift rod.

7 Speedometer cable

The speedometer cable is a conventional inner/outer driven cable. It is fixed at the gearbox by a 'clamp' screw and at the speedometer head by a knurled nut, on the outer cable. It is easily replaced. The whole cable has to be replaced, 'inners' and 'outers' are not available separately. Make sure it passes through its original passage. Speedometer failure is inevitably a broken speedo cable. Fluttering and whining is quite common and a sign of impending cable failure.

8 Fault finding

1 Faults can be sharply divided into two main groups: Some definite failure with the transmission not working: Noises implying some component worn, damaged, or out of place.

2 The failures can usually be tracked down by commonsense and remembering the circumstances in which they appeared. Thus if the car will not go at all a mechanical failure will occur in different circumstances to a broken linkage from the gear lever!

3 If there is a definite fault within the transmission then it has got to be removed and dismantled to repair it, so further diagnosis can wait till the parts can be examined.

4 But if the problem is a strange noise the decision must be taken whether in the first place it is abnormal, and if so whether it warrants action.

5 Noises can be traced to a certain extent by doing the test sequence as follows:

6 Find the speed and type of driving that makes the noise. If the noise occurs with engine running, car stationary, clutch disengaged, gear engaged: The noise is not in the transmission. If it goes after the clutch is engaged in neutral, halted, it is the clutch.

7 If the noise can be heard faintly in neutral, clutch engaged, it is in the gearbox. It will presumably get worse on the move, especially in some particular gear.

8 Final drive noises are only heard on the move. They will only vary with speed and load, whatever gear is engaged.

9 Noise when pulling is likely to be either the adjustment of preload of the differential bearings, or the crown wheel and pinion backlash.

10 Gear noise when free-wheeling is likely to be the relative positions of crown wheel and pinion.

11 Noise on corners implies excessive tightness or excessive play of the bevel side gears or idler pinions in the differential.

12 In general, whining is gear teeth at the incorrect distance apart. Roaring or rushing or moaning is bearings. Thumping or grating noises suggest a link out of a gear tooth.

13 If subdued whining comes on gradually, there is a good chance the transmission will last a long time to come.

14 Whining or moaning appearing suddenly, or becoming loud, should be examined quickly.

15 If the thumping, or grating noises appear, stop at once. If bits of metal are loose inside, the whole transmission, including the casing, could quickly be wrecked.

16 Synchromesh wear is obvious. You just 'beat' the gears and crashing occurs.

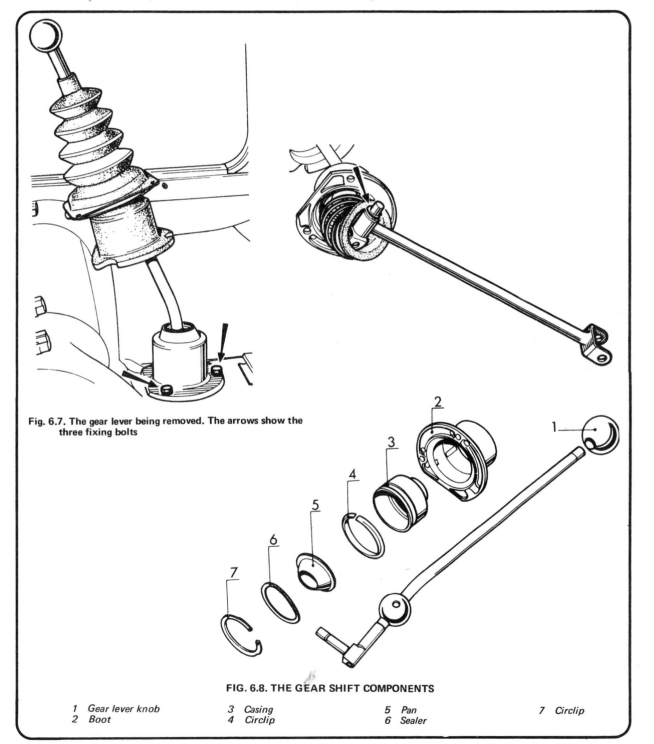

Fig. 6.7. The gear lever being removed. The arrows show the three fixing bolts

FIG. 6.8. THE GEAR SHIFT COMPONENTS

1 Gear lever knob	3 Casing	5 Pan	7 Circlip
2 Boot	4 Circlip	6 Sealer	

Chapter 7 Drive shafts, hubs, wheels and tyres

Contents

Specifications

Drive shaft type

Outer joint	BED in steel or BED in cast iron
Inner joint	SPIDER
Inner joint oil	Supplied by Renault
Front hub bearings	2 ball journal bearings
Rear hub bearings	2 taper roller bearings

Torque wrench settings

	lbf ft	Nm
Front suspension		
Stub axle nut	115	156
Suspension upper balljoint	35	48
Track rod end balljoint	25	34
Roadwheel	45 to 60	61 to 82
Rear Suspension		
Stub axle nut (initial setting)	25	34

Wheels

Pressed steel disc without centre holes, 3 stud fixing ... ... (R 1177 has 'Gordini' type wheels without knave plate)	13 inch diameter, 4½ in. B rim width

Tyres

Saloons	145 x 13 radial ply
Estate	155 x 13 radial ply

Tyre pressure

All models -	Front	21 psi
	Rear	24 psi

These pressures are only a guide. Check with the individual tyre manufacturer.

1 General description

The drive shafts fitted to the Renault 12 drive the front wheels direct from the final drive in the transmission casing. They also undergo the steering movement of the car with the front wheels. Consequently they are fitted with universal joints at the outer (wheel) end and sliding joints at their inner (transmission) end. They are effectively single units, the joints being totally integral with the shafts. Little maintenance can be done on them and when worn out they must be renewed as a whole, although they can obviously be renewed singly.

The front hubs, encased in the stub axle carrier are unusual in that they are two ball journal bearings. The rear hubs are conventional in being two taper roller bearings.

The wheels and tyres are normal for Renault by being their familiar three stud fixing and radial ply fitting respectively.

2 Drive shafts - disconnection and replacement

1 To be able to remove the transmission unit, the drive shafts have to be disconnected at the inner end and the top suspension ball joint at the outer end has to be forced from its mounting point.

2 Before attempting to work on the drive shafts it is desirable to purchase a special tool kit, which is inexpensive, from your Renault garage. This kit enables the drive shaft roll pins to be driven out, and refitted. There is no other way of doing it short of manufacturing your own version of these tools.

3 Under special tool number B.Vi.31b are these three drifts for extracting the roll pins (5 mm), which hold the splines in place on the final drive. With the car jacked up, road wheels removed and safely supported on stands drive out the inner roll pins. You will find these located very close to the transmission case,

between that and the rubber bellows on the drive shaft. With the appropriate drift drive the pins downwards and throw the two pins (one inside the other) away. Never re-use old roll pins. (photos)

4   Place a brace, a tyre lever would do, to hold the hub (between the wheel studs) and remove the stub axle nut and washer. 90 lb f ft torque was used to do it up!

5   Take off the brake caliper and hang up safely. See Chapter 8.

6   Using a ball joint remover (a cheap, useful tool) disconnect the steering arm ball joint at the suspension stub axle carrier but leave it hanging loosely in its place with the nut still attached. Then disconnect the upper suspension ball joint completely. Turn the steering to full lock to give good access.

7   Support the lower suspension arm with a block of wood and then disconnect the steering arm. Pull the drive shaft out gently from the transmission spline. (photo)

8   For total safety Renault's special puller/pusher is needed to drive the shaft out of the hub. (T.AV. 235) Borrow this if you can and push the shaft out. Reconnect the top suspension ball joint to avoid strain on the ball joints whilst the shaft is out. (It is possible, that is to say it has been done, to drive out the drive shaft with a hammer and then to drive the hub back onto the new shaft. This will automatically necessitate a new shaft because the stub axle is always damaged; Use the proper tool!)

9   Replacement is an exact reverse procedure. Use the tool T.AV 236 to pull the 'new' drive shaft back through the stub axle carrier, having smeared the splines with molybdenum grease. Torque the stub axle nut to 90 lb ft.

10   When driving in a new set of roll pins (always use new ones) use a different and appropriate drift from the tool kit. Grease the splines with Castrol LM Grease. Tap in the large roll pin first, having lined up the splines on the shaft with those on the transmission so that the four holes are all aligned. Then place the second one inside the first with its slot opposite the other, and drive in. Smear the ends of the roll pins once in position with vaseline or very heavy grease.

11   Top up the transmission unit with oil.

Note: It is only economic to purchase the tools T.AV 235 and 236 if more than one shaft is going to be replaced during work on the car. It is unlikely to be economic to purchase the three legged puller for this purpose.

2.3a A long parallel pin punch to remove the roll pin

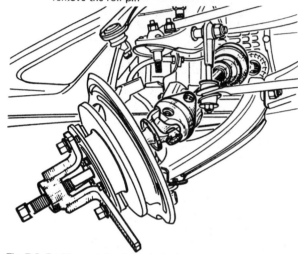

Fig. 7.2. Pushing out the drive shaft through the front hub using the special Renault pusher/puller (T. AV 235)

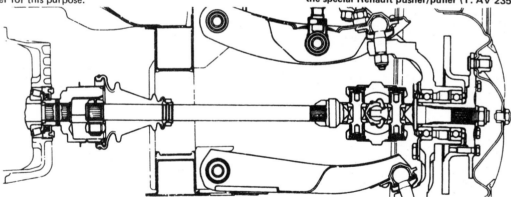

Fig. 7.1. Cross sectioned front axle and drive shaft (right)

3   Drive shaft joints - dismantling and assembly

As has been stated in the General Description, there is very little maintenance which can be carried out on the drive shaft joints. The outer universal joints are sealed at manufacture and cannot under any circumstances be replaced because the joint itself is not available separately. It is unwise to attempt any work on these joints. The inner joints can be dismantled by the do-it-yourself mechanic but he will find that he is unable to reassemble them. No matter which type of shaft is fitted special tools are needed to effect a repair. Even replacing the rubber bellows and relubricating the inner joint is beyond the use of

ordinary tools. Under all circumstances it is more efficient to remove the drive shaft and then take it to a Renault garage to have them effect any repair or maintenance. With the specific special tools available to them all repairs to the inner joint can be carried out very quickly by an experienced man, and this will always be more efficient and safer than attempting it yourself.

For SPIDER joints it is possible to have the bellows, yoke and spider itself replaced, together or separately. Experience shows that unless the bellows is punctured and lubricant allowed to escape and joint to become dry, the outer universal joint wears at a far greater rate than the inner, consequently the shaft is nearly always replaced before the total life of the inner joint is reached.

2.3b This shows the two roll pin holes
in the ends of the shafts

2.7 Line up the roll pin holes before
pushing on the splines

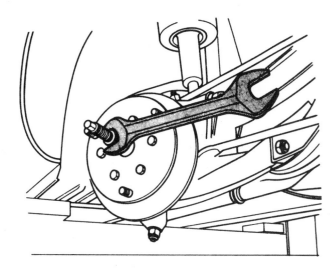

Fig. 7.3. Pulling the drive shaft back through the hub using the official tool'(T. AV 236)

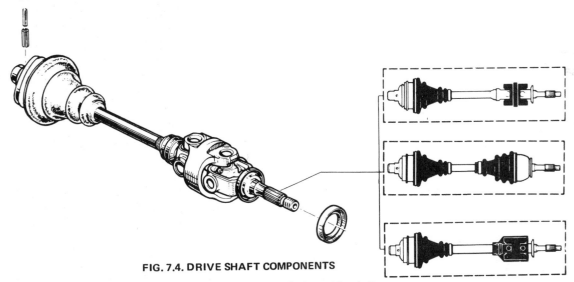

FIG. 7.4. DRIVE SHAFT COMPONENTS

Inset: The three possible profiles of a front drive shaft

4　Front hub bearings - removal and replacement

1　Front hub bearing removal is no easy task. It is as involved as that of removing a drive shaft.

2　Jack up the car, support firmly and then remove the road wheel, 'hang up' the caliper and remove the hub/disc as described in Chapter 8.

3　Disconnect the steering arm ball joint and the upper and lower suspension ball joints at the stub axle carrier with a ball joint remover, and remove the stub axle carrier. Retain the rear closure plate. Rest the lower suspension arm and drive shaft on a wooden block.

4　The outer bearing race is still located on the hub/disc whilst the inner bearing is in the stub axle carrier. The hub/disc bearing will have to be pulled off with a three legged puller. Do not mess with hammers and drifts. Get the proper puller. Retain the distance piece. The stub axle carrier bearing can be pressed or drifted out. First remove and then retain the grease seal.

5　Preferably using a press but the jaws of a vice suitably padded will do, press on a new bearing to the hub/disc. The sealed side of the bearing should face the hub. A tube of 35 mm (1.3/8 inch) internal diameter will help.

6　Use a 68 mm (2.11/16 inch) external diameter tube to press in a new bearing into the stub axle carrier. Again the jaws of a vice will suffice.

7　Place the hub/disc, its new bearing and the distance piece already fitted flat on a bench. Lightly pack the stub axle carrier with high melting point grease and then drift, with a rawhide hammer, the whole assembly onto the hub/disc. Make sure it is 'square' and do not use undue force.

8　Fit the rear closure plate using some sealing adhesive - good quality gasket cement. (Bolt up when the dust shield and caliper are re-installed).

9 Now refit the stub axle carrier and hub/disc. First connect the lower suspension arm ball joint and then follow the procedure through as if just refitting a drive shaft as described in Section 2.

10 Check the front wheel track.

5 Rear hub bearings - removal, replacement and adjustment

1 Only ever replace the inner and outer rear hub bearings as a pair.

2 Remove the brake drum as described in Section 4, Chapter 8.

3 Remove the grease seal from the drum and have a new one ready for replacement. A screwdriver will easily remove this.

4 Tap the two outer bearing housings out of the drum using a large screwdriver and hammer, from the other side of the drum

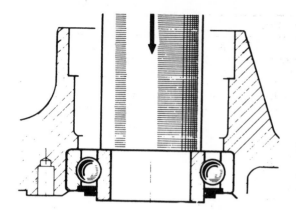

Fig. 7.6. Driving out the inner bearing from the stub axle carrier

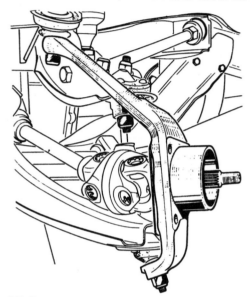

Fig. 7.5. Removing a stub axle carrier, the front hub/disc has been removed

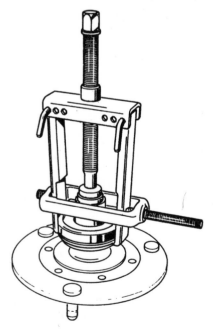

Fig. 7.7. Pulling off the outer bearing from the hub/disc

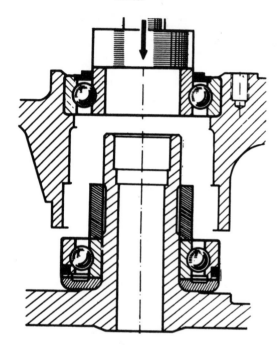

Fig. 7.8. The top arrow shows the inner bearing being driven into the stub axle carrier. The new bearing is pressed onto the hub/disc which is then pressed into the stub axle carrier through the outer bearing

to the bearing. The roller bearing race of the outer bearing is already loose. Extract the inner bearing roller race using a bearing extractor. This could be a simple two legged extractor.

5 Replacement of the races and housing is an obvious reversed sequence to their removal. Tap the inner bearing race onto the stub axle using a suitably sized socket and very carefully ease in the outer housings into the drum.

6 Refit the brake drum, 'D' washer and nut, then tighten the nut to a torque of 25lbf ft (34 Nm) whilst turning the drum.

7 Back off the nut ¼ turn, then pull on the brake drum to take up all the end-play in the outboard direction. Now tighten the nut to obtain 0.01 to 0.08 mm (0.001 to 0.004 in) total end-play. This will be difficult to judge accurately unless a dial gauge is available, but end-play should *just* be detectable when correctly set.

8 Fit the nut locking cap and a new split pin. Fill the grease cap 2/3 full with a general-purpose wheel bearing grease and carefully tap it into position.

9 Finally, adjust the rear brake shoes as described in Chapter 8, Section 4.

6 Wheels

Because of the design of the suspension of the car the strength and the trueness of the road wheels is critical, particularly at the front. A great deal of excessively fast wear on the wheel bearings and universal joints can be attributed to buckled and deformed wheels. Check every 3000 miles or when there is a sudden difference of feeling at the steering wheel that the wheels are not buckled or dented. Check also that the front wheels are balanced. (Remember that the wheels do not have holes in their centres, consequently not all electronic balancing machines can be used on these wheels.) If any deformity is noticed the wheel concerned should be replaced by new. Do not attempt to 'repair' wheel rims.

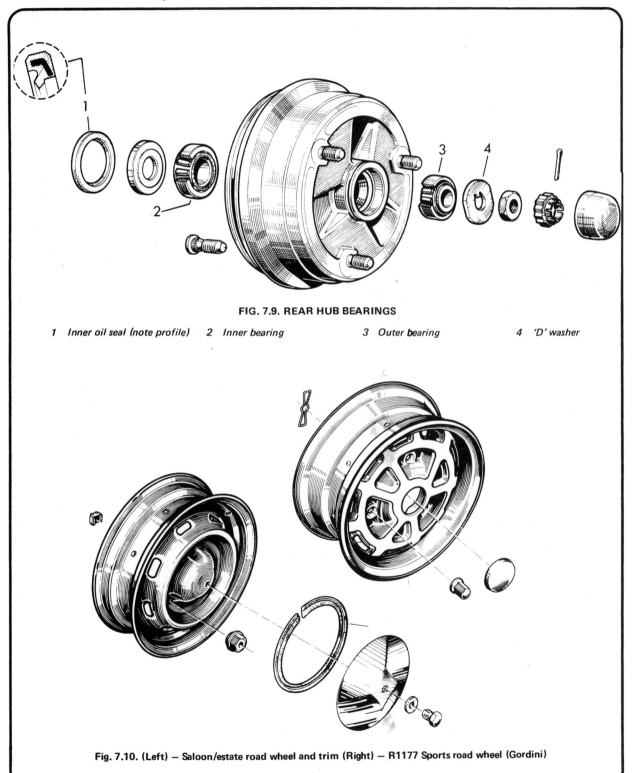

FIG. 7.9. REAR HUB BEARINGS

1 Inner oil seal (note profile)   2 Inner bearing   3 Outer bearing   4 'D' washer

Fig. 7.10. (Left) — Saloon/estate road wheel and trim (Right) — R1177 Sports road wheel (Gordini)

If the front wheels are balanced on the car, make sure that the balancing machine is not of the type which drives the roadwheels electrically.

Only the type of equipment should be used which relies upon the car transmission driving the roadwheels with the engine running.

Failure to observe the foregoing may cause damage to the driveshafts and final drive.

It is permissible for the rear wheels to be balanced on the car with an electrically driven machine.

7 Tyres

In the same way that the condition and suitability of the wheels fitted is critical so it is with the tyres. It is always wise to fit radial ply tyres on all wheels of these cars. Tyre wear is not great under any circumstances but the front tyres will wear faster than the rear. Do not fit oversize tyres. The wheel rims are not able to take a larger section tyre. See the Specifications for suitability of tyres. Tyre pressures are critical too.

EXAMPLE 1

Difference in actual depth of cut and high

Difference tabulated cutting speeds 287-26

To the lower cutting speed add 1% of 26 fo

$$328 + (26 \times \frac{75}{100}) = 342.5$$

Difference in tabulated feed rate and actu
add 15% to the factorised cutting speed 34
The tool nose radius is greater than .040"
398.88 x .9 for 'POOR' rigidity of compone

CONVERT TO R.P.M.

Determine mean diameter of face   Inner Dia

Mean Diam

$$\frac{3.82 \times 308.25}{2.781} = 423.4$$ Apply maximum 1

Therefore use 381 R.P.M. and .0125" INS p

FORM GROOVE

Width of Groove .250", Depth of groove
Feed Rate and Cutting Speed from Table 3.
Applying .9 Factor   for poor rig
.0035" x .9 = .00315   205 x 9

CONVERTING TO R.P.M.

Calculate mean diameter. Inner Diameter
Mean Diameter = 3.4"

$$\frac{3.82 \times 184.5}{3.4} = \underline{207.3 \text{ R.P.M.}}$$

Match 207.3 R.P.M. to Machine. Apply max

Match .00315 ins. min to machine. Apply

Chapter 8 Braking system

Contents

Specifications

Type	Front disc brakes, rear drum brakes. Handbrake operates two independent cables, one to each rear wheel. Servo assistance is fitted to R1171, R1330 and R1177 models
Hydraulic fluid	Specifications SAE J1703e - Castrol Girling Universal Brake and Clutch Fluid.

Disc brakes

Disc diameter	9 inch (228 mm)
Disc thickness	.393 inch (10 mm)
Pad thickness (including backing)	35/64 inch (14 mm)
Caliper piston bore	1.7/8 inch (48 mm)

Drum brakes

Drum diameter	7.086 inch (180 mm)
Lining width	1.9/16 inch (40 mm)
Lining thickness	9/32 inch (7 mm)
Wheel cylinder diameter	.812 inch (20.6 mm)
Maximum drum diameter after regrind	7.126 inch (181 mm)

Master cylinder

Diameter	.748 inch (19 mm)
Stroke	1.3/16 inch (30 mm)
Clearance between piston and pushrod	.196 inch (5 mm)

Brake limiter	560 psi ± 28 psi
Servo unit	Master Vac

Torque wrench settings

	lbf ft	Nm
Bleed screws	7	10
Flexible hose to caliper	15	20
Rigid pipe unions (steel)	10	14
(copper)	9	12
Caliper mounting bolts	50	68
Disc to hub bolts	15	20
Stub axle nut	115	156
Brake servo mounting nuts	10	14

1 General description

The Renault 12 is fitted with disc brakes on the front wheels, and drum brakes on the rear. These are hydraulically operated from a single circuit system which is servo assisted on most models.

The calipers are of the floating type with a cylinder in one side only. Incorporated in the hydraulic pressure line to the rear brakes only is a fluid pressure regulating valve which reduces the braking force on the rear wheels in certain light load applications.

The handbrake operates on the rear drum brakes only and is actuated by cables from an umbrella type or centrally mounted ratchet lever inside the car.

The vacuum servo is fitted as standard on certain models and uses manifold depression from the engine intake manifold to boost hydraulic pressure with lower pedal pressures.

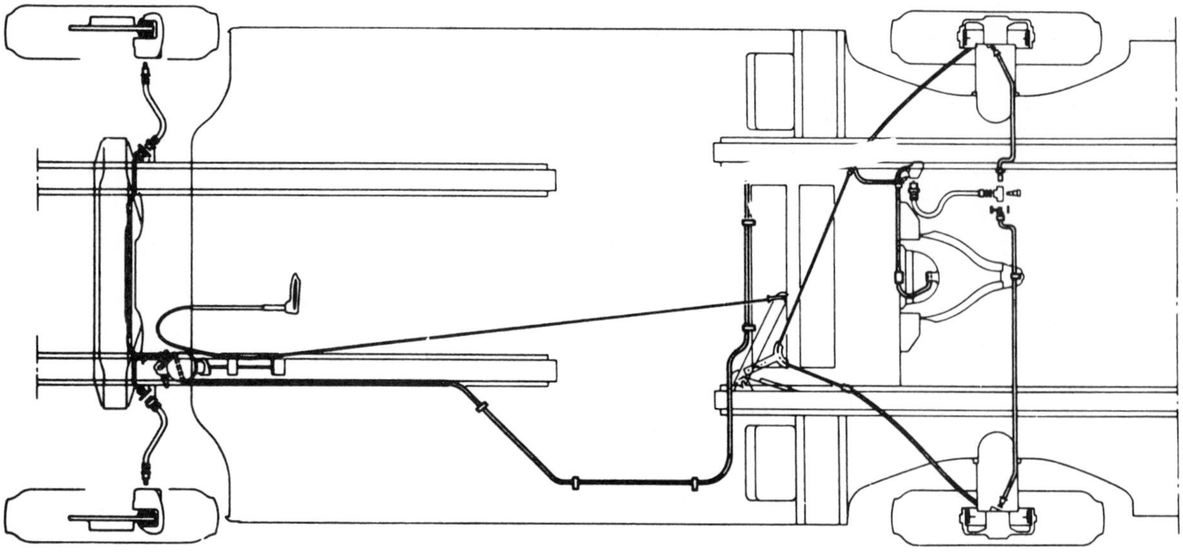

Fig. 8.1. The brake pipe single circuit layout for a left hand drive car (RHD is simply a mirror image)

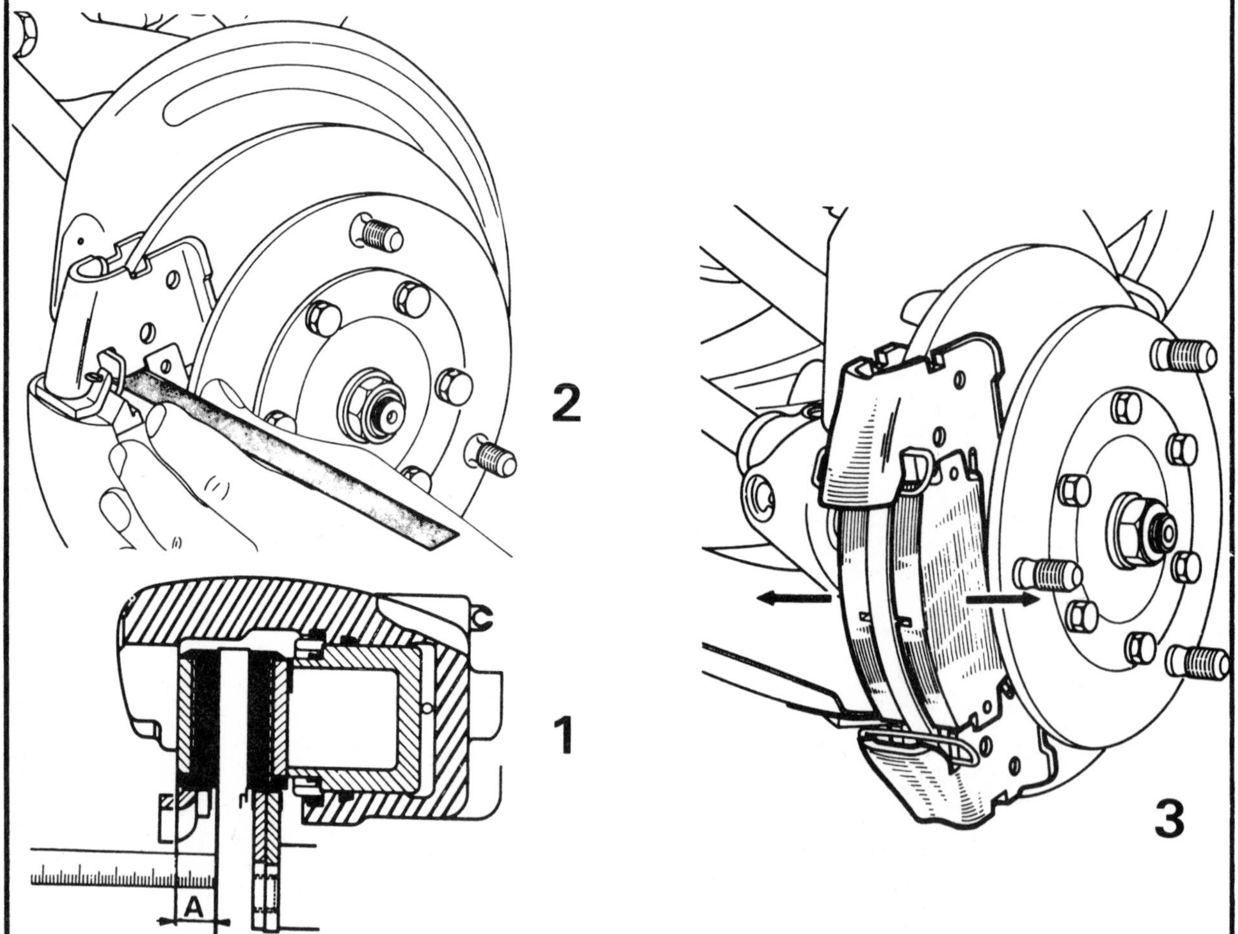

Fig. 8.2. The front disc brake pad arrangement
1 Measuring pad wear — A = 7 mm (9/32 in) minimum of friction material plus backing plate.
2 Extracting caliper locking block clips
3 Removing pads from caliper support bracket

2 Front brake disc pads - removal, inspection and replacement

1 Before dismantling any parts of the brakes they should be thoroughly cleaned, using a brush to remove mud. Do not use petrol, paraffin or any other solvents which could cause deterioration to the friction pads or piston seals.

2 Jack up the car and remove the wheel.

3 Inspection does not necessitate the removal of the disc pads themselves. The pads abut the disc surface at all times. Therefore it is possible to put the end of a steel rule (the measure must start at the end of the rule) into the recess above the caliper and the tops of the pads. It should then be evident where the outer edge of the pad comes to, on the rule, from the surface of the disc outwards. The total thickness of the pad, and its backing, must not be less than 7 mm (9/32 in). If less than this figure the pads must be renewed.

4 To remove the pads take out the two clips which hold the caliper locking blocks in place. (photos) Hold the caliper and pull out the locking blocks, with a pair of pliers if necessary, and swing the caliper out to one side out of the way, and then hang with a piece of string without straining the flexible hose.

5 The pads may be taken out of the caliper support bracket. If they are not being renewed note which side they come from so they may be put back in the same place. The pad friction material plus the backing should be no less than 7 mm (9/32 in). If the pads are not worn out but have a black and shiny surface it is helpful to roughen them up a little on some emery cloth before replacing them. Disc pads last normally about 12,000 miles.

6 Behind the pads on the carrier bracket are two pad anchor springs. Remove these and clean them up after ensuring that they are intact. Renew them otherwise.

7 Check the disc and caliper before replacing the original on new pads. See Section 6.

8 Replacement of the pads and calipers is a reversal of the removal procedure, but when fitting new pads certain additional matters must be attended to.

9 Make sure that the new pads are exactly similar to the ones taken off. Push back the piston in the caliper with a suitable blunt instrument to provide the necessary clearance for the new thicker pads.

10 Make sure the pads are the correct way up. The drilling on the back is downwards.

11 Refit the pads into the carrier, after the two pad anchor springs. The longest spring goes on the outside whilst the shortest on the inside. (photos)

12 Fit one side of the caliper between the spring and the keyway on the caliper bracket and then fit the other side of the caliper by compressing both springs. (photo)

13 Push in the first locking block. Using a screwdriver press in the other keyway and then push in the second locking block. (photos)

14 Refit the four spring clips with their flat portion facing the caliper bracket.

15 Refit the road wheel, lower the car and pump the brake pedal.

NOTE: Disc pads must be renewed in sets. Always renew pads on both front wheels - never just one.

2.4a Lock block clips

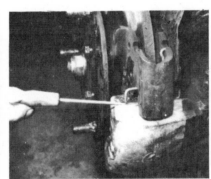
2.4b Spring clips for anti-rattle

2.11a Note the pad anchor spring pad

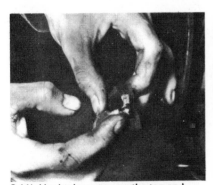
2.11b Use brake grease on the top and bottom of the edge of the pad

2.12 Pads installed, caliper being pushed on

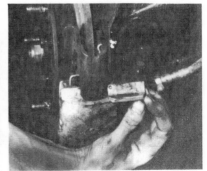
2.13a Slide in the lock blocks

104

2.13b Use a screwdriver to ease the gap

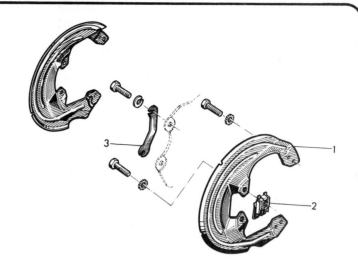

FIG. 8.3a. THE FRONT DISC DUST SHIELDS

1 Dust shield (they are handed)
2 Captive nut   3   Shim

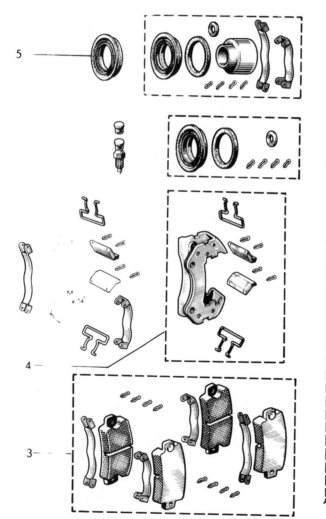

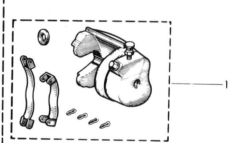

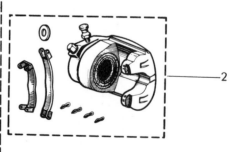

FIG. 8.3b. THE COMPONENTS OF THE DISC CALIPER

1 Left hand caliper body   2   Right hand caliper body   3   Pads and anti-rattle springs   4   Caliper bracket
(axle set)   5   Piston and seals

3 Rear brake drum and shoes - removal, inspection and replacement

1 Jack up the car and remove the road wheel. Block the relevant wheel and release the handbrake.

2 Slacken off the adjusters and then remove the rear drum hub grease cap with a pair of small Stilsons or punch. Wipe any excess grease away from the castellated nut and split pin and pull out the split pin. Undo and remove the locking nut, and D washer. With luck the drum/hub will pull off the stub axle easily together with most of the bearings, inners and outers. If this is not possible a road wheel can be replaced on the hub and this used for something to pull on. Do not waggle the wheel though. Failing both these possibilities a three-legged puller will have to be used fixed to the wheel studs and pushing on the centre of the stub axle. This puller will have to be hired or borrowed. (photos)

3 With the drum removed brush out any dust and examine the rubbing surface for any signs of pitting or deep scoring. The surface should be smooth and bright but minor hairline scores are of no consequence and could have been caused by grit or brake shoes with linings just worn to the rivets. A drum that is obviously badly worn should be renewed. A perfectly satisfactory replacement can sometimes be obtained from a breaker. It is no economy having drums turned up on a lathe (unless you can have it done for nothing!). Also, as the radius is altered if the rubbing surfaces are machined out, standard shoes will not match properly until a lot of bedding in has taken place and re-radiused the linings.

4 The brake shoes should be examined next. There should be no signs of contamination by oil and the linings should be above the heads of the rivets. If the level is close (less than 1/32 inch) it is worth changing them. If there are signs of oil contamination they should be renewed also and the source of oil leakage found before it ruins the new ones as well.

5 To remove the shoes (having, of course, removed the drum) use a screwdriver to push one end of the top inner spring, which pulls the two shoes towards each other, to hold-in the two pistons of the wheel cylinder, back through its locating hole in the shoe. This should loosen the spring at the top, the two shoes and the lower shorter spring. Ease each shoe in turn towards the outer rim of the backing plate and then out and away from the anti-rattle clip. Disconnect the lower shorter spring from the shoes. (photo)

6 Remove the steady bar from between the two shoes and then remove the one loose shoe. The other shoe is attached by a stud and circlip to the handbrake pressure arm. Remove the circlip with pliers and then slip off the second shoe.

Do not press the brake pedal and use some sort of cylinder holding device to stop the pistons easing out (if possible).

7 Before fitting new shoes check that the wheel cylinder is not leaking and is securely bolted on. Also see that the hydraulic piston moves freely.

8 Replacing the brake shoes is almost an exact reversal of removal. Refit the one shoe to the handbrake pressure arm and secure with the circlip. Now place both shoes under the anti-rattle clips and affix the lower retention spring in place. Now place the steady bar in place. Place the end of the spring which you originally pushed in towards the backing plate to release the brake shoes in its position under the shoe and hooked in. Wedge it there with a Phillips screwdriver or similar tool. This just holds the little clip firm. With a pair of Stilsons grip the other end of the top spring and squeezing the two shoes together onto the piston faces with the other hand, drag the spring over the other shoe and slot in the curved end into the hole in the shoe. This is quite difficult but not dangerous. It will soon be seen exactly where to grip the spring to do this. Be patient and be sure not to damage the wheel cylinder rubber seals. (photo)

9 When replacing the drums try to make sure the drums go back on in the original positions. See Chapter 7 to check on the tightening of the rear/hub bearing.

10 When the drum has been replaced and the brakes adjusted

(Section 4), operate the brakes to check that they do not bind. It is possible for light binding to occur initially, in which case they should be checked again after a few miles' motoring.

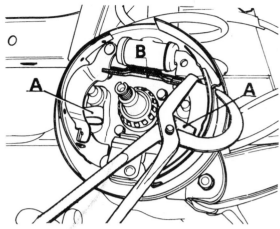

FIG. 8.4. REMOVING THE REAR DRUM BRAKE SHOES

A Anti-rattle clips   B Hydraulic piston

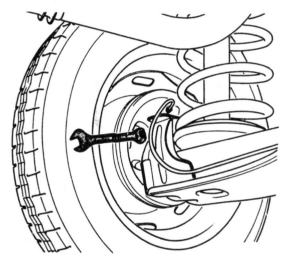

Fig. 8.5. Adjusting the rear drum brakes

3.2a Tap off the grease cap

3.2b Do not damage its edge

3.2c Nut locking mechanism

3.2d 'D' washer; in fact a lip washer

3.2e The oil seal in the drum should keep the drum clean

3.5 Note the position of the spring - in and out

3.8 The anti-rattle clip slips in

4 Brake adjustment

1   Only the rear drum brakes need manual adjustment. This should also take up the 'day-to-day' adjustment of the handbrake. The front disc brakes, are of course, self adjusting. It is necessary only to have the correct sized metric spanner to turn the square headed adjuster although the job is always better done with the correct Renault brake spanner which can cover all four sides of this adjuster. The adjusters seize easily and soon become chewed-up if the incorrect tool is used. To this end it is wise to lubricate the adjusters with some penetrating oil in advance of the time you wish to do the task. Soak the adjuster with this fluid at the back of the backing plate. All four adjusters are exposed to road dirt!

2   Jack up each wheel individually having loosened the hub cap and wheel nuts. Release the handbrake.

3   Remove the wheel and turn the drum with the wheel studs. If it revolves easily the drums are in need of reasonable adjustment. Place the adjusting spanner on each adjuster in turn, loosen it by turning and then revolve the drum very slowly and tighten up the adjuster until the drum is just locked by the shoe. Slacken it off fractionally so that the drum rotates, just, under slight, but not binding, friction. Proceed with the other adjuster on that backing plate. Then go on and do the other wheel. Never adjust only one wheel.

4   Road test the car and check that it pulls up firmly and straight, without an increase in foot pressure. The pedal should not need pumping.

5 Handbrake adjustment and cable renewal

Two types of actuating mechanisms have been fitted. Early models (R1170 Vehicle No. 1 to 503103, R1171 all models, R1330 Vehicle No. 1 to 41501) were fitted with an umbrella type dashboard mounted mechanism. It is more complex than the later fitted floor mounted lever type. (All vehicles after the last numbers given previously plus all R1177 vehicles). Handbrake adjustment must always take place after rear drum brake adjustment, NEVER before and then only to take up cable stretch.

1   Early type, umbrella adjustment: Raise the rear of the vehicle and then release the handbrake. Unlock the handbrake adjusting rod (fits into the 'U' shaped cable puller/compensator) and then tighten the inner nut until the brake drums just contact the rear drums. Rotate the rear wheels as you would for hydraulic drum adjustment. Use the second, outer, nut to lock the inner nut on the adjusting rod when all is correct.

2   The umbrella type operates through two cables. The primary cable (nearest the control lever) is attached to the 'umbrella' by a plastic guide tube and a Renault type roll pin. Should the cable break or fray or the lever need replacement, both the cable and the lever must be removed.

3   Free the cable at the compensating lever under the car. Then where the umbrella carriage bolts to the floor, remove the two nuts from underneath, and detach the cable outer from its clips. Remove the two handbrake lever securing screws, adjacent to the face of the lever itself and pull out the under carriage, cable and lever assembly complete.

4   To remove the cable from the lever, push the plastic guide tube towards the lever after punching out the roll pin. Now free the cable. The lever and its ratchet clip are easily dismantled. Reassembly is a direct reverse process. Always grease lightly the ratchet and the inner cable.

5   The secondary (or rear cable) is released from its 'U' shaped cable puller by slackening off fully the adjustment and pulling through the threaded rod. To remove the two drum ends you must remove the drums themselves (see Section 3) and then disconnect it from the cable stop on the trailing shoe. Feed the inner and outer stop, plus spring through the back plate. Replacement is again a straight reverse procedure.

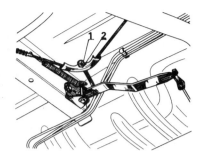

FIG. 8.6. THE HANDBRAKE CABLE ADJUSTMENT

1 Locknut   *2 Adjuster nut*

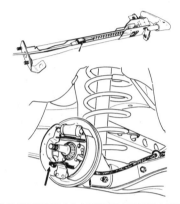

FIG. 8.7. UMBRELLA TYPE HANDBRAKE CABLES

Top: Primary/front   *Lower: Secondary/rear*

6   Always adjust the cable after the rear brake shoes have been adjusted.

7   Later type, centre lever adjustment: This type is adjusted by exactly the same method as the early type using very similar components at this point. See paragraph 1.

8   The centre lever and short primary cable are again interconnected. To remove one or other, unscrew inside the car, the two fixings for the lever plate having slackened off the adjustment. Pull the lever, when released, upwards and pull off the circlip which locates the cable to the lever with a fulcrum pin. Pull the lever mechanism away.

9   Underneath the car the fixing plate of the lever should be hanging. Undo the adjusting rod puller and pull both fixing and primary cable away.

10 Replacement of this cable and lever are a simple reverse process, whilst the removal and replacement of the rear cable are exactly as described for the early umbrella type, paragraph 5.

11 Always grease the cables and replace all bodyshell sealing and grommets where found.

12 Adjust the rear brakes THEN the cable.

---

6   Calipers, discs, pistons and seals - inspection and renewal

1   Unbolt the caliper from the car as described in Section 2. Then remove totally by undoing the flexible hose from the caliper end. This is simpler than removing from the bodywork. Let the hydraulic fluid drain into a container.

2   With a brake caliper, if the piston is only partially seized it should be possible to force it right out under pressure from an air line on the hydraulic fluid inlet. With an air line at a petrol station this should be fairly easy but on a foot pump it will be necessary to make up a suitable air tight adaptor.

3   If the piston is seized solid it is more than likely that you will be unable to get the piston out without damaging the caliper

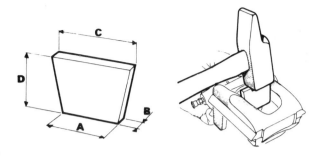

Fig.8.6a Wedge for spreading caliper bracket legs

A 51.5 mm (2 1/32 in)   B 8 mm (5/16 in)
C 56 mm (2 7/32 in)   D 35 mm (1 3/8 in)

or piston. However it is worthwhile having a go. Pull out the rubber dust seal and leave the whole assembly to soak in methylated spirits for a time. If this does not soften things up then a new caliper assembly will have to be bought.

4   Assuming the pistons have been removed without difficulty, clean them thoroughly with methylated spirit and remove the seal from the annular groove in the cylinder bore. Any hard residue deposits may be removed with careful use of some 600 grit wet and dry paper. If there are any ridges or scores in the cylinder or on the piston the parts must be renewed. To renew the cylinder, it must be separated from the caliper bracket. To do this, spread the legs of the bracket (using a wedge) just enough to slide the cylinder from its grooves. Make a wedge in accordance with the diagram (Fig. 8.6a).

5   Fit new seals in the cylinder groove, lubricate the cylinder and piston with hydraulic fluid and replace the piston. Fit the dust seal so that it fits in the caliper groove and on to the piston.

6   When the caliper has been reassembled and fitted back to the car bleed the hydraulic system as described in Section 10.

7   Discs do not last forever. Under ideal conditions and with proper and regular maintenance of caliper pistons and brake pads they will last a long time. Under other circumstances they can warp, wear irregularly, get rusted and pitted, develop score lines and as a result provide poor braking and rapid consumption of pads. Remember, disc brakes are only better than drum brakes if they are in good condition.

8   A disc in good condition should have a smooth, shiny bright surface on the pad contact area. Do not hope to improve a deteriorated disc by the burnishing effect of new pads! Another fault which a disc may have, even though the surfaces are good, is a warp (or run-out). This means it does not run true. If bad it can be seen when the wheel is spun. However, to measure the run-out accurately a clock gauge pointer should be set against one face. The deviation should not exceed 0.15 mm/.006 ins. If you do not possess a clock gauge it is worth holding a steel pointer firmly on a nearby support with the point up to the disc face. Variations can be detected in this way also. Remember that the wheel bearings must be completely devoid of any end float in order to check disc run out. Worn or maladjusted bearings can be a contributory factor in disc deterioration.

9   To renovate a disc calls for either re-facing or renewal and for this they must be taken off as described next. The cost of re-facing should be checked against the cost of a new disc. Remember also that the thickness of the disc should not be less than 10 mm/.39 inches. If it is very deeply scored or pitted, or the run out is excessive the only remedy may be a new one. If the disc is too thin it loses some of its capability to disperse heat and its rigidity.

10 To remove a disc, a difficult task, first remove the road wheel and unbolt the caliper. Hang the caliper up so that the flexible hose is not strained.

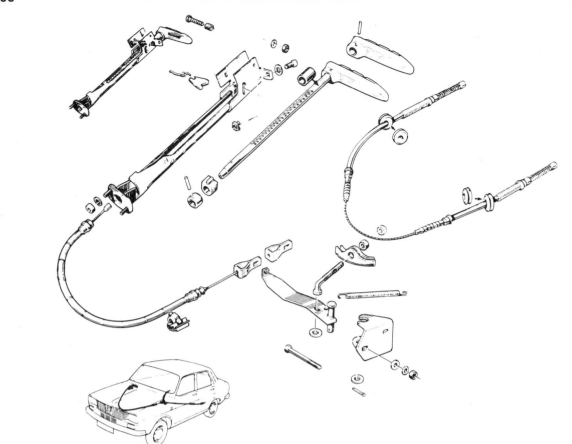

Fig.8.8. Components of the early type umbrella handbrake mechanism (R1170 to Vehicle No. 503103, R1171s, and R1330 to Vehicle No. 41501)

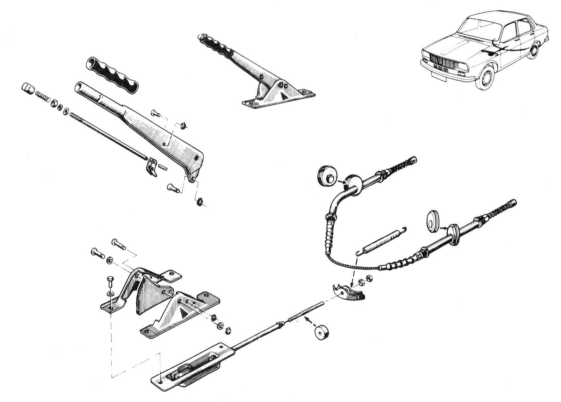

Fig. 8.9. Components of the later type floor mounted handbrake mechanism (R1170 from Vehicle No. 503104, R1330 from Vehicle No. 41502 and R1177)

11 Remove the caliper bracket by removing the two deflector securing bolts and then the two bracket to stub axle carrier bolts. Free the bracket but retain the adjusting shim between the bracket and the stub axle carrier.

12 Unscrew three of the six disc to hub securing screws. Obtain three other 8 mm setscrews about two inches long and three pieces of steel rod about 4 mm in diameter, two inches long.

13 Place one piece of rod in each of the drillings from which the bolts have just been removed. Then screw in a new setscrew pushing them through to the face of the stub axle carrier.

14 Remove the stub axle nut (90 lb f ft is needed). Hold the hub with a tyre lever placed appropriately across the wheel studs.

15 Now progressively tighten the three setscrews and push the hub/disc off the stub axle carrier. It is not easy and quite a crude but effective method.

16 Once off the disc can be separated from the hub quite easily. Hold the disc in padded jaws of a strong vice.

17 Replacement is almost a direct reverse motion of the removal except that hub/disc must be replaced using the method described in Chapter 7 for refitting a drive shaft.

Note: Only use high tension bolts for the hub to disc fitment. (Y3 should be stamped on their heads).

18 When replacing the caliper carrier bracket the distance between the caliper bracket and disc must be correct, hence the shim, so that the pads sit equally. See Fig. 8.10a and measure 'A'. Then see the table coming next - if 'A' measures:

0.91 to 1.55 mm (.036" to .061"), fit a shim 1.2 mm (.048") thick.

1.56 to 1.78 mm (.062" to .070"), fit a shim 1 mm (.40") thick.

1.79 to 2.06 mm (.071" to .081"), fit a shim 0.8 mm (.032") thick.

2.07 to 2.58 mm (.082" to .101"), fit a shim 0.6 mm (.024") thick.

2.59 to 3.45 mm (.102" to .136"), remove the shim.

When a caliper bracket is changed, fit a shim 0.6 mm (.024"), and check the measurement at 'A'.

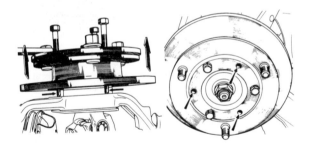

Fig. 8.10. The proper method of removing a disc/hub. The top illustration shows the three bolts removed, the lower shows the steel spacers pressing through with the bolts replaced

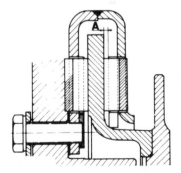

Fig. 8.10a Caliper bracket-to-disc clearance setting diagram. For values of A see text

7 Rear wheel cylinders and back plates - inspection and overhaul

1 If it is suspected that one or more of the wheel cylinders is malfunctioning, jack up the suspect wheel and remove the brake drum as described in Section 3.

2 Inspect for signs of fluid leakage around the wheel cylinder and if there are any, proceed as described in paragraph 6.

3 Next get someone to release the handbrake and then to press the brake pedal very gently and a small amount. Watch the wheel cylinder and see that the pistons move out a little. On no account let them come right out or it will need reassembly and bleeding. On releasing the pedal pressure, make sure that the retraction springs on the shoes move the piston back into position without delay. If both pistons move all is well in the cylinder. If only one piston moves, only one shoe has been effective and repair is necessary.

4 If there is a leak, or the piston does not move (or only moves very slowly under excessive pressure) then the rubber piston seals will need renewal at least.

5 Seal the reservoir cap and remove the brake shoes as described in Section 3.

6 Disconnect the brake fluid pipes where they enter the cylinder and plug the ends of the lines to minimise loss of fluid.

7 Remove the cylinder from the backing plate by undoing the two setscrews from the rear side of the backing plate. Remove them and push the cylinder through and away. Do not attempt any cylinder repair with it still in place on the car. It may be necessary to loosen the backing plate to get at the two setscrews.

8 Then pull out the piston, complete with seal and the spring. Examine the piston and cylinder for signs of wear or scoring and if there are any the whole assembly must be renewed. If they are in good condition only the seal needs renewal. Pull the old one off the piston and thoroughly clean the whole assembly using clean hydraulic fluid or methylated spirit.

9 Fit the new seal to the piston so that the lip faces away from the centre of the piston.

10 Lubricate the components in hydraulic fluid before reassembly which is carried out in the reverse order. Make sure the lip of the seal on the piston enters the cylinder first.

11 Replace the cylinder back on the backing plate correctly.

12 Reconnect the hydraulic pipe, replace the brake shoes and drum as described in Section 3. Bleed the hydraulic system as described in Section 10.

Special Note: The wheel cylinders are never interchangeable wheel for wheel. They can only be fitted in one place, one way up. Because of the various size changes that have taken place in wheel cylinders be absolutely sure any replacement cylinders or cylinder kits are of the correct size and type.

13 The rear back plate is easily removed once the brake drum, shoes and wheel cylinder are removed although it is not strictly necessary to remove the cylinder. The normal reason for removing the back plate is one of the adjusters seizing solid. Little but renewal can be done once this has happened.

14 Disconnect the rigid fluid pipe from the wheel cylinder and then thread the handbrake cable, once disconnected from the pressure arm, through the back plate.

15 Undo the four securing screws and pull off the back plate.

16 Replacement is an exact reversal of the removal sequence. Add a sealing compound like gasket cement to the rear abutting face of the back plate. Always bleed the brakes and oil the adjusters.

8 Master cylinder - removal, overhaul, reassembly

1 If the wheel hydraulic cylinders are in order and there are no leaks elsewhere, yet the brake pedal still does not hold under sustained pressure then the master cylinder seals may be presumed to be ineffective. To renew them the master cylinder must be removed. For servo equipped cars see Section 11 first. This is important.

2   Disconnect the master cylinder pushrod from the brake pedal by removing the clevis pin.

3   Unscrew the hydraulic pipe unions and push the pipes to one side.

4   Remove the two nuts and washers holding the master cylinder to the bulkhead, one inside the car the other under the bonnet, and lift the unit away wrapped in a piece of rag. This will stop fluid dripping out onto the paintwork. Then empty the contents of the reservoir into a clean container. Remove the reservoir.

5   Replacement is a reversal of the removal procedure, after which the braking system must be completely bled. Make sure the master cylinder is 'sealed' to the bulkhead.

6   If overhaul is desired, the fitting of new seals, first remove the reservoir. This screws into the top.

7   Dismantle and reassemble in the same way as you would a wheel cylinder, with the same care and cleanliness. Note however the additional final circlip which holds the piston and spring and seals in the cylinder.

8   Adjust the brake pedal rod as described in Section 12.

9   Completely bleed the hydraulic system.

Fig. 8.11. Components of the rear wheel hydraulic cylinder
The dark shading shows the rubber seals and the light shading the pistons and cylinders

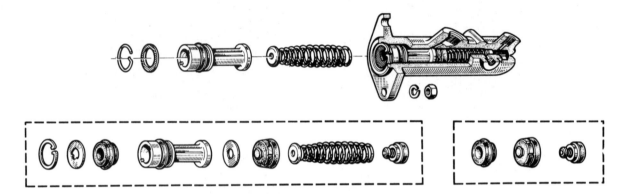

Fig. 8.12. The components of the master cylinder. The two boxed insets show the components available in a repair kit

9   Hydraulic pipes and pressure limiter valve

1   Periodically and certainly well in advance of the MOT test, if due, all brake pipes, connections and unions should be completely and carefully examined. Fig.8.1 shows the composition of all such pipes and unions in the system.

2   Examine first all the unions for signs of leaks. Then look at the flexible hoses for signs of fraying and chafing (as well as for leaks). This is only a preliminary inspection of the flexible hoses as exterior condition does not necessarily indicate interior condition which will be considered later.

3   The steel pipes must be examined equally carefully. They must be thoroughly cleaned and examined for signs of dents or other percussive damage, rust and corrosion. Rust and corrosion should be scraped off and, if the depth of pitting in the pipes is significant, they will need renewal. This is most likely in those areas underneath the chassis and along the rear suspension arms where the pipes are exposed to the full force of road and weather conditions.

4   If any section of pipe is to be removed, first of all take off the fluid reservoir cap, line it with a piece of polythene film to make it airtight and screw it back on. This will minimise the amount of fluid dripping out of the system when the pipes are removed.

5   Rigid pipe removal is usually quite straightforward. The unions at each end are undone and the pipe drawn out of the connection. The clips which may hold it to the car body are bent back and it is then removed. Underneath the car exposed unions can be particularly stubborn, defying the efforts of an open ended spanner. As few people will have the special split ring spanner required, a self-grip wrench (Mole) is the only answer. If the pipe is being renewed new unions will be provided. If not then one will have to put up with the possibility of burring over the flats on the union and use a self-grip wrench for replacement also.

6   Flexible hoses are always fitted to a rigid support bracket where they join a rigid pipe, the bracket being fixed to the chassis or rear suspension arm. The rigid pipe unions must first be removed from the flexible union. Then the locknut securing the flexible pipe to the bracket must be unscrewed, releasing the end of the pipe from the bracket. As these connections are usually exposed they are more often than not rusted up and a penetrating fluid is virtually essential to aid removal (try Plus-Gas). When undoing them, both halves must be supported as the bracket is not strong enough to support the torque required to undo the nut and can easily be snapped off.

7   Once the flexible hose is removed examine the internal bore. If clear of fluid it should be possible to see through it. Any specks of rubber which come out, or signs of restriction in the bore, mean that the inner lining is breaking up and tha pipe must be renewed.

8   Rigid pipes which need replacement can usually be purchased at any local garage where they have the pipe, unions and special tools to make them up. All that they need to know is the pipe length required and the type of flare used at the ends of the pipe. These may be different at each end of the same pipe. Always screw hydraulic unions and fittings into position by hand initially to check that the threads are compatible. Do not overtighten and only use spanners of short length.

9   Replacement of pipes is a straightforward reversal of the

removal procedure. It is best to get all the sets (bends) in the pipe made preparatory to installation. Also any acute bends should be put in by the garage on a bending machine otherwise there is the possibility of kinking them and restricting the bore area and fluid flow.

10 With the pipes replaced, remove the polythene from the reservoir cap and bleed the system as described in Section 10.

11 Connected into the hydraulic pipe system is the brake pressure limiter valve which limits pressure to the rear wheels to stop them locking up before the front. It operates in a similar manner to a rear wheel cylinder and can be removed in a similar manner but not overhauled. If it leaks, renew it. Its operating mechanism consists of a compact system of rods, and is again straightforward to renew if damaged. The system is both hydraulic and mechanical. When the car brakes hard, the rear of it raises as the nose dips taking away adhesion from the rear wheels because of an effective release of weight. To stop the rear wheels locking under the lack of adhesion, a rod passes from the rear suspension 'A' arm and actuates the pressure limiter to the extent that the correct pressure of fluid always passes from it to the rear brakes. Simply, as the 'A' bracket rises, so the rod cuts off fluid pressure in the valve and so to the rear brakes. (photos)

12 When overhaul and replacement has taken place, to either or both, the valve and rods, reassembly is simple. However, adjustment is not. ALWAYS take the vehicle to a Renault dealer, no other, to have the pressure adjustment undertaken. An hydraulic fluid gauge is necessary.

13 Never use the vehicle without this valve in proper operation.

9.11a The brake pressure limiter mechanism on the 'A' bracket

9.11b The valve

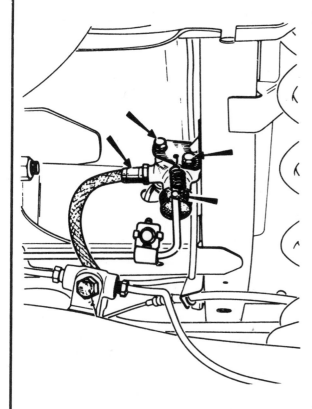
Fig. 8.13. The fixing of the rear wheel brake limiter valve

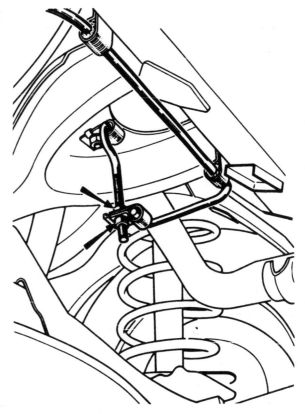
Fig. 8.14. The suspension operated rod mechanism for the brake pressure limiter switch

10 Bleeding the brakes

1 If the hydraulic system has air in it, operation will be spongy and imprecise. Air will get in whenever the system is dismantled, or if it runs low. The latter is likely to happen as the brakes wear, and the pistons move further out in the wheel cylinders. Air can leak into the system, sometimes through a fault too slight to let fluid out. In this latter case it indicates a general overhaul of the system is needed. Bleeding is also used at the 30,000 miles task, to change the brake fluid.

2 You will need:

a) An assistant to pump the pedal
b) A good supply of new hydraulic fluid
c) An empty glass jar
d) A plastic or rubber pipe to fit the bleed nipple
e) A spanner for the nipple

3 Top up the master cylinder, and put fluid in the bleed jar to a depth of about ½ inch.

4 Start at the nipple furthest away from the master cylinder; ie. rear brake, passenger side, and work nearer.

5 Clean the nipple and put the pipe on it.

6 Tell your assistant to give a few quick strokes to pump up pressure, and then hold the pedal on.

7 Slacken the nipple, about ½ or 1 turn, till the fluid or air begins to come out. This is usually quite apparent either as bubbles or dirt in the clean fluid in the jar.

8 As soon as the flow starts, tell the assistant to keep pumping the pedal everytime it gets to the end of its travel, and tell you all the time where the pedal is; 'down, up' etc.

9 As soon as air has stopped coming out shut the bleed nipple; do so as the assistant is pushing the pedal down. Do not go on too long, lest the reservoir is emptied, and more air pumped in. About 15 pedal pumps is safe.

10 Refill the reservoir, and repeat at the other wheels. Also keep going on the original wheel after refilling the reservoir if dirty fluid is still coming out, to get rid of all the old.

11 Bleeding is greatly speeded, and can be done by one person, if spring loaded valves are fitted to the nipples. These are available from accessory shops.

12 Keep hydraulic fluid clear of the car's paint. It ruins it. Throw old fluid away. It attracts damp, so deteriorates in use.

13 If there is difficulty in getting air out of the system, then each time the assistant releases the pedal, close the nipple, so no back flow can take place.

11 Servo unit

1 The servo unit is bolted to the bulkhead on a special bracket and comes between the brake pedal and the master cylinder. The master is, therefore, removed from the servo unit not the bulkhead. The servo unit uses inlet manifold vacuum to provide boosted pressure on the master cylinder piston. (photo)

2 Maintenance and adjustments are minimal. There is an air filter round the pushrod from the brake pedal. Overhaul kits are not readily available and in the case of suspected malfunction it must be renewed complete. However check the following paragraphs very carefully first.

3 Poor braking can come on gradually, so escape notice. If the pedal pressure seems high the servo action should be checked as follows.

4 Do a brake test from about 25 mph, on a smooth, level and traffic free road. The car should pull up straight, and it should be possible to lock the wheels, leaving black tyre marks.

5 Switch off the engine. Apply the brakes about six times to deplete the vacuum reserve.

6 Press the pedal down, and hold the brakes on lightly. Start the engine; the pedal will tend to fall away from the foot: less pressure will be needed to hold the brakes applied. If this effect

is not felt the servo is not giving assistance.

7 Start up. Run the engine at medium speed, to build up depression. Switch off the engine and close the throttle. Wait for 90 seconds. Then try the brakes. There should be enough vacuum for two or three applications of the brakes. If the depression has been lost either the check valve is faulty, or there is a leak.

8 To double check for a leak replace the manifold hose and its clips.

9 To renew the non-return valve, leave the servo unit in position in the vehicle. Disconnect the vacuum inlet hose from the servo unit.

10 Pull and twist the non-return valve out of engagement with its rubber sealing washer.

11 Renew the valve and sealing washer if required. Refitting will be eased if both components are first lubricated with clean brake fluid.

12 Apart from the air filter, non-return valve and vacuum inlet hose which should be checked as described, the servo unit will have to be renewed as an assembly. Disconnect its pushrod from the brake pedal, undo the four nuts which locate it to its bracket, disconnect the fluid and vacuum pipes and remove the unit complete with master cylinder from the car leaving the pipes, and its brackets, behind. Now remove the master cylinder.

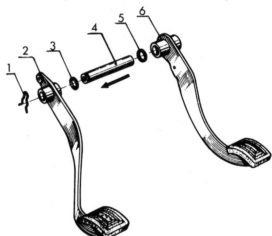

FIG. 8.15. THE BRAKE AND CLUTCH PEDAL MECHANISM

1 Circlip   4 Pedal shaft
2 Clutch pedal   5 Spacer
3 Spacer   6 Brake pedal
The arrow indicates the direction of removal

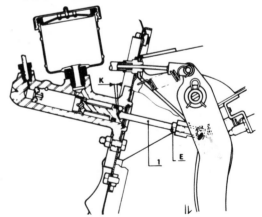

FIG. 8.16. CROSS SECTION OF THE BRAKE PEDAL AND MASTER CYLINDER WITH FLUID RESERVOIR

1 Pedal push rod   E is the adjusting nut
K Free play distance = 5 mm (0.196 in.)

12 Brake and clutch pedals and adjustments

1   The brake and clutch pedals pivot on the same shaft and must, therefore, be considered together. The shaft runs through bronze bushes, one located in each pedal and is located by a circlip and a roll pin. The bushes, but usually the shaft, wear and cause sloppy action of both pedals.

2   To remove the shaft, unclip both return springs from the pedals. (This disconnects the clutch cable). Remove the split pin from the brake pedal to master cylinder pushrod hinge pin and remove the pin.

3   Remove the circlip from the clutch side of the shaft and pull away the clutch pedal towards the left.

4   Now drive out the shaft, with a 'soft' drift through the brake pedal noting how the washers fall.

5   Replacement is a reversal of the removal procedure but grease the shaft first and relocate all the washers and pins properly.

6   Clutch pedal adjustment is not strictly necessary, for cable adjustment only should be made. See Chapter 5.

7   Brake pedal/pushrod adjustment, however, must be made. Renault state that the clearance should be 5 mm (0.196 inch) between the pushrod end and the inner face of the master cylinder or servo unit. This is impractical to measure, therefore this clearance must be judged by watching the 'loose' movement of the pushrod when the pedal is lightly pressed before it "clicks" with the inner face. If desired press the pedal in, then put a pencil mark on the pushrod at the point it disappears through the bulkhead. Release it and measure the difference. Adjust the pushrod and lock it with the nut, when clearance is correct.

13 Brake light switch

1   The brake light switch is mechanically rather than hydraulically operated. It is attached to the steering column support bracket just above the brake pedal and is affixed by a through bolt. As the pedal is pressed down, so it pivots up and presses the brake light switch.

2   If the switch fails it must be renewed. Disconnect the feed wires and withdraw the through bolt. Replacement is a simple reverse procedure.

11.1 The brake servo is no more difficult to remove than the ordinary master cylinder

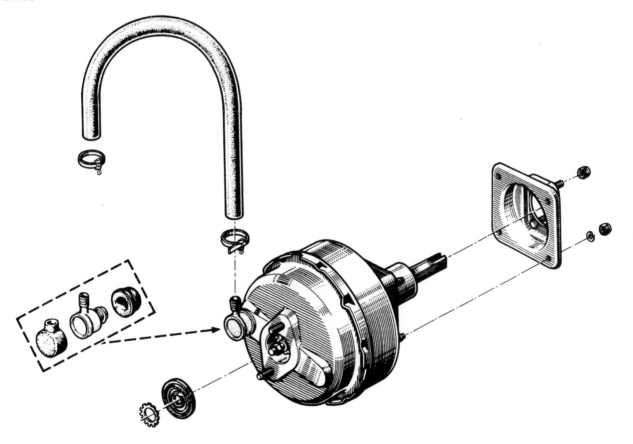

Fig. 8.17. The brake servo and its mounting bracket

14 Fault finding

Before diagnosing faults in the brake system check that any irregularities are not caused by:

1 Uneven and incorrect tyre pressures
2 Incorrect 'mix' of radial and cross-ply tyres
3 Wear in the steering mechanism
4 Defects in the suspension and shock absorbers
5 Misalignment of the body frame

Symptom	Reason/s	Remedy
Pedal travels a long way before the brakes operate	Brake shoes set too far from drums, or badly worn linings/pads	Check rear brake adjustment (where applicable). Check disc pad thicknesses. Check rear brake linings for wear. Adjust/renew as applicable.
Stopping ability poor, even though pedal pressure is firm	Linings and/or drums badly worn or scored One or more wheel hydraulic cylinders seized, resulting in some brake shoes not pressing against the drums (or pads against discs) Brake linings contaminated with oil	Dismantle, inspect and renew as required. Dismantle and inspect wheel cylinders. Renew as necessary. Renew linings and repair source of oil contamination.
	Wrong type of linings fitted	Verify type of material which is correct for the car and fit it.
	Brake shoes wrongly assembled Servo booster unit inoperative	Check for correct assembly. Check manifold vacuum pipe overhaul servo.
Car veers to one side when the brakes are applied	Brake linings on one side are contaminated with oil/grease/hydraulic fluid Hydraulic wheel cylinder on one side partially or fully seized A mixture of lining materials fitted between sides Unequal wear between sides caused by partially seized wheel cylinders	Renew linings and stop leak. Inspect wheel cylinders for correct operation and renew as necessary. Standardise on types of linings fitted. Check wheel cylinders and renew linings and drums as required.
Pedal feels spongy when the brakes applied	Air is present in the hydraulic system	Bleed the hydraulic system and check for any signs of leakage.
Pedal feels springy when the brakes are applied	Brake linings not bedded into the drums (after fitting new ones)	Allow time for new linings to bed in after which it will certainly be necessary to adjust the shoes to the drums as pedal travel will have increased.
	Master cylinder or brake backplate mounting bolts loose	Retighten mounting bolts.
Brakes overheating	Brakes used too severely Brakes binding	Drive less hard. Check rear drum adjuster. Check master cylinder free play.
Pedal travels right down with little or no resistance and brakes are virtually non-operative	Leak in hydraulic system resulting in lack of pressure for operating wheel cylinders If no signs of leakage are apparent the master cylinder internal seals are failing to sustain pressure	Examine the whole of the hydraulic system and locate and repair source of leaks. Test after repairing each and every leak source. Overhaul master cylinder. If indications are that seals have failed for reasons other than wear all the wheel cylinder seals should be checked also and the system completely replenished with the correct fluid.
Pedal creeps down when held on	Hydraulic leak	If no visible leak, master cylinder cups are being by-passed and need renewal.
Brake juddering	Disc/drum out of true Backplate loose Lining dust or road dirt inside rear drums	Measure and replace. Tighten. Clean out drums.

Chapter 9 Electrical system

Contents

Specifications

Battery

Voltage	12 DC
Capacity	40 ampere/hours
Polarity	Negative (−) earth
Manufacture (original equipment)	Fulmen AS810 or Tudor 6RF4

Alternator ... ... SEV, Ducellier or Paris-Rhone

Voltage	12v AC (rectified)
Regulator	Separate fitting, of appropriate SEV, Ducellier or Paris-Rhone manufacture

Starter motor

Type	Pre-engaged with solenoid engagement control
Voltage	12v DC
Manufacture	Ducellier 6187 or Paris-Rhone D8 E81
Commutator segment insulation undercut	.5 mm (.020 mm)

	Commutator dia.		Brush length	
	Nominal	Min.	Nominal	Min.
Ducellier type	33.5 mm (1.319 in)	33 mm (1.300 in)	15 mm (19/32 in)	7.5 mm (19/64 in)
Paris-Rhone type	36.5 mm (1.7/16 in)	34 mm (1.11/32 in)	14 mm (35/64 in)	8 mm (5/16 in)

Oil pressure switch ... ... Jaeger, points open under 5 psi

Water temperature switch ... ... Jaeger, contacts close at 115°C + or −5' (239°F + or − 41')

Windscreen wiper motor ... ... 2 speed: SEV 116 006 or Bosch WS490! REZA or Femsa

Flasher unit

Type	Klaxon 30 860 40/45W or Scintex 30630-6
or	Cartier 161

Stoplight switch ... ... Torix or LMP, mechanical type

Fuses

One fuse (15 amp) protecting	Interior light and wiper motor
One fuse (15 amp) protecting	Instrument panel, indicators, stop lights, heater fan

Ignition starter switch ... ... Neiman 23000

Headlamps ... ...   Cibie rectangular 72 20 056

Bulbs
Headlights (main and dipped beam) ... ...   12v 45/40 W headlight bulb socket 45 t 41
Front sidelights ... ...   12v 5W socket R19, BA15S/19
Front and rear direction indicators.. ... ...   12v 21W type P25–1, BAY15S/19
Rear sidelights and stop lights ... ...   12v 21/5W type P25–2, BAY 15S/19
Side repeater lights ... ...   12v 4W bulb
                                       Type T8
                                       Socket BA9s
Interior light ... ...   12v 7W festoon 10 x 39
Warning lights and instrument panel lights ... ...   12v 2W type T8, BA9/S socket
Glove box, rear luggage compartment lights ... ...   12v 5W type CU, festoon 11 x 35

1 General description

The electrical system operates at 12 volts DC and the major components, excluding the ignition circuits are:—
Battery, 12 volt negative earth.
Generator, alternator, driven by a V belt from the crankshaft.
Regulator.
Starter motor, pre-engaged, mounted at the right rear of the engine under the manifolds.
The battery supplies current for the ignition, lighting and other circuits and provides a reserve of power when the current consumed by the equipment exceeds the production of the generator.
The starter motor places very heavy demands on the power reserve. The generator uses engine power to produce electricity to re-charge the battery and the rate of charge is automatically controlled by a regulator. This regulator keeps the power output of the generator within its capacity (an uncontrolled generator can burn itself out) and adjusts the voltage and current output depending on the state of the battery charge and the electrical demands being made on the system at any one time.

2 Battery - maintenance, removal and replacement

1 Any new battery, if properly looked after, will last for two years at least (provided also that the generator and regulator are in correct order).
2 The principal maintenance requirements are cleanliness and regular topping up of the electrolyte level with distilled water. Each week the battery cell cover or caps should be removed and just enough water added, if needed, to cover the tops of the separators. Do not overfill with the idea of the topping up lasting longer - it will only dilute the electrolyte and with the level high the likelihood of it 'gassing' out is increased. This is the moisture one can see on the top of a battery. 'Little and often is the rule'.
3 Wipe the top of the battery carefully at the same time removing all traces of moisture. Paper handkerchiefs are ideal for the job.
4 Every three months disconnect the battery terminals and wash both the posts and lead connectors with a washing soda solution. This will remove any corrosion deposits. Dry them off and smear liberally with petroleum jelly - not grease, before reconnection.
5 Battery removal is simply a matter of disconnecting the lead terminal clamps, slackening the battery retaining clamp and lifting it out. Always undo the earth terminal clamp first and when reconnecting replace it last. In this way there is no danger of short circuiting the other terminal to earth. Always carry and place the battery in an upright position so as to prevent spillage of the electrolyte.

6 If a significant quantity of electrolyte is lost through spillage it will not suffice merely to refill with distilled water. Have the battery drained, and refilled by your dealer.

3 Battery - charging

1 In winter certain conditions may result in the battery being used in excess of the generator's ability to recharge it in the running time available. This situation does not occur however on cars fitted with alternators which have a much higher rate of output at low revolutions.
2 Where necessary therefore, an external charging source is needed to keep the battery power reserve at the proper level. If batteries are being charged from an external source a hydrometer is used to check the electrolyte specific gravity. Once the fully charged reading is obtained charging should not continue for a period in excess of four hours. Most battery chargers are set to charge at 3–4 amps initially and as the battery charge builds up this reduces automatically to 1–2 amps. The table below gives details of the specific gravity readings, at 21°C/70°F. Do not take readings just after topping up, just after using the starter motor, or when the electrolyte is too cold or too warm. The variation is SG readings is .004 for every 6°C/10°F charge - the higher readings being for the higher temperatures.

Specific gravity	Battery state of charge
1.28	100%
1.25	75%
1.22	50%
1.19	25%
1.16	Very low
1.11	Discharged completely

4 Generator (alternator) - description and precautions

All models imported to the United Kingdom are fitted with alternators in place of the more generally wellknown DC dynamos. The alternator generates alternating current (AC) which is rectified by diodes into DC and is the current needed for battery storage.
The regulator is a transistorized unit which is permanently sealed and required no attention. It will last indefinitely provided no mistakes are made in wiring connections. It is mounted on the left side inner wing.
Apart from the renewal of the rotor slip ring brushes and rotor shaft bearings, there are no other parts which need periodic inspection. All other items are sealed assemblies and must be replaced if indications are that they are faulty.
If there are indications that the charging system is malfunctioning in any way, care must be taken to diagnose faults

properly, otherwise damage of a serious and expensive nature may occur to parts which are in fact quite serviceable.

The following basic requirements must be observed at all times, therefore, if damage is to be prevented:

1   ALL alternator systems use a NEGATIVE earth. Even the simple mistake of connecting a battery the wrong way round could burn out the alternator diodes in a few seconds.

2   Before disconnecting any wires in the system the engine and ignition circuits should be switched off. This will minimise accidental short circuits.

3   The alternator must NEVER be run with the output wire disconnected.

4   Always disconnect the battery from the car's electrical system if an outside charging source is being used.

5   Do not use test wire connections that could move accidentally and short circuit against nearby terminals. Short circuits will not blow fuses - they will blow diodes or transistors.

6   Always disconnect the battery cables and alternator output wires before any electric welding work is done on the car body.

Fault diagnosis on alternator charging systems requires sophisticated test equipment and even with this the action required to rectify any fault is limited to the renewal of one or two components. Knowing what the fault is is only of academic interest in these circumstances.

7   Rotor slip ring brushes are easily removed and replaced, however the rotor shaft bearings should be left to an auto electrician. (photo)

8   The slip ring brushes are secured to a special plate screwed to the brush end cover. Unscrew the plate and renew complete. Brush length should be at least 2/3 of their original length to warrant continued use. Compare them with new brushes as a guide. Note that in the Ducellier alternator the brushes are not located in a separate carrier but in the end housing. The brushes and wires are still retained by screws.

4.7 The alternator brush holder - two small screws for fitting

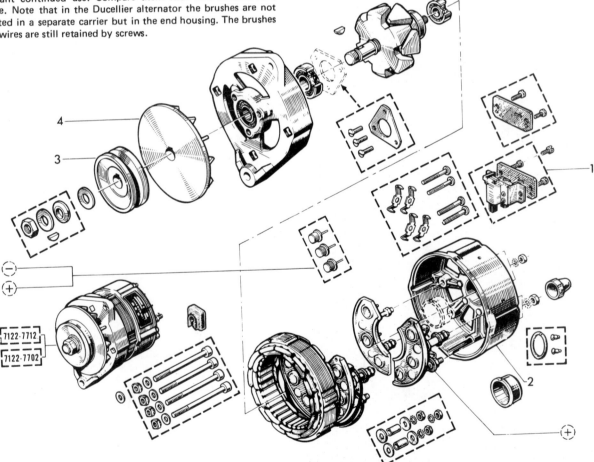

FIG. 9.1. THE SEV ALTERNATOR COMPONENTS

1   Brush holder   2   Main casing   3   Pulley   4   Fan

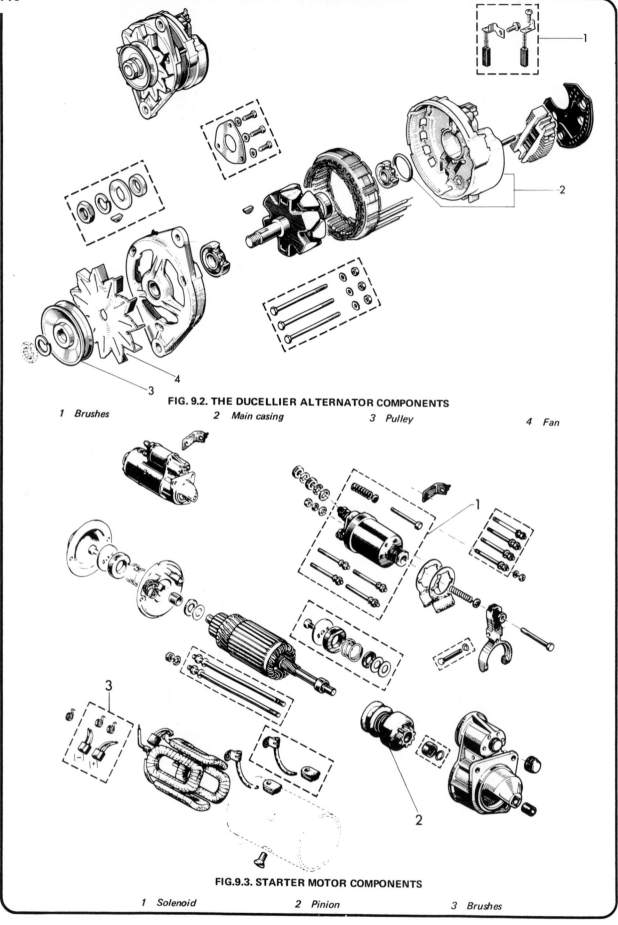

FIG. 9.2. THE DUCELLIER ALTERNATOR COMPONENTS

1 *Brushes*   2 *Main casing*   3 *Pulley*   4 *Fan*

FIG.9.3. STARTER MOTOR COMPONENTS

1 *Solenoid*   2 *Pinion*   3 *Brushes*

5   Generators - removal and replacement

1   The generator is held by a pivot bolt on the left side of the cylinder head and a lower slotted brace which allows it to be positioned in order to adjust the fan belt tension.

2   Remove the nuts holding the two leads or withdraw the plug connections on an alternator.

3   Slacken the nut on the slotted brace and the upper pivot bolt, move the generator inwards and disengage the fan belt.

4   Remove the slotted brace securing bolt.

5   Remove the pivot bolt completely and lift the generator away.

6   Replacement is a reversal of this procedure. Tension the fan belt by pulling the generator away from the crankcase. A lever can be used on a dynamo but with an alternator the case is more fragile so leverage should not be used. Then tighten the locknut on the brace followed by the pivot bolt. (photo)

7   The generator mounting bracket and the slotted brace are bolted to the cylinder head. They are held by four and two setscrews respectively, consequently they are straightforward to remove once the generator has been removed.

5.6   The fan belt adjuster

6   Starter motor - removal and replacement

1   Removal of the starter motor is a lousy job and takes time because of all the other things that have to be taken away first. If you are removing it because it does not work (and if it does not work you can do nothing except remove it first) make quite sure first that it is not just a disconnected lead. One of the leads to the starter is a straight bullet connector and it may be loose or dirty. You will have to feel round behind the exhaust shield plate to get to it. It cannot be seen.

2   Having decided to remove the starter first remove the carburettor air cleaner.

3   Remove the two bolts holding the heat shield over the starter motor. Then disconnect the leads from the starter solenoid.

4   The three starter mounting bolts have to be undone. The upper two are not too inaccessible. The lower one needs a long socket extension and a universal joint adaptor. It must be got at from underneath.

5   The starter motor can be drawn back and out from the side with the exhaust pipe out of the way.

6   The starter is replaced in the same way.

7   Starter motor - testing, dismantling and fitting new solenoid and carbon brushes

Two types of solenoid enactivated pre-engaged starter motors have been used, either Paris Rhone or Ducellier. Both are very similar in concept. Little can be done successfully at home other than solenoid and brush renewal.

1   With the starter removed clamp it in a vice and connect up to it two wires of heavy capacity. They need not be like the wires on the car because it is going to be run without a load on. One of the wires should be connected to the large terminal from which the battery lead was disconnected and the other to the small connection terminal. If battery power is applied and the solenoid does not throw the drive pinion forward then the solenoid at least is faulty.

2   Next connect the wires so that one is to the other large terminal on the solenoid and the other to the body of the starter motor. If the motor turns you may have reasonable assurance that it will work in the car. If it does not, dismantling may reveal the need for new carbon brushes or skimming of the commutator in a similar manner to the dynamo.

3   A faulty solenoid must be renewed complete. Undo the nut securing the lead from the starter and the three or four through bolts holding it to the pinion end frame. After unhooking it from the pinion lever it can be removed. A new one may be fitted in the reverse order. (photo)

4   To examine the brushes the commutator end bracket with the brush holders must be removed after undoing the nuts on the through bolts. Do not lose the fibre and steel thrust washers between the bracket and the shaft.

5   If the brushes are renewed only, make sure that the starter is tested again after reassembly as described earlier. If it still does not turn then there must be something wrong with either the armature or the field coils and it should be checked and repaired by specialists.

7.3 Easy solenoid removal

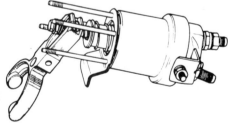

Fig.9.4. The fixings of the solenoid (starter motor)

Fig.9.5. The brushes in place in the brush carrier for the starter motor

8 Fuses

1   There are two fuses, in one fuse box on the inner wing under the bonnet. One fuse protects the interior light and the windscreen wiper. The other protects the instrument panel, stop lights, heater and direction indicators. The fuses are the weakest link in the circuit and any fault causing a short circuit will therefore blow the fuse rather than cause burning and a possible fire at the fault point. (photo)

2   If a fused item of electrical equipment fails to operate first check the appropriate fuse. If the fuse has blown the first thing to do is to find out why, otherwise it will merely blow again - (fuses can fail with old age but this is the exception rather than the rule). Having found the faulty fuse, switch off all electrical equipment and then fit a new fuse. From the Specifications note which circuits are served by the blown fuse and then start to switch each one on separately in turn. (It may be necessary for the ignition circuit to be turned on at the same time). The fuse should blow again when the faulty item is switched on. If the fuse does not blow immediately, start again only this time leave the circuits switched on and build up the cumulative total on the fuse. If and when it blows you will have an indication of which circuits may be causing the problem. It may take a little longer to isolate the fault which may not be serious at this stage. If the new fuse does not blow until the car is moving then look for a loose piece of wire which only causes a short circuit when moved.

8.1 Never drive without the proper fuses

9 Direction indicators

1   The direction indicators at the front have single filament bulbs with offset bayonet caps. To change a bulb on a front lamp remove the screws securing the lens and take off the lens and sealing gasket to get access to the bulb. At the rear the indicator bulb is a single filament and is housed in the single reflector. To replace the rear bulb remove the lens securing screw, remove the lens and then gain access to the bulb.

Some models have been fitted with front wing side repeater lights. These are conventional in fixture and similar to the front flasher light unit.

2   Failure of one or more of the indicator lights may be caused by a blown bulb. If the bulb is good the most likely reason otherwise is a bad earth connection from either the bulb to the bulb holder (corrosion caused by damp is a common cause) or from the bulb holder to the body frame. Check all these before assuming the flasher unit or switch is at fault. The flasher unit sits under the facia adjacent to the steering column. If each pair of terminals on the flasher unit is bridged then it can be seen whether the lamps light. It is then best to try and borrow a flasher unit known to be good to check whether the fault lies there. If the switch is suspect it will be an expensive replacement as there is no hope of a repair should it prove to be faulty. It is a combination switch with the lighting dip switch.

3   To remove this switch remove the bottom steering column cover (two Phillips screws countersunk). Disconnect the junction blocks and the other connections. Unscrew the three switch securing screws from the switch bracket to the steering column and remove th switch. (photo)

4   Replace the switch in a reverse sequence. Check the wiring connection with the appropriate illustration.

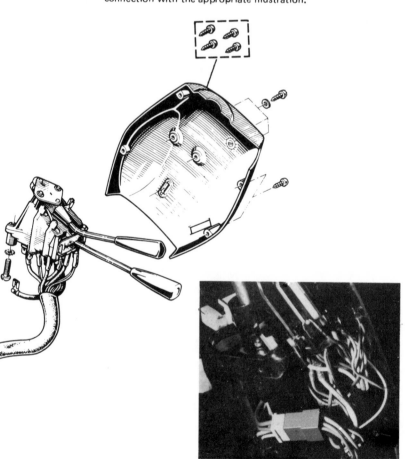

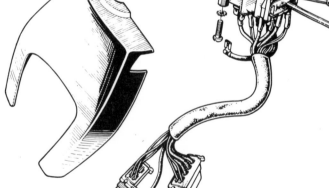

Fig.9.6. The combination lighting switch and cowling covers

9.3 The wiring shown is cluttered. In fact each steering connection is unique.

10 Windscreen wipers

1 Failure or malfunction will be due to a blown fuse, burnt out motor, or wear in the mechanical linkage causing stiffness or jamming. The latter fault could also be caused by incorrect mounting or a distorted support bracket.

2 To remove the wiper blades simply flick them round and pull them off in the conventional manner. They must be renewed when they leave a clear screen streaky. Always purchase the genuine fitment - there are few substitutes that work. (photo)

3 Remove the wiper blades and then spring forward the arms away from the screen. The arm is a push-on sprung fit, simply pull it off. Refitment is straightforward. Always make sure the sweep is correct - set the motor in the 'Park' position before fitting - then check. (photo)

4 If wiper failure has occurred pull off the blades and arms and then remove the spindle outer securing nut which sits below the base of the wiper arm. Never remove the wiper motor without the mechanism, it solves nothing. Proceed as follows:

5 Remove the heater controls (see Chapter 2).

6 Unclip the rubber air flap behind the control. Unscrew the two screws which locate the wiper motor plate.

7 Pull the plate back, and pull the wiper spindles through at the end of the plate. Wriggle the winder mechanism to the left of the steering column.

8 The motor is secured to the plate by three screws. The motor drive is located to the 'master' link by one shaft nut. Undo the shaft nut first, then the three securing screws.

9 Check the operation of the spindles. They go rusty and therefore seize very quickly. The individual spindles are available as a spare. Retain the small fixing circlips.

10 Failure of the motor, even brush deterioration, is rare. If this does happen, either exchange the motor or have it rebuilt by an auto electrician - its an intricate mechanism with its 'Park' facility.

11 Replacement of the motor and mechanism is fiddly, yet is a reverse procedure to their removal. Before tightening the spindle securing nuts check the proper operation.

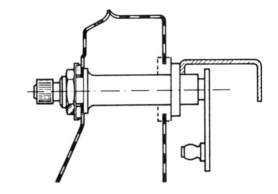

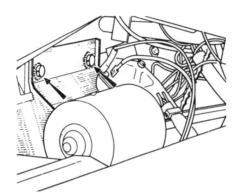

Fig.9.7. Cross section of the windscreen wiper spindle fixture (top) fixing screws of the wiper motor (lower)

Fig.9.8. Cross section of the windscreen wiper arm fixing

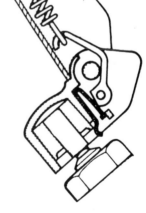

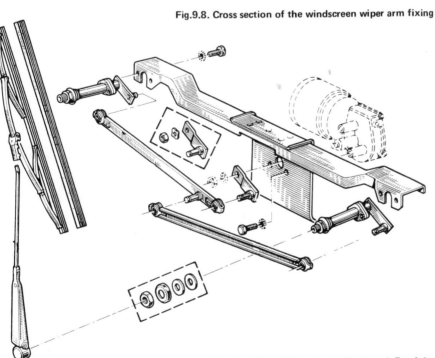

Fig.9.9. The wiper mechanism (The SEV system is illustrated, Bosch is very similar)

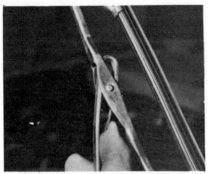

10.2 The unusual wiper blade fitting

10.3 The arm pulls off on splines

11 Windscreen washer

1   The screen washer is a manually operated pump (not R1177) mounted on the dashboard with a flexible pressure bulb. The unit contains two one-way valves so that when the bulb is pressed water is forced out to the screen through two valves and when it is released more liquid is drawn through the other valve from the reservoir hanging on the side of the engine compartment.
2   Malfunction is usually due to blocked jets on the screen delivery nozzles. These can be cleared with fine wire. Other causes of failure are usually due to blocked pipes, kinked pipes or disconnected pipes. The latter is usually apparent when the pump is operated.
3   If the pump is proved unserviceable it must be renewed.
4   The R1177 is electrically operated by a small pump attached to the reservoir. It is easy to check the operation of this pump, once the wiring is checked. Renew the pump if faulty, spares are not available.

12 Lights (front) and main light switch

1   The headlamp assemblies must be removed to change the bulbs. To remove the headlamp unit first remove the headlamp surround by unscrewing the two top locating screws and pulling it away from the bottom lugs. Bulb removal is described shortly. (photo)
2   The basic headlight is of the pre-focus type fitted with a replaceable bulb held by spring clips. With the thumb of the left hand push upwards the metal clip on the top left hand side of the lamp unit retainer and with the right hand pull the lamp away from this retainer hinging it at the opposite edge. Lift out the lamp by releasing the hook from the wire bracket at this hinging point. Pull off the electrical connector(s) from the bulb. The bulb may be released from the lamp by pressing down the two retaining springs and extracting it. (photos)

3   Check the condition of the bulbs once removed and replace if doubtful. Any discolouring is an indication of present or potential malfunction. Make sure you purchase the correct type of bulb. Take the old bulb along to the stores and match it with the replacement.
Special Note: If there is any kind of malfunction of the headlights always check the earth strap.
4   Headlamp adjustment should be undertaken only with the proper optical equipment. This is therefore best left to your local Renault garage. Fitted to the headlight units is a small switch below the bulb orifice which allows differing beam dipping direction. Make sure this is in the correct position under all circumstances. Full instructions should be stuck to the rear of the unit. Also check the side level switch for proper operation.
5   It is possible to adjust the direction and height of the headlights with a small screwdriver. Always adjust on main beam, and blank off one headlight while the other is being adjusted. Headlamp rims do not have to be removed on all models to adjust in an emergency. Place the vehicle 25 feet, square, away from a wall and turn the adjusting screws in either direction until the lamp is adjusted. Then do the other one. When finally adjusted oil the adjusting screws (they often rust solid). (photo)
6   The headlight holders are illustrated.
7   Front side/flasher units are illustrated; they are conventional and easy to repair. (photo)
8   The lighting switch is a 'twist and flick' affair on the steering column. If there is any failure the whole switch must be renewed. See Chapter 12 for its removal and replacement.

13 Lights - rear

1   The direction indicator bulb and the stop tail light bulb are housed in a common cluster. Remove the single lens fixed with three screws. The bulbs can then be removed. The stop/tail lamp bulb is a double filament one with offset bayonet pins. It is the same as the side/flasher bulb used at the front. (photo)
2   The registration plate light is conventional. On the saloon models it is a screw in fixing in the rear bumper accessible from above. On the estate there are two black plastic lamps on the tailgate either side of the number plate. See the appropriate illustrations.
3   Most models are equipped with reversing lights attached to the rear bodywork below the rear lights (integral with the rear lights on R1177 and on the tailgate R1171 and R1330). In all cases they are a conventional fitting and are removed/replaced as for the rear lights.

14 Interior lights

1   There is one centre roof interior light. The light has an integral switch which can be hand operated - it has three positions - "off", "on" and "on" when a front door is open.
2   If there is any failure the conventional checks should be made. First the bulb, then the switch etc. The lens clips on.
3   If the lamp does not illuminate when a front door is open check the courtesy switch in the front door pillar. It too is a 'push-in' clip. Check its earth first.
4   All instrument panel lights are described in the instrument panel section.

15 Instrument panel and instruments, to include the switches

1   It is not necessary to remove the dashboard/facia to remove the instrument panel nor the otherway round, although it is desirable when removing the facia.
2   Instrument panels are junction connected, printed circuitry which is both clear and simple and of great advantage to the home mechanic. The R1170, R1171 and R1330 share the same panel whilst the R1177 is different. Effectively the R1177 panel

combines the two outer R1170 instruments/dials and adds an electronic tachometer to make three dials. All types are similar in principle and in terms of removal and replacement.

3 Always disconnect the battery. See Fig.9.6 and remove the two junction blocks and the speedometer cable. Check there are no further electrical connections.

4 Lift the two top locating clips and pull the panel out freeing the bottom mounting lugs. Replacement is an exact reverse procedure. Changing a malfunctioning instrument or warning bulb is simple. The bulbs are a push-in push-out fit. Instruments cannot be repaired at home. Once removed have an instrument specialist look at it or purchase a new part. Both will be expensive. (photos)

5 Instrument glass is integral for all three instruments. It is 'notched' in the panel, spring it out. On the reverse of the panel unscrew the appropriate fixings and take care with the instrument. Remove the appropriate printed circuit.

6 Replacement is an exact reverse procedure.

16 Horns and switch

1 The horns are located behind the grille panels under the front bumper at each side of the car. They are accessible from inside the front wings.

There is no facility for adjustment or repair. If it has failed it must be renewed. As they are reliable instruments always check the horn push (much less reliable) and the wiring.

2 The horn push is part of the expensive combination light and flasher switch. This is described in Section 12. No repair facility is possible.

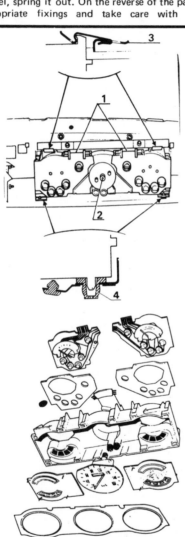

FIG.9.10. THE REAR AND THE COMPONENTS OF THE INSTRUMENT CLUSTER (NOT R1177)

1 Locating lips	3 Top clips
2 Speedo cable	4 Locating sockets

(R1177 is very similar except that there are three instrument pods)

12.1 Remove the outer grille cover for any work on the headlamps

12.2a Special bulb clip. Always clean the contacts

12.2b The bulb is held by two 'push' springs

12.2c Check that the bulb will clip correctly

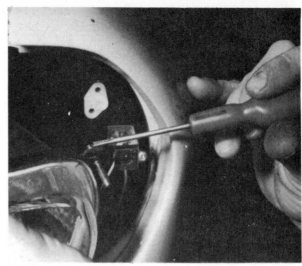

12.5 The adjusting screws always seize!

12.7 One single (left), one double (right) filament bulbs

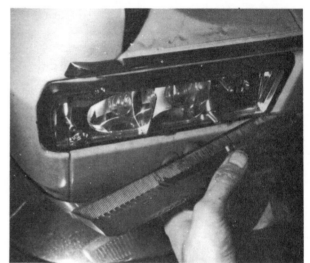

13.1 The total rear lens is expensive

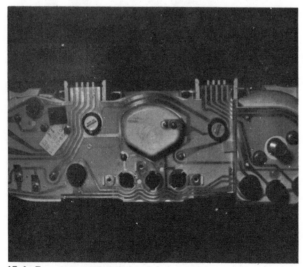

15.4a Easy to use printed circuitry

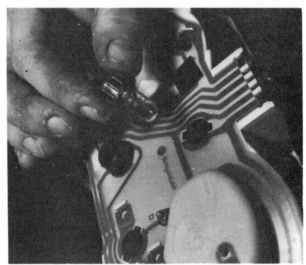

15.4b Panel bulb changing is a simple pull-out/ push-in fit.

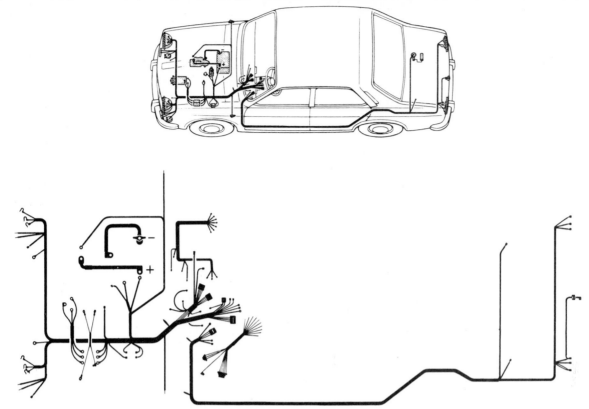

Fig.9.11. The wiring loom location for R1170 to Veh. no.503103, all R1171 and R1330 to Veh. no.4151

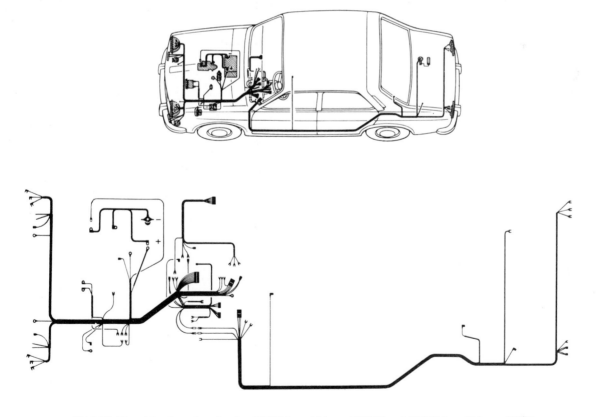

Fig.9.12. The wiring loom location for R1170 from Veh. no.503104 and R1330 from Veh. no.41502

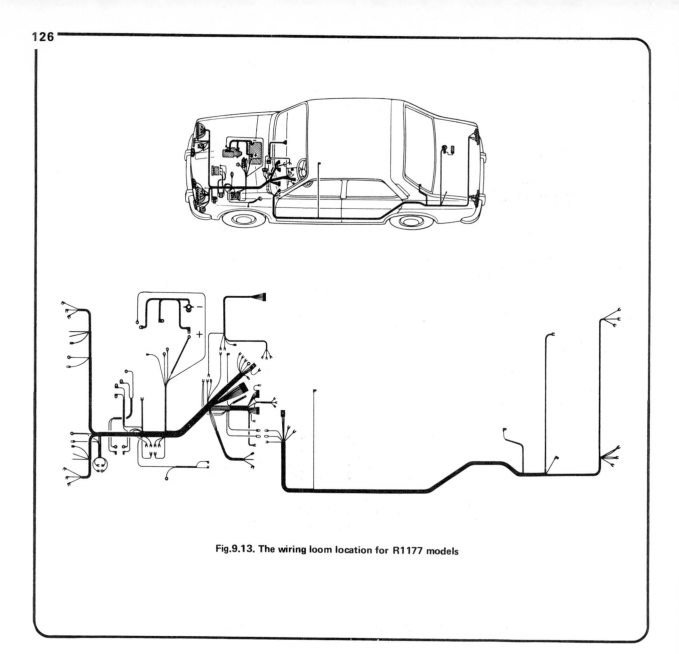

Fig.9.13. The wiring loom location for R1177 models

ELECTRICAL WIRING

Note: Drawings and information in connection with wiring with relevant colour codes in respect of sundry components, instruments, switches etc (Figs. No. 9-14 — 9-35) is given on the following pages–127 to 134 inclusive.

FIG. 9.14. INSTRUMENT PANEL

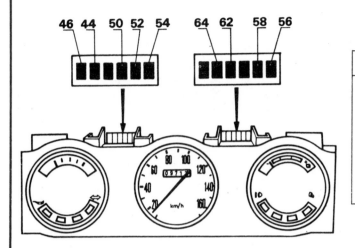

No.	Description	Colour
44	Oil pressure switch	Pink
46	Water temperature switch	Green
50	Choke warning light	Red
52	Direction indicator tell-tale	Black
54	Instrument panel earth	Yellow
56	Handbrake warning light	Black
58	Feed to instrument panel	Grey
62	Headlight main beam warning light	Blue
64	Instrument panel lighting	White
112	Fuel gauge	Black

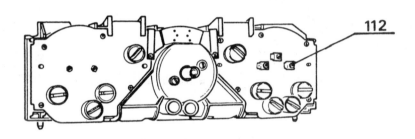

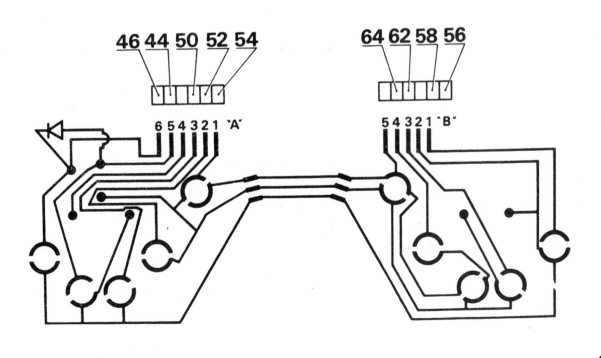

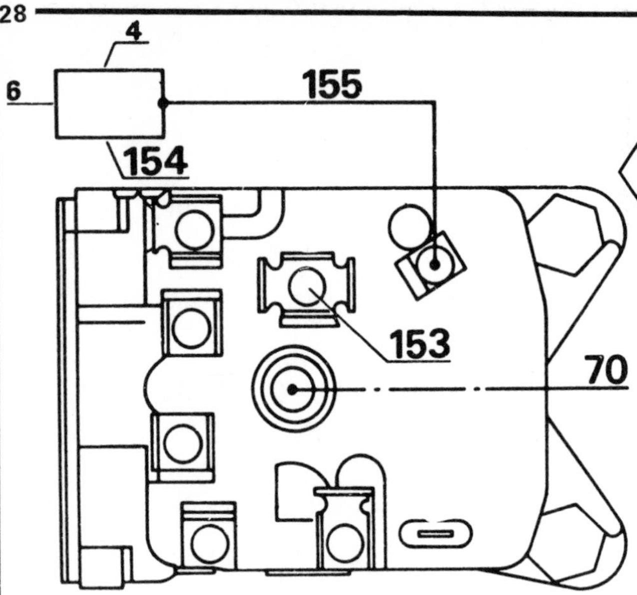

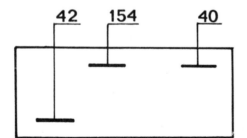

FIG. 9.15. COMBINATION LIGHTING SWITCH

No.	Description	Colour
4	Feed to junction plate on combination lighting switch	White
6	Feed to Neiman	Beige
70	Retaining wire	Grey
153	Feed to instrument panel rheostat	White
154	Feed to parking lights	Blue
155	Feed to combination lighting switch	Blue

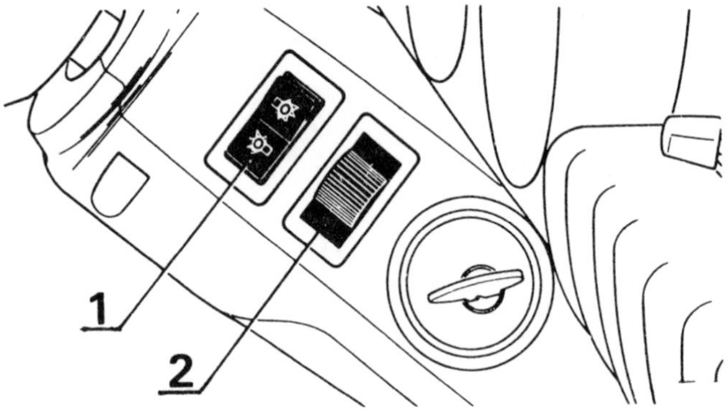

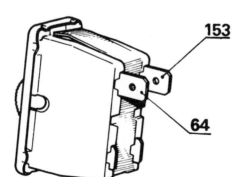

FIG. 9.16. INSTRUMENT PANEL SWITCHES

1 – Parking lights switch
2 – Instrument panel lighting switch

FIG. 9.17. PARKING LIGHTS SWITCH

No.	Description	Colour
40	Left hand parking light	Black
42	Right hand parking light	Black (maroon)
154	Feed to switch	Blue

FIG. 9.18. INSTRUMENT PANEL LIGHTING RHEOSTAT

No.	Description	Colour
64	Instrument panel lighting	White
153	Feed to rheostat	White

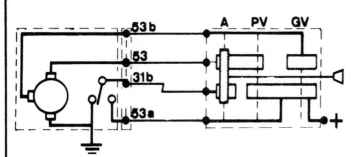

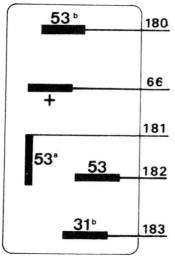

FIG. 9.19. WINDSCREEN WIPER

No.	Description	Colour
66	Feed to windscreen wiper switch	Pink
180		(red)
181		(blue)
182	Windscreen wiper motor	(green)
183		(black)

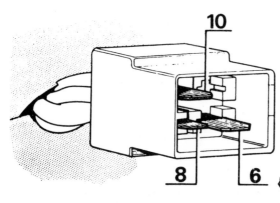

FIG. 9.20. IGNITION STARTER SWITCH

No.	Description	Colour
6	Feed to Neiman	Beige
8	Starter relay	Grey
10	Feed to fuse (after Neiman)	Red
170		Red
171	Ignition starter switch	Blue
172		Green
173		Yellow

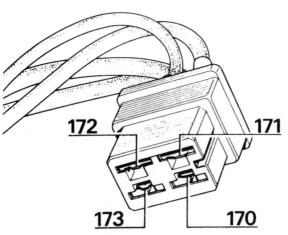

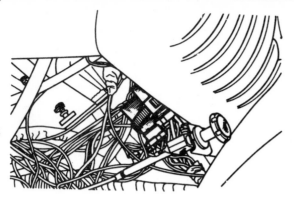

FIG. 9.21. JUNCTION BLOCKS

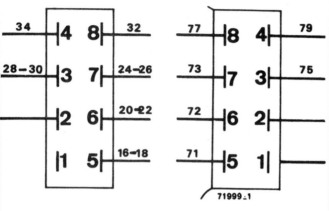

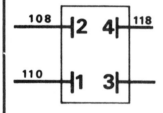

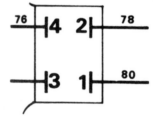

71999·1

No.	Description	Colour
16	Left hand main beam	Green
18	Right hand main beam	Green
20	Left hand dipped beam	Pink
22	Right hand dipped beam	Pink
24	Left hand horn	Grey
26	Right hand horn	Grey
28	Left hand front sidelight	White
30	Right hand front sidelight	White
32	Left hand front direction Indicator	Blue
34	Right hand front direction Indicator	Red
71	Feed to headlights	Blue
72	Feed to dipped beams	Red
73	Horns	White
75	Feed to front side lights	White
76	Feed to rear lights	Blue
78	Feed to left hand rear direction indicator	Blue
79	Feed to right hand front direction indicator	Red
80	Feed to right hand rear direction indicator	Red
108	Left hand rear direction indicator	Blue
110	Right hand rear direction indicator	Red
118	Feed to rear lights	White

FIG. 9.22. JUNCTION PLATES

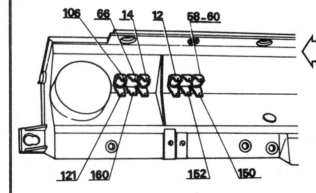

No.	Description	Colour
12	Feed to junction plate (after switch)	Red
14	Feed to junction plate (direct)	Blue
58	Feed to instrument panel	Grey
60	Feed to heater	Grey
66	Feed to windscreen wiper switch	Pink
106	Rear luggage compartment light	Blue
121	Feed to interior light	White
150	Feed to stop light switch	Grey
152	Feed to flasher unit	Grey
160	Feed to cigar lighter	White

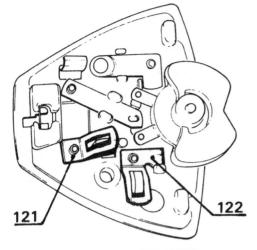

No.	Description	Colour
121	Feed to interior light	White (blue)
122	Return to earth (ground)	White

FIG. 9.23. INTERIOR LIGHT

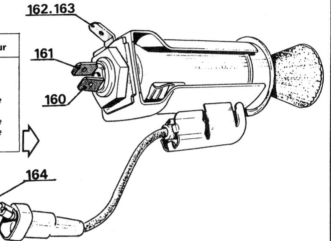

No.	Description	Colour
160	Feed to cigar lighter	Blue
161	Feed to glove compartment light	Blue
162	Cigar lighter earth (ground)	White
163	Glove compartment light earth (ground)	White
164	Cigar lighter illumination	White

FIG. 9.24. CIGAR LIGHTER

No.	Description	Colour
52	Direction indicator tell-tale	Black
74	Feed to change-over switch	Green
152	Feed to flasher unit	Grey

FIG. 9.25. FLASHER UNIT

No.	Description	Colour
10	Feed to fuse after Neiman	Red
12	Feed to junction plate (after Neiman)	Red
14	Feed to junction plate (direct)	Blue
48	Ignition coil	Grey
151	Feed to fuses (direct)	Blue

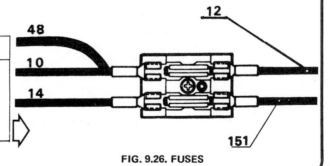

FIG. 9.26. FUSES

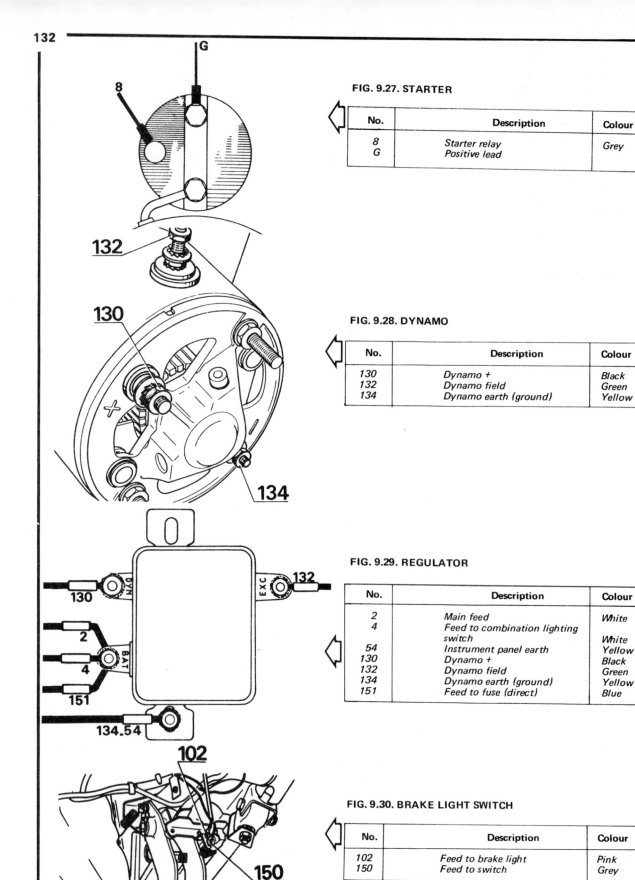

FIG. 9.27. STARTER

No.	Description	Colour
8	Starter relay	
G	Positive lead	Grey

FIG. 9.28. DYNAMO

No.	Description	Colour
130	Dynamo +	Black
132	Dynamo field	Green
134	Dynamo earth (ground)	Yellow

FIG. 9.29. REGULATOR

No.	Description	Colour
2	Main feed	White
4	Feed to combination lighting switch	White
54	Instrument panel earth	Yellow
130	Dynamo +	Black
132	Dynamo field	Green
134	Dynamo earth (ground)	Yellow
151	Feed to fuse (direct)	Blue

FIG. 9.30. BRAKE LIGHT SWITCH

No.	Description	Colour
102	Feed to brake light	Pink
150	Feed to switch	Grey

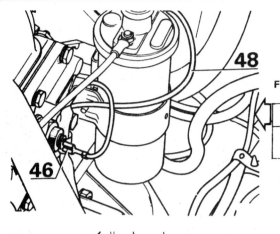

FIG. 9.31. IGNITION COIL AND WATER TEMPERATURE SWITCH

No.	Description	Colour
46	Water temperature switch	Green
48	Ignition coil	Grey (red)

FIG. 9.32. OIL PRESSURE SWITCH

No.	Description	Colour
44	Oil pressure switch	Pink

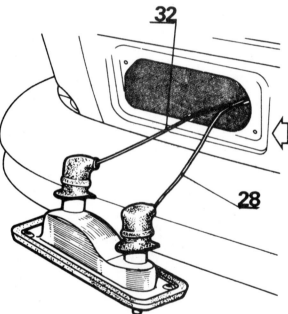

FIG. 9.33. FRONT SIDE LIGHTS

Left hand

No.	Description	Colour
28	Front left hand sidelight	White
32	Front left hand flasher	Blue

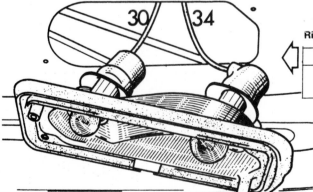

Right hand

No.	Description	Colour
30	Front right hand sidelight	White
34	Front right hand flasher	Red

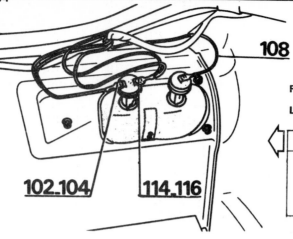

108

102.104 **114.116**

FIG. 9.34. REAR LIGHTS

Left hand side

No.	Description	Colour
102	Feed to brake light	Pink
104	Right hand brake light	Black
108	Left hand rear flasher	Blue
114	License plate light	White
116	Left hand rear light	White

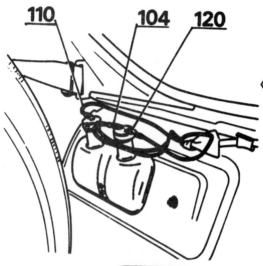

110 **104** **120**

Right hand side

No.	Description	Colour
104	Right hand brake light	Black
110	Right hand rear flasher	Red
120	Right hand rear light	White

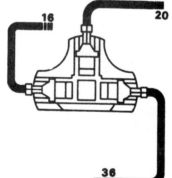

16 **20**

36

FIG. 9.35. HEADLIGHTS

Left hand side

No.	Description	Colour
16	Left hand main beam	Green
20	Left hand dipped beam	Pink
36	Left hand headlight earth (ground)	Grey

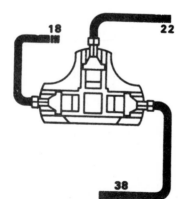

18 **22**

38

Right hand side

No.	Description	Colour
18	Right hand main beam	Green
22	Right hand dipped beam	Pink
38	Right hand headlight earth (ground)	Grey

Chapter 10 Suspension and steering

Contents

Specification

Front suspension	Independent by wishbones and coil springs, hydraulic telescopic shock absorbers, anti-roll bar
Rear suspension	Non-independent, pressed steel beam axle, two longitudinal tie-rods and an A bracket (central triangle) to assure its lateral positioning, anti-roll bar, coil springs and telescopic shock absorbers
Front springs	7.1 coils, wire diameter ½ inch (12.6 mm)
Rear springs	6 coils, wire diameter 31/64 inch (12.4 mm)

*R1171/R1330 plus 5% increase in flexibility rate of rear springs

Front anti-roll bar	17 mm diameter all models

| Rear anti-roll bar ... ... | 14 mm diameter R1170/R1177 |
| Rear anti-roll bar ... ... | 16 mm diameter R1171/R1330 |

Steering

Type	Rack and pinion
Turns from lock to lock	3.5
Ratio	20 to 1
Camber angle	1° 30' (laden)
Castor angle (nominal)	4° (laden)
Kingpin angle	8° (laden)
Toe-out (total)	1 to 4 mm (1/32 to 5/32 in)

Torque wrench settings

	lbf ft	Nm
Front suspension and steering		
Shock absorber lower mounting	45	61
Upper ball joint	35	48
Lower ball joint	35	48
Track rod end ball joints	25	34
Stub axle nut	115	156
Steering wheel nut	35	48
Steering shaft universal joint nut	25	34
Steering arm bolts	25	34
Anti-roll bar mounting	60	82
Lower wishbone pivot bolts	80	109
Upper wishbone pivot bolts	75	102
Steering box mounting bolts	20	27
Steering shaft flexible coupling	10	14
Rack end fitting	30	41
Castor tie rod to upper wishbone	30	41
Rear suspension		
Shock absorber lower mounting	20	27
Side arm pivot bolts	25	34
'A' bracket double pivot nuts	80	109
'A' bracket single pivot nuts	35	48
'A' bracket centre bearing nuts	10	14

1 General description and inspection of components

1 The suspension and steering of the Renault 12 is nothing startling when many manufacturers are now using hydraulic and air suspension systems although it was a slight departure from Renault's previous designs, and it is very effective.

The front suspension features double wishbones with ball joints at their outer ends locating on the 'stub axle' carrier. Telescopic hydraulic shock absorbers sitting inside coil springs are located on a pan on the top wishbone and again on the inside of the top inner wing of the front of the bodywork. Consequently unlike other earlier front wheel drive Renaults the monocoque construction of the bodywork is used to mount some of the suspension. An anti-roll bar connects the outer ends of the upper wishbone, and is itself located in its centre on two brackets to the bodyshell. Camber and castor angles are not adjustable.

The rear suspension is not independent. It consists of a pressed steel beam axle, from each end come stub axles to mount the rear road wheels. The beam axle is mounted in three places to the bodyshell; by two longitudinal tie rods at its outer ends and an 'A' bracket in the centre. Coil springs are mounted on special pans on the longitudinal arms at their lower end and are again fixed at their upper ends to the bodyshell. Telescopic hydraulic shock absorbers sit inside the springs. The longitudinal tie rods are affixed to the underside of the beam axle while the 'A' bracket is affixed to the top side. An anti-roll bar is used.

The usual Renault type of rack and pinion steering is used except that on these cars it sits behind the engine very close to the bulkhead. A jointed steering column is used allowing it to be described as 'collapsible'.

For maximum life of the vehicle and greatest passenger safety constant suspension and steering inspection should take place. These vehicles work their 'chassis' hard. Follow the Routine Maintenance checks thoroughly.

2 Inspect the outside of the shock absorbers for leaks and check their operation by bouncing.

3 With the car parked on level ground check that it sits level from left to right, and does not appear to be drooping at one end, particularly down at the back.

4 Examine all the rubber bushes of the suspension arms. The rubber should be firm, not softened by oil or cracked by weathering. The pin pivotted in the bush should be held central, and not able to make metal to metal contact.

5 Check the outside of the springs. If rusting, they should be sprayed with oil.

6 Check the tightness of all nuts, particularly those holding the front suspension ball joints to the uprights, and the shock absorbers to their fixings.

7 Grip the top of each wheel, in turn, and rock vigorously. Any looseness in the bearings, or the suspension can be felt, or failed rubber bushes giving metal to metal contact heard.

8 Free wheel slowly with the engine switched off, and listen for unusual noises.

9 The rubber boots of the ball joints that exclude dirt and water should be inspected to ensure they are properly in position, and not torn. If dirt or water gets into such a joint, it is ruined in a few hundred miles. The joint should be removed and a new boot fitted without delay.

10 Check the steering for wear. An assistant should wiggle the steering wheel to and fro, just hard enough to make the front wheels move. Watch the ball joints. There should be no visible free movement. Then grasp a front wheel with the hands at 3 and 9 o'clock on the wheel. Work at the wheel hard, to twist it. The rocking should shift the steering wheel but no lost motion should be felt.

11 There are also ball joints at the outer end of the track rods, where these join to the upright. But these are so well shielded and lubricated that no wear should develop there for considerable mileages.

12 If the steering rack/track rod gaiters fail disconnect the appropriate side and renew the gaiter immediately.

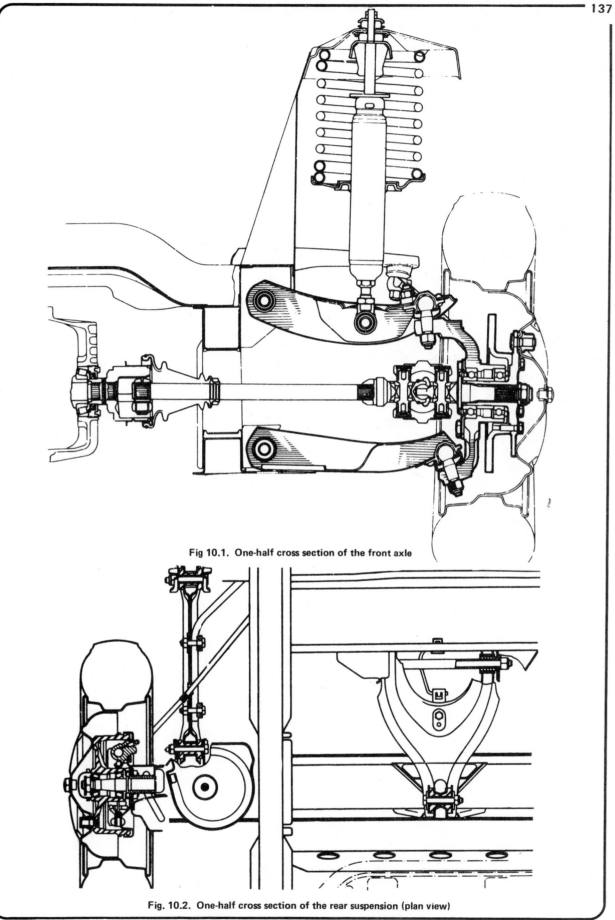

Fig 10.1. One-half cross section of the front axle

Fig. 10.2. One-half cross section of the rear suspension (plan view)

2 Front anti-roll bar - removal and replacement

1   The front anti-roll bar is often removed to give access to other parts of the car. Whenever it is always check the condition of its rubber bushes. Renew if they are suspect.

2   It is easiest if the vehicle is over a pit when removing the anti-roll bar to replace the bushes or to replace other suspension parts, although it matters little. Make sure the vehicle is properly secure on stands (if available) or on the ground with the handbrake on. It is not always necessary to remove the front wheels.

3   Remove the four bolts or nuts, and washers, which locate the anti-roll bar at its centre section under the car, and pull off the two clamps. Remove the two rubber bushes. That is all that need be done to replace these bushes. Return new bushes and refix the clamps. (photo)

4   To remove the bar completely undo the upper bolt of the top link on the wishbone. This is easier at this stage than removing the lower link bolt at the anti-roll bar end. Inspect the two rubber tubular bushes at the bottom end of the link. If the top link inserted bush is weak the top link must be renewed. (photo)

5   Replace in a reverse sequence but check that the bushes and their cups are located correctly.

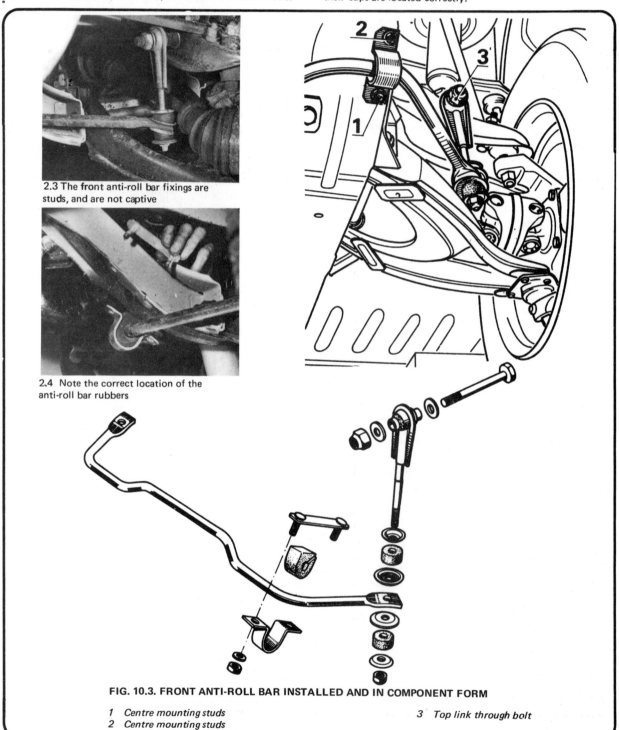

2.3 The front anti-roll bar fixings are studs, and are not captive

2.4 Note the correct location of the anti-roll bar rubbers

FIG. 10.3. FRONT ANTI-ROLL BAR INSTALLED AND IN COMPONENT FORM

1   Centre mounting studs
2   Centre mounting studs

3   Top link through bolt

3 Rear anti-roll bar - removal and replacement

1 The rear anti-roll bar is fixed only at its outer ends to the longitudinal arms. Jack up the rear of the car and support on axle stands allowing the axle to hang loose, and at the same height throughout its length. (photo)

2 Remove the four fixing bolts and their cap fixings. The anti-roll bar should now come away. Feed it over the exhaust.

3 Replace in a reverse sequence but remember to have the rear axle beam equally placed at each end. The anti-roll bar bolts solid to the suspension arms.

3.1 Two captive bolts only

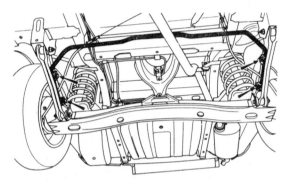

Fig.10.4. Rear anti-roll bar showing four fixing points

4.5 Grip the lower end of the shock absorber to undo lock nut

4 Front shock absorber and coil spring - removal and replacement

1 It is not possible to remove a front shock absorber without its coil spring, although they are easily separated. Fortunately it is not too difficult nor dangerous provided the right tools are to hand. Always renew shock absorbers and springs in pairs.

2 Jack up and support the side being repaired. Remove the road wheel. Clean the majority of the road dirt away from the spring, and shock absorber mountings. Soak the lower end with penetrating fluid. Lift the bonnet.

3 Obtain a spring compressing tool. These are now readily available and not too expensive. They consist of a threaded rod with a hooked end. A moving hook then slides up the rod, motivated by a large nut and washer. Clamp the pair of these to the spring (there is not too much room to work) and just tighten each one. Place the hooks as near to the top and bottom of the spring as is possible. Tighten each progressively and the spring will be seen to compress. Stop tightening once the spring is 'loose', away from its mounting pads.

4 With a pair of mole grips (self grip wrench) hold the top flat of the upper shock absorber mounting under the bonnet. Unlock the nut below it and remove the upper half bushes of this mounting.

5 At the bottom end of the shock absorber hold the nut close to the body of the shock absorber and then unlock the one below it. Now turn the first one and the body will unscrew from the bottom mounting bracket. (photo)

6 Compress the shock absorber by hand about two inches and then feed the shock absorber and coil spring still compressed away and over the front suspension.

7 Replacement is a straight reverse process. Check that the mounting bushes are in their correct sequence. 'Pump' by hand (vertically) new shock absorbers before fitting. The coil spring must be fitted 'compressed'.

8 If a new spring is to be fitted carefully compress it with the help of the two clamps and a large vice. Go very carefully because they can 'spring'. The spring 'top' has a flat locating area, the 'bottom' has a spiral locating area.

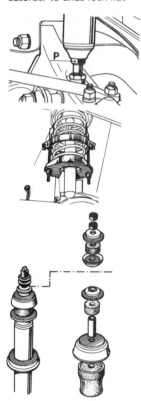

Fig.10.5. Front coil spring and shock absorber removal P - locking point to loose bottom mounting. Note Renault type spring compressor and washer positions for shock absorber

5 Suspension ball joints - removal and replacement

1   The four suspension ball joints, two on each side of the front suspension, at the outer end of the upper wishbone and lower suspension arm are sealed for life. They therefore need replacing rather than servicing.

However, it is possible to purchase a new rubber bellows kit if one should fail but the ball joint remains in good condition. Carry out the following work as for ball joint removal but only go so far to enable the old bellows to be cut off and the new one fitted. Repack the ball joint with high melting point grease and take care fitting the circlip. Your own conclusions must be drawn as to its efficiency once everything is dismantled!

2   Top ball joints: Jack up the car and place on axle stands. Turn the steering to left lock when working on a right hand ball joint and vice versa.

3   Using a patent ball joint remover split the top ball joint. To free the ball joint from the upright finally obtain a small wooden wedge. With a tyre lever or strong screwdriver lever on the wedge under the upper suspension arm on top of the drive shaft outer joint. The ball joint should then free.

4   The original ball joints are rivetted onto the wishbones. These rivets will have to be drilled out. Clean up the rivet heads with a wire brush and file a good flat onto their heads. Use an electric drill if possible. Be patient and very careful. It is not a 'rush' job. Do not attempt to drill from below and try not to drill into the wishbone itself. If done carefully it is not necessary to remove the wishbone from the vehicle.

5   When purchasing new ball joints make sure that the CORRECT fixing setscrews and nuts, to replace the rivets, are supplied. This is important.

6   Replace the new ball joint into its correct seating and place the setscrews from below up through the ball joint and then wishbone. Tighten the nyloc nuts firmly.

7   Replace all the parts in an opposite procedure to their removal. Be sure that the ball joints are finally tight onto the upright when the car is resting on all four wheels.

8   It is advisable to have the car re-tracked if a ball joint is replaced. Have this done by a Renault agent.

9   Lower ball joints: Unfortunately changing a lower ball joint is more involved. Once having compressed the coil spring it should be possible to undertake this on the car but it is too involved and potentially dangerous. Remove the lower wishbone from the car. See the next Section. Remove and then replace the ball, using the same method as described in paragraphs 4 to 7.

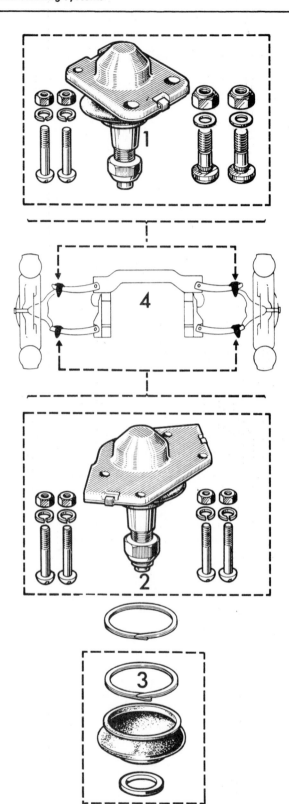

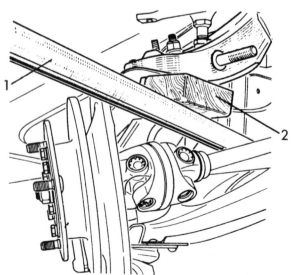

FIG.10.7. TOP BALL JOINT DISLOCATION

1   Lever   2   Wooden fulcrum block

FIG.10.6. TOP AND BOTTOM BALL JOINT RENEWAL KITS

1   Top kit   2   Bottom kit
3   Bellows kit   4   Location diagram

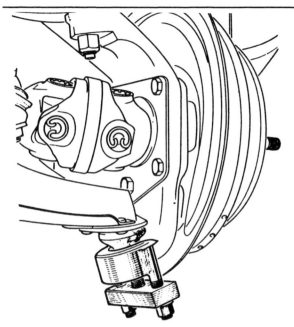

Fig.10.8. Lower ball joint removal using patent ball joint remover

---

6 Front axle - removal and replacement

---

1 Do not play with the front suspension without necessity. Replace worn bushes and ball joints as they occur but in the case of accident damage, before removing any 'broken' components check most carefully the condition of the bodyshell mountings. If in any doubt have a Renault body specialist look at it first. Only he is sure that the 'chassis' is straight should repair work commence.

2 Upper wishbone and tie-rods: Jack up the appropriate side of the car, support on axle stands and remove the road wheel. Clean all the road dirt off first.

3 Disconnect and remove the anti-roll bar as described in Section 2.

4 Disconnect the castor tie-rod connected to the top wishbone with one bolt and to the chassis with a shock absorber type mounting.

5 Disconnect the steering arm ball joint but do not remove its

nut. Use a ball joint extractor.

6 Release fully the upper ball joint as described in Section 5, paragraph 3.

7 Remove the steering arm ball joint nut and release it fully.

8 From the top eye of the stub axle carrier fix a piece of wire to hold it to the bodywork so that the driveshaft is not strained nor is the flexible brake pipe.

9 Unlock the lower shock absorber mounting as described in Section 4, paragraph 5.

10 The final fixing, the inner end of the top wishbone, pivots on a steel bolt through a rubber/metal bonded bush. Try to release the inner nut facing the bulkhead first. Once this is removed it should be possible to tap the steel bolt through the wishbone using a short steel drift. Once this is through, the wishbone will release. (photo)

11 Because the top wishbone is a pressed steel fitting it should be possible to check easily for damage. Wrinkles and bowing will indicate. Never try to repair a wishbone, always renew.

12 Refitting a new bush is possible, but not at home. A press is needed for removal and replacement. Have this done by a competent repair shop. The new bush must protrude 6 mm (15/64 inch) each side of the wishbone. Always renew the steel fixing pivot bolt at the same time.

13 Replacement is a reverse procedure but fix the lower shock absorber to the wishbone before pressing the pivot pin through. Grease the pin. Check the torque wrench settings. Have the car re-tracked and checked for alignment.

14 Lower suspension wishbone: Set up the car as in paragraph 2.

15 Disconnect the lower ball joint with a patent ball joint remover.

16 Undo the lower pivot pin and remove the inner nut. With a pair of mole grips gripping the head of the other nut or by using a short steel drift pull out or drive out the pivot pin (forwards).

17 The wishbone is now away.

18 Replacement of the bushes can only be dealt with by competent repair shop, not at home. Make sure the new bushes are 151 mm (5 5/16 inch) apart between them when installed.

19 Replacement is a straight reverse procedure. Grease the pivot pin and use nyloc nuts. Renew the pin if new bushes are fitted. Have the alignment of the front suspension checked.

WARNING: If the castor tie rod has been removed and replaced it must be reset by a Renault Agency. This is critical for safe running.

20 Stub axle carrier: From what has just preceded this, stub axle carrier removal should be straightforward. See Chapter 7 for its description.

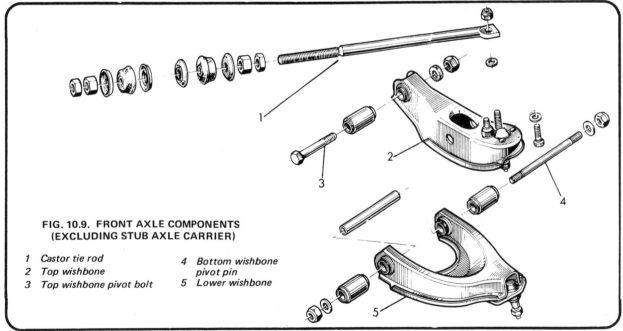

FIG. 10.9. FRONT AXLE COMPONENTS (EXCLUDING STUB AXLE CARRIER)

1   Castor tie rod
2   Top wishbone
3   Top wishbone pivot bolt
4   Bottom wishbone pivot pin
5   Lower wishbone

6.10 Both pivot pins must come out forwards

7.4 Top rear shock absorber mounting. Mole grip the top

7 Rear shock absorber and coil spring - removal and replacement

1   Although the coil spring and shock absorber are individual separate components it is not possible to remove one without the other. Again with the proper tool it is an easy operation. Always renew springs and shock absorbers in pairs.

2   Support the bodyshell on the appropriate side once having jacked up the rear of the car. Leave the other road wheel on the ground. Remove the road wheel.

3   Use the same spring compressing tool as described in Section 4, and fit it to the coil spring. Open the boot lid or tailgate. Using the jack supplied with the car, raise the axle beam directly under the orifice for the lower shock absorber mounting. As the spring compresses 'catch it up' with the spring compressing tool. When it is compressed by about ¼ to 1/3 of its length having tightened the clamp, lower the car jack. The spring will now be loose.

4   Inside the boot lid/tailgate grip the top of the shock absorber with a pair of mole grips and undo the locknut below it. Release the nut. (photo)

5   Release the lower end of the shock absorber using a flat spanner (open-ended) just below the body of the shock absorber above the axle beam and a tubular spanner from below and through the axle beam. This is fairly tricky but not difficult with patience.

6   The coil spring should then feed off the shock absorber forwards and the shock absorber can then follow it.

7   As can be appreciated removing the other side's spring and shock absorber once one side is removed, calls for careful juggling and supports. It is however possible, but to be avoided.

8   Replacement is a straight reverse process. Check the bushes of the shock absorber for correct location.

9   Always have the spring compressed safely before refitment. When renewing springs check that the 'flat' locating area of the coil is on the top. 'Pump' new shock absorbers vertically by hand before refitting.

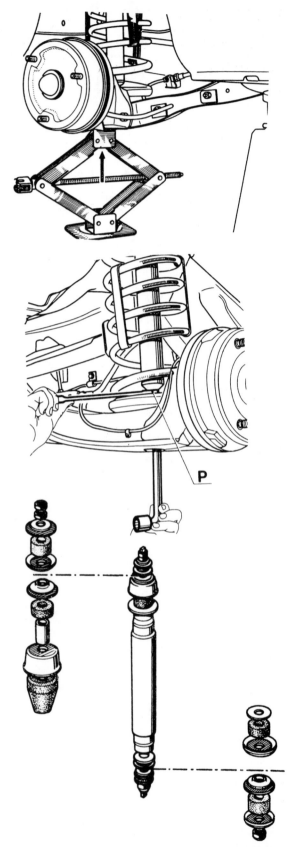

Fig.10.10. Rear coil spring and shock absorber removal P locating point to hold bottom mounting. Note different spring clips and washer position of the shock absorber rubbers

8   Rear axle - removal and replacement

1   Check the instructions given in Section 6, paragraph 1.

2   'A' bracket: Raise the rear of the car, both wheels off the ground and support the bodyshell on axle stands.

3   Disconnect the brake pressure limiter valve (see Chapter 8).

4   Undo the two nuts on the clamp locating the 'A' bracket to the beam axle. The clamp is like a 'U' bolt. Leave the pin on the beam axle with its bush.

5   Undo the right hand side nut on the 'A' bracket 'chassis' pivot pin. Drift it through the hole in the 'chassis' to the left with a short steel drift. The 'A' bracket is now free.

6   Renewal of the two bushes on the 'A' bracket is not possible at home. Have them pressed out and new ones pressed in at a competent repair specialist. The total 'outer' dimension from the two outer edges of the bushes once installed must be 243 mm (9.9/16 inch).

7   The single bush still located on the axle beam is held by a through bolt and nut. Undo this and renew the bush easily.

8   Place the 'A' bracket in position for refitting. Grease the pivot pin and locate in a reverse sequence at each end. Do not finally tighten the long pivot pin until the car rests on the ground on its all four wheels.

9   Longitudinal tie-rods: Jack up the rear of the car and support the bodyshell on axle stands. Remove the road wheels.

10 Remove the rear anti-roll bar (see Section 3).

11 Remove the brake drum and disconnect the handbrake cable and withdraw the cable through the tie-rod. See Chapter 8.

12 Undo the two fixing bolts, one at each end of the tie-rod, one on the chassis, the other on the beam axle. Allow the tie-rod to drop down and out.

13 Renewable bushes are NOT fitted to the tie-rods. A new tie-rod must be purchased.

14 Replacement is a straight reverse procedure. Grease the pivot/fixing bolts. Adjust the rear brakes.

15 Beam axle: See paragraphs 1 to 3, 5 to 7 of Section 7 but repeat for both sides of the car. See paragraphs 3 and 4 ('A' bracket) and 11 of this Section.

16 Disconnect the rigid brake pipes at the brake back plates and tape over their ends to stop dirt entering. Free the 3 way banjo unit from the axle beam, using a tubular spanner through the axle.

17 Undo the axle beam to tie-rod fixing bolts only once you have placed the car jack on blocks up the axle beam. It should now be free and can be lowered away.

18 For brake plate and hub bearing removal see Chapters 8 and 7 respectively.

19 Replacement is a reverse procedure. Grease all the pivot pins, and do not finally tighten anything until the car rests on all four road wheels. Bleed the brakes. Check the operation of the brake pressure limiter valve.

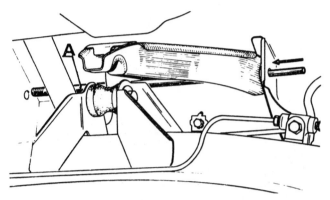

Fig.10.12. Long pivot pin (A) must be extracted to the left through the hole in the chassis

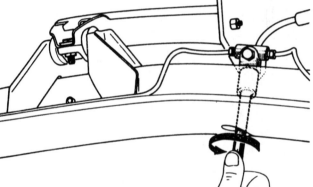

Fig.10.13. 3 way brake pipe banjo. Fixing bolt through the beam axle

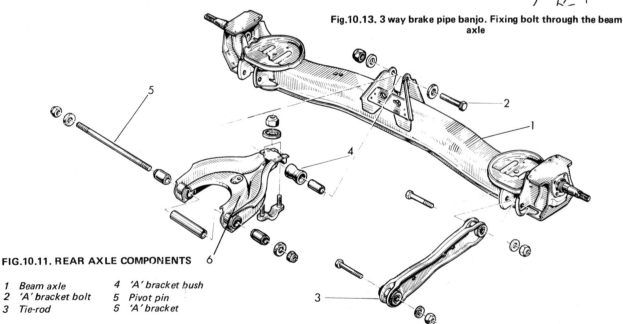

FIG.10.11. REAR AXLE COMPONENTS

1 Beam axle	4 'A' bracket bush
2 'A' bracket bolt	5 Pivot pin
3 Tie-rod	5 'A' bracket

9 Steering rack - removal and replacement

1   Do not undertake any steering repairs lightly. Any Renault garage will avoid setting up the steering if they possibly can!

2   Open the bonnet and remove the battery and the battery tray. The tray is fixed by three screws. Undo two of the four bolts locating the flexible coupling to the steering rack and lower column.

3   Undo the bolts which connect the inner ends of the track rods to the steering rack at the end of the rack gaiters. You may struggle getting the two bolts through.

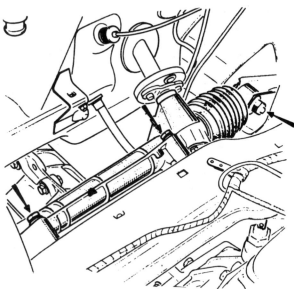

Fig.10.14. Steering rack mounting points

4   Scribe round the steering rack where it mounts onto the bodyshell crossmember if the same rack is to be refitted. The rack mounting is drilled with eccentrics to allow for height adjustment. Do not disturb the locking plates. If the rack is to be renewed it does not matter. Undo the four bolts locating the rack to the crossmember and remove.

5   Remember the rack cannot be overhauled, only renewed.

6   Replacement is a straight reverse procedure but lightly grease all the mounting bolts. If the position of the rack has been disturbed be prepared to spend some money having it set up. Always have the car checked at a Renault garage (only) for wheel tracking etc. Check the condition of the rack bellows/ gaiters and the flexible coupling. (Rivets may have been used as original equipment, bolts are supplied with the repair kit). Renew if necessary. See Section 12.

10 Steering wheel and column - removal and replacement

1   Always disconnect the battery.

2   From underneath the steering wheel unscrew the top embellisher securing screws. Remove the top embellisher. (The bottom half of the embellisher is located by two screws from the top!, but cannot be released until the wheel is removed).

3   Undo the steering wheel shaft nut. If necessary 'knock' it and then drift it round.

4   Remove the top and bottom covers of the combination light switches. See Chapter 9.

5   Pull off the steering wheel. It should pull off the splines fairly easily. Note its positioning on the splines with a scribe mark for accurate refitting.

6   To remove the column means that you must also remove the trim and the column mounting bracket. Disconnect the brake

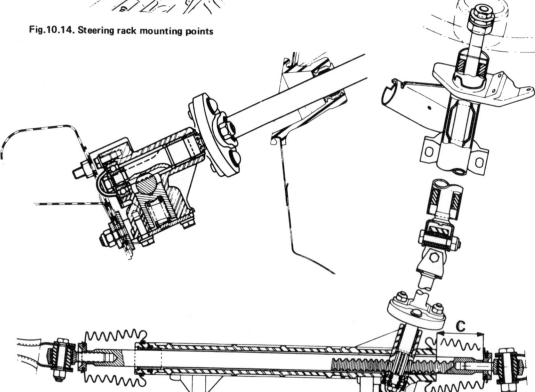

FIG.10.15. A CROSS SECTION OF THE STEERING MECHANISM
C = 65 mm (2 9/16 in.) = steering centre point (manual transmission). Inset: through cross section of the rack
C = 61 mm (2 13/32 in.) = steering centre point with automatic transmission.

light switch and the ignition starter switch. See Chapter 8 and 4 respectively. Then remove the combination lighting switch and the flasher unit. On some later models there may be further obvious switches to disconnect.

7 Disconnect the master cylinder (do not remove totally) and brake pedal (see Chapter 8), and the clutch cable and clutch pedal (see Chapter 5).

8 Disconnect the universal joint upper hinge pin on the steering column shaft inside the car and then undo the two nuts on the steering column support bracket securing bolts. The column and its mounting bracket should now be free.

9 To overhaul the steering column bushes, insert and turn the ignition key into 'ON' and pull the inner column out from below. Drift out the top bush once you have picked out the snap ring. The bottom bush is split and can be picked out.

10 Smear the new bushes with high melting point grease. Drift in the top one, into its recesses and refit the snap ring. Place the inner shaft back into the column, fit both the split bushes over the shaft just in the column and then push them into their recesses by pushing on the lower end of the shaft.

11 Replacement of the column and column mounting bracket is a straight reverse procedure. Tighten the lower universal joint hinge pin first then turn the steering a ¼ of a turn and tighten the upper. Check for switch operation and adjust the brake and clutch pedals accordingly.

12 It may seem simple at first to renew the column bushes with the column mounting still in the car. It is not simple. Remove the column first.

13 Check for steeing wheel setting when the rack is centred (see Fig. 10.15).

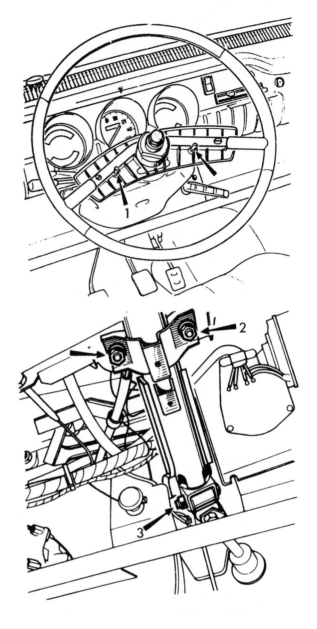

FIG.10.18. STEERING WHEEL AND COLUMN REMOVAL

1 Embellisher screws
2 Top column mounting bracket
3 Universal joint bolt

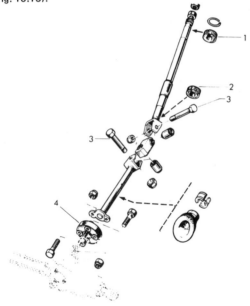

FIG.10.16. INNER STEERING COLUMN COMPONENTS

1 Top bush (solid)   3 Universal joint bolts
2 Bottom bush (split)   4 Flexible joint

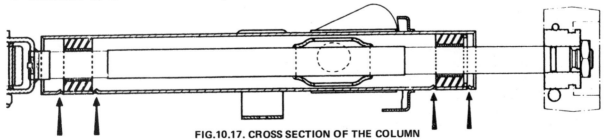

FIG.10.17. CROSS SECTION OF THE COLUMN

Left side is the bottom of the column. Arrows show bush locating indentations

11 Steering track rods and ball joints - removal and replacement

1   To remove either one of the steering track rods do not remove the rack.

2   No repair is available for the track rod arms or ball joints if they are worn or damaged except the renewal of the rubber dust cover which can be done on the car. They should be cut off the ball joint, once it is disconnected and a new one fitted with a piece of tube of 37 mm diameter. Grease the joint first with high melting point grease.

3   Undo the track rod at the steering rack as described in Section 9.

4   Using a patent ball joint remover disconnect the outer ball joint at the stub axle carrier (upright). Remove the track rod.

5   If in any doubt as to the straightness of a steering arm have it checked by a Renault agent. Never replace with a bent arm and note that the arms are not interchangeable. Right hand side arms have an indentation on the underside below the inner hinge pin end. Left hand side arms are smooth.

6   If the inner bushes through which the steering arm pins pass are worn they should be pressed out and new ones pressed in. This cannot be undertaken at home successfully and should be given to a Renault agent. Unscrew these eyes from the steering rack.

7   Replacement is again a reversal of the removal sequence.

12 Steering geometry and wheel alignment

Such is the complexity of steering and suspension adjustment and its relative importance to the total correct functioning of the vehicle it is advised that any adjustment of this type be made by the local Renault garage which will be equipped with the necessary optical and measuring jigs. If any major suspension or steering part is removed and/or replaced it is absolutely necessary to have the vehicle checked. The following measurements may be necessary depending on what has been removed. See the Specifications for their tolerances. To some extent you will be in the hands of the Renault garage as to what they will actually measure, but each component mentioned in the Specifications when removed will place the vehicle in need of one or more measurement checking. Tell the garage to make the relevant check and to report on any adjustment found to be necessary.

a)   The camber angle (which cannot in fact be altered)
b)   The castor angle
c)   The steering rack height setting
d)   The front axle toe-out/toe-in
e)   The position of the wheels in relation to the steering centre point.

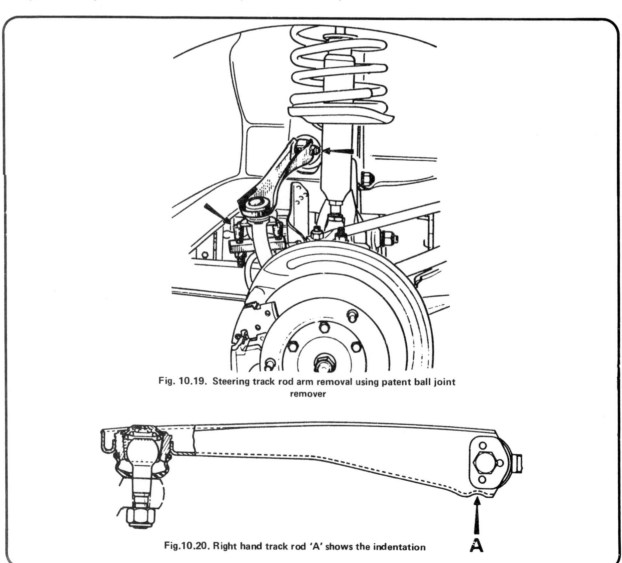

Fig. 10.19. Steering track rod arm removal using patent ball joint remover

Fig.10.20. Right hand track rod 'A' shows the indentation

Chapter 11 Bodywork

Contents

Specifications

Renault 12 saloons:

R1170 and R1177 ... ... All welded monocoque construction of 4 door design. Forward hinging bonnet and boot lid
Bonnet, boot lid, doors and front wings only are bolted to the monocoque

Renault 12 estate:

R1171 and then R1330 ... ... As for the saloon except rear bodywork extended to include a rear vertical opening tailgate, with rear window in the tailgate

Underseal ... ... All models are factory undersealed

Paintwork ... ... For reference to paintwork of individual vehicles, see the paint code for specific type. (See Ordering Spare Parts)

Trim ... ... All trim, mainly non-corrosive metal or plastic construction can be glued or pinned to the bodywork

---

1 General description

The bodyshell is integral with the chassis and is an all steel welded monocoque construction. Only the doors, bonnet, boot-lid and the front wings are detachable. The bodyshell is welded to reinforced box sections to make it integral with the chassis members. All engine, transmission and running gear are bolted to the bodyshell. Soundproofing and vibration insulation are used extensively.

2 Maintenance - bodywork

1 The body is easy to keep clean due to its shape. The general condition of a car's bodywork is the one thing that significantly affects its value. Maintenance is easy but needs to be regular and particular. Neglect, particularly after minor damage, can lead quickly to further deterioration and costly repair bills. It is important also to keep watch on those parts of the car not immediately visible, for instance, the underside, inside all the

wheel arches and the engine compartment.

2   The basic maintenance routine for the bodywork is washing - preferably with a lot of water, from a hose. This will remove all the solids which may have stuck to the car. It is important to flush these off in such a way as to prevent grit from scratching the finish. The wheel arches and underbody need washing in the same way to remove any accumulated mud which will retain moisture and rust. Paradoxically enough, the best time to clean the underbody and wheel arches is in wet weather when the mud is thoroughly wet and soft. In very wet weather the underbody is usually cleaned of large accumulations automatically and this is a good time for inspection.

3   Periodically it is a good idea to have the whole of the under-side of the car steam cleaned, engine compartment included, so that a thorough inspection can be carried out to see what minor repairs and renovations are necessary. Steam cleaning is available at many garages and is necessary for removal of accumulations of oily grime which sometimes cakes thick in certain areas near the engine and transmission. The facilities are usually available at commercial vehicle garages but if not there are one or two excellent grease solvents available which can be brush applied. The dirt can then be hosed off.

4   After washing paintwork, wipe it with a chamois leather to give an unspotted clear finish. A coat of protective wax polish will give added protection against chemical pollutants in the air. If the paintwork sheen has dulled or oxidised, use a cleaner/polisher combination to restore the brilliance of the shine. This requires a little more effort, but is usually caused because regular washing has been neglected. Always check that door and ventilator opening drain holes and pipes are completely clear so that water can drain out.

5   Bright work should be treated the same way as paintwork. Windscreens and windows can be kept clear of the smeary film which often appears if a little ammonia is added to the water. Never use any form of wax or chromium polish on glass.

3   Maintenance - body interior

1   Floor mats should be brushed or vacuum cleaned regularly to keep them free of grit. If they are badly stained remove them from the car for scrubbing or sponging and make quite sure they are dry before replacement. Seats (not nylon 'cloth') and interior trim panels can be kept clean by a wipe over with a damp cloth. If they do become stained (which can be more apparent on light coloured upholstery) use a little liquid detergent and a soft nail-brush to scour the grime out of the grain of the material. Nylon 'cloth' seats must be treated with respect. Use a little warm soapy water on stains but watch for 'watermarks', otherwise brush gently. Serious stains may respond to a 'dry cleaning' agent. Do not forget to keep the roof lining clean in the same way as the upholstery. When using liquid cleaners inside the car do not over-wet the surfaces being cleaned. Excessive damp could get into the seams and padded interior causing stains, offensive odours or even rot. If the inside of the car gets wet accidentally, it is worthwhile taking some trouble to dry it out properly, particularly where carpets are involved. Do NOT leave oil or electric heaters inside the car for this purpose.

4   Minor body repairs

1   A car which does not suffer some minor damage to the bodywork from time to time is the exception rather than the rule. Even presuming the gatepost is never scraped or the door opened against a wall or high kerb, there is always the likelihood of gravel and grit being thrown up and chipping the surface, particularly at the lower edges of the doors and sills.

2   If the damage is merely a paint scrape which has not reached the metal base, delay is not critical, but where bare metal is exposed action must be taken immediately before rust sets in. Before taking any repainting action, however, always check with a Renault garage (with your car's paint number) the type of

paint which is used on your car. It need not necessarily be cellulose!

3   The average owner will normally keep the following 'first aid' materials available which can give a professional finish for minor jobs:

a) Matching paint in liquid form - often complete with brush attached to the lid inside. Aerosols are extravagant. Spraying from aerosols is generally less perfect than the makers would have one expect.
b) Thinners for the paint (for brush application).
c) Cellulose stopper (a filling compound for small paint chips).
d) Cellulose primer (a thickish grey coloured base which can be applied as an undercoat in several coats and rubbed down to give a perfect paint base).
e) Proprietary resin filler paste (for larger areas of in-filling).
f) Rust-inhibiting primer (a zinc based paint).
g) "Wet or dry" paper grades 220 and 400.

4   Where the damage is superficial (i.e. not down to the bare metal and not dented) fill the scratch or chip with stopper sufficient to smooth the area, rub down with paper and apply the matching paint.

5   Where the bodywork is scratched down to the metal, but not dented, clean the metal surface thoroughly and apply the primer (it does not need to be a rust-inhibitor if the metal is clean and dry), and then build up the scratched part to the level of the surrounding paintwork with the stopper. When the primer/stopper is hard it can be rubbed down with "wet or dry" paper. Keep applying primer and rubbing it down until no surface blemish can be felt. Then apply the colour, thinned if necessary. Apply as many coats and rub down as necessary.

6   Rub down each coat before applying the next. It is likely three coats of the colour paint will be needed to get enough thickness for polishing.

7   If the bodywork is dented, first beat out the dent as near as possible to conform with the original contour. Avoid using steel hammers - use hardwood mallets or similar and always support the back of the panel being beaten with a hardwood or metal 'dolly'. In areas where severe creasing and buckling has occurred it will be virtually impossible to reform the metal to the original shape. In such instances a decision should be made whether or not to cut out the damaged piece or attempt to re-contour over it with filler paste. In large areas where the metal panel is seriously damaged or rusted, the repais is to be considered major and it is often better to replace a panel or sill section with the appropriate part supplied as a spare. When using filler paste in largish   quantities, make sure the directions are carefully followed. It is false economy to try and rush the job as the correct hardening time must be allowed between stages or before finishing. With thick application the filler usually has to be applied in layers - allowing time for each layer to harden.

8   Sometimes the original paint colour will have faded and it will be difficult to obtain an exact colour match. In such instances it is a good scheme to select a complete panel - such as a door, or boot lid, and paint the whole panel. Differences will be less apparent where there are obvious divisions between the original and repainted areas.

9   Do not expect to be able to prepare, fill, rub down and paint a section of damaged bodywork in one day and expect good results. It cannot be done. Give plenty of time for each success-ive application of filler and primers to harden before rubbing it down and applying the next coat.

10 Do not think that it is necessary, or even desirable to spray the paint on. To get a satisfactory result requires good equip-ment and experience. Yet a coachbuilder's finish is easily got by brush painting. The secret is the preparation and final polishing. All undercoats must be rubbed down with wet "wet or dry" paper of grade about 220, to remove all traces of the original damage, the edge of the filler, and the brush marks in the under-coat. Paint on a coat of top, the coloured paint, brushing it out with criss-cross brushing to get it even. Brushing paint type

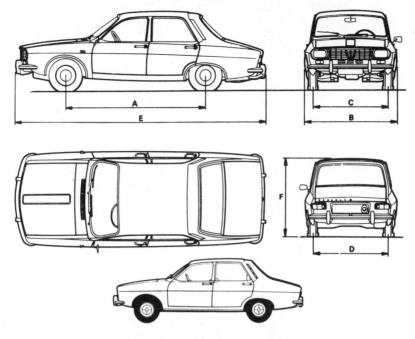

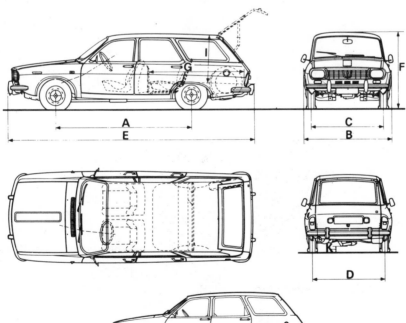

FIG.11.1. OUTLINE DIMENSIONS OF THE SALOON

Wheelbase	A	8 feet	2441 mm
Overall width	B	5 feet 4.3/8''	1636 mm
Front track	C	4 feet 3.5/8''	1312 mm
Rear track	D	4 feet 3.5/8''	1312 mm
Overall length	E	14 feet 2.7/8''	4340 mm
Height when empty	F	4 feet 8.1/2''	1434 mm

FIG.11.2. OUTLINE DIMENSION OF THE ESTATE

Wheelbase	A	8 feet	2441 mm
Overall width	B	5 feet 4,3/8''	1636 mm
Front track	C	4 feet 3,5/8''	1312 mm
Rear track	D	4 feet 3,5/8 ''	1312 mm
Overall length	E	14 ft 4 in.	4404 mm
Height	F When empty	4 feet 7 in.	1455 mm

This sequence of photographs deals with the repair of the dent and scratch (above rear lamp) shown in this photo. The procedure will be similar for the repair of a hole. It should be noted that the procedures given here are simplified - more explicit instructions will be found in the text

In the case of a dent the first job - after removing surrounding trim - is to hammer out the dent where access is possible. This will minimise filling. Here, the large dent having been hammered out, the damaged area is being made slightly concave

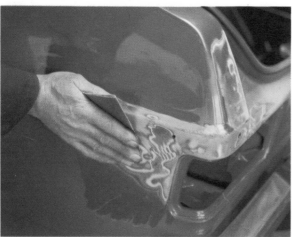

Now all paint must be removed from the damaged area, by rubbing with coarse abrasive paper. Alternatively, a wire brush or abrasive pad can be used in a power drill. Where the repair area meets good paintwork, the edge pf the paintwork should be 'feathered', using a finer grade of abrasive paper

In the case of a hole caused by rusting, all damaged sheet-metal should be cut away before proceeding to this stage. Here, the damaged area is being treated with rust remover and inhibitor before being filled

Mix the body filler according to its manufacturer's instructions. In the case of corrosion damage, it will be necessary to block off any large holes before filling - this can be done with zinc gauze or aluminium tape. Make sure the area is absolutely clean before ...

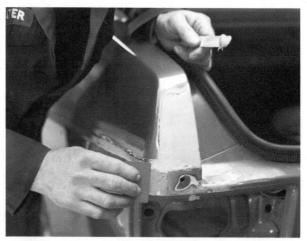

... applying the filler. Filler should be applied with a flexible applicator, as shown, for best results: the wooden spatula being used for confined areas. Apply thin layers of filler at 20-minute intervals, until the surface of the filler is slightly proud of the surrounding bodywork

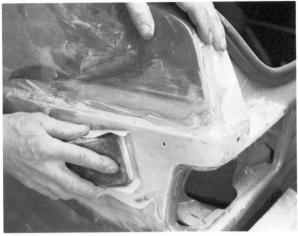

Initial shaping can be done with a Surform plane or Dreadnought file. Then, using progressively finer grades of wet-and-dry paper, wrapped around a sanding block, and copious amounts of clean water, rub-down the filler until really smooth and flat. Again, feather the edges of adjoining paintwork

The whole repair area can now be sprayed or brush-painted with primer. If spraying, ensure adjoining areas are protected from over-spray. Note that at least one-inch of the surrounding sound paintwork should be coated with primer. Primer has a 'thick' consistency, so will fill small imperfections

Again, using plenty of water, rub down the primer with a fine grade of wet-and-dry paper (400 grade is probably best) until it is really smooth and well blended into the surrounding paint-work. Any remaining imperfections can now be filled by carefully applied knifing stopper paste

When the stopper has hardened, rub-down the repair area again before applying the final coat of primer. Before rubbing-down this last coat of primer, ensure the repair area is blemish-free - use more stopper if necessary. To ensure that the surface of the primer is really smooth use some finishing compound

The top coat can now be applied. When working out of doors, pick a dry, warm and wind-free day. Ensure surrounding areas are protected from over-spray. Agitate the aerosol thoroughly, then spray the centre of the repair area, working outwards with a circular motion. Apply the paint as several thin coats.

After a period of about two-weeks, which the paint needs to harden fully, the surface of the repaired area can be 'cut' with a mild cutting compound prior to wax polishing. When carrying out bodywork repairs, remember that the quality of the finished job is proportional to the time and effort expended

thinners must be used as paint prepared for spraying will dry too fast, and go tacky before it is brushed smoothly out. This coat of the top paint cannot be the final one as it cannot be put on thick enough without risk of weeping. Some areas will be so thin the undercoat will be visible immediately after painting. Anyway a good thickness of paint is needed for the polishing. So allow this coat to harden for 24 hours. Then lightly rub it down with wet "wet or dry" paper of about 380 - 400 grade. It must be rubbed matt all over for the final coat to key in, and to get rid of brush marks. Extend the rubbing down into the surrounding original paint if patching part of a panel. Then put on the top coat. Do not take it beyond the area rubbed down. Brush the edges out thin to blend in well, leaving about 1/8 inch still matt. Take great care with this. Dry weather, without any wind to stir up dust is needed. Again, when hard after 24 hours, rub down very gently with grade 400 wet "wet or dry" just enough to take off the tops of the brush marks, and any blobs of dust. Then polish up with "rubbing compound" and abrasive paste. Then give the paint a few days to really harden, and polish with car polish; a cleaner or restorer, not a wax. Metal polish is excellent for this. Incidentally metal polish can often be used for polishing out minor scratches that have marked the paint but not got down to the undercoat.

11 If you do apply the paint by spraying, then the guidance for rubbing down is still the same. The "orange peel" effect of one coat must be removed before the next coat is applied. Also polishing will be needed after the final coat, preceded by the gentle rub to get off the top of its lumps.

5 Major body repairs

1 Where serious damage has occurred or large areas need renewal due to neglect, new sections or panels will need welding in and this is best left to professionals. If the damage is due to impact it will also be necessary to check the alignment of the body structure.

If, however, this damage is confined to the front wings, doors, bonnet or boot lid/tailgate, their replacement is well within the ability of the home mechanic. See paragraph 3 for front wing replacement and the relevant sections for the other panels.

2 If a body is left misaligned it is first of all dangerous as the car will not handle properly - and secondly, uneven stresses will be imposed on the steering, engine and transmission, causing abnormal wear or complete failure. Tyre wear will also be excessive.

3 Both front wings are easily removed and replaced. Special care must be taken on the fitting stage if a really good 'invisible' job is to be done. Remove the front bumper (Section 14) and the headlamp rim and headlamp. Disconnect the battery and pop off any trim.

4 Jack up that side of the car, chock well, remove the road wheel.

5 Remove the special body screws from along the top of the wing under the bonnet (there's one under the rubber pad under the windscreen), the joint between the wing and the front cross panel from under the wing and the front door pillar (open the door but do not remove it), and lastly from the sill. Gently tap the wing away for it must be rusted in place.

6 A sealing compound is used on all edges and this should still be fairly pliable.

7 Clean off the old sealing compound with a knife. Check that the inner wing is in good enough condition before replacing with a new one.

8 If replacing with a new wing it is wise to underseal the new wing before it is placed on the car.

9 Place a thin strip of sealing compound (black soft setting sealing putty is most suitable) on the fixing edges of the inner wing and after making sure that the setscrew holes are clear press over the wing so that the sealing strip oozes equally on its three edges. Place all the fixing bolts in their holes and screw in a few turns so that the wing is fixed but not tightened all round. Then

progressively tighten the wing onto the shell making sure that it is done equally and in the correct profile.

10 Once you are happy that it is properly fixed peel off and flatten any excess sealing putty. Smooth off the channel at the leading edge.

11 It is best to do any spraying on new wings before they are fitted.

12 Replace the parts removed for the wing removal.

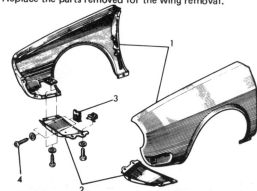

FIG.11.3. FRONT WING ATTACHMENTS

1 Wing panel	3 Captive nut
2 Lower inner panel	4 Sheet metal screw

6 Body corrosion

1 The ultimate scrapping of a car is usually due to rust, rather than it becoming uneconomic to renew mechanical parts.

2 The rust grows from two origins: From the underneath unprotected after the underseal and paint were blasted off by road grit: From inside, where damp has collected inside hollow body sections, without a chance to drain, and no rust protection to the metal.

3 The corrosion is particularly prone to start at welded joints in the body, as there are stresses left in after the heat of welding has cooled. These seams are also traps for the damp, and difficult to rustproof.

4 Salt on the roads in winter promotes this horror. It is hygroscopic; it attracts damp, so the car stays damp even in a garage. It is also an electrolyte when wet, so promotes violent corrosion. If the car has been used on salty roads it must be desalted as soon as possible. A couple of days rain after a thaw clears the roads, and then driving the car in wet does this naturally. The damage is worse if a car is not used for some time after getting salty.

5 Check the underneath for rust every six months. It should be done just before the winter, so that the car is prepared for its ravages whilst dry and free of salt. Then it needs doing in the spring to remove the winter's damage.

6 The bodywork should be explored and all hollow sections found. Into these a rust inhibitor should be injected; aerosols like Supertrol 001, or Di-Nitrol 3B are good. Areas easier of access can be wetted by the inhibitor bought more cheaply as a liquid and applied by paint brush. An example are the insides of the doors, which can be reached by removing the panel linings. If hollow sections are sealed, it pays to drill a hole, spray in the aerosol, and then seal with the underneath paint smeared over the hole.

7 The underneath needs painting, and where abraded by grit flung up by the wheels, this must be one of the special thick resilient paints. "Adup" bronze super seal is recommended. It is compatible with the Supertrol 001 and De-Nitrol 33B inhibitors; So if these are put on first the two between them make a good job in getting into corners. The "Adup" underneath paint can be used as ordinary paint on sheltered areas. On those showered by grit from the wheels, thick layers need to be applied. At the mudguards the underneath paint wants to be brought nearly round the edges so that these are protected, the corners being particularly vulnerable.

7 Windscreen and fixed glass - removal and replacement

1 Make sure you know what kind of glass is fitted. Toughened safety glass will stand a certain amount of impact blows without breaking but any other kind will crack at least and only carefully applied sustained pressure may be used with safety. The windscreen is described here, but the rear screen and fixed side windows of the estate are removed and replaced in a similar manner. Vehicles fitted with heated rear windows require special care. Consult a specialist before undertaking any work. These screens are expensive!

2 After taking off the windscreen wiper arms, loosen the rubber sealing strip on the inside of the car where it fits over the edge of the window frame. Use a piece of wood for this. Anything sharp may rip the rubber weatherstrip. The screen can be pushed out, weatherstrip attached, if pressure is applied at the top corners. Two people are needed on this to prevent the glass falling out. Push evenly and protect your hands to avoid accidents. Remove the finisher strip from the weatherstrip.

When fitting a screen first make sure that the window frame edges are even and smooth. Examine the edges of the screen to see that it is ground smooth and no chips or cracks are visible. Any such cracks could be the source of a much bigger one. The rubber weatherstrip should be perfectly clean. No traces of sealing compound should remain on rubber, glass or metal. If the sealing strip is old, brittle or hard, it is advisable to fit a new one even though they are not cheap.

4 Fit the weatherstrip to the screen first so that the joint comes midway along the top edge.

5 Next fit the decorative moulding into the weatherstrip. This is done by first feeding fine cord into the slot (use a piece of thin tubing as a guide and time saver) and leave the ends overlapping sufficiently to grip later. The two halves of the moulding are then put in place and the cord drawn out so that the edge of the strip locks them into place.

6 Apply suitable sealing compound to the weatherstrip where it will seat onto the metal window frame and also onto the outside faces of the frame at the lower corners.

7 Fit a piece of really strong thin cord into the frame channel of the weatherstrip as already described and then offer up the screen to the aperture. A second person is essential for this.

8 When you are sure that the screen is centrally positioned, pull the cord out so that the lip of the weatherstrip is drawn over the inner edges of the frame flange. One of the most frequent difficulties in this job is that the cord breaks. This is often because of sharp or uneven edges on the frame flange so a little extra time in preparation will pay off.

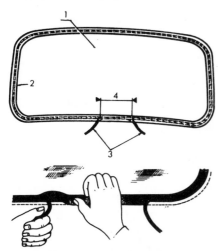

FIG.11.4. WINDSCREEN FITTING

1 Glass	3 String ends
2 Rubber seal	4 4'' string overlap

8 Door lining trim panels

1 It is necessary to remove the trim panels to get at the door lock mechanism, the window winder mechanism and the door glass.

2 Front doors: Remove the elbow rest secured by two visible screws. Flip back the cover on the window winder handle and undo the securing nut, and remove the winder. Retain the 'flat' spring.

3 Push up the door catch remote lever button and release its clip. Unscrew the two embellisher plate fixing screws. Unclip, at the top edge, the plate and remove.

4 Insert a thin piece of wood or tyre lever between the trim panel and the door halfway down its leading edge and 'pop' out the whole panel. Free its top edge carefully from the lip. Ignore the glued panel.

5 Removal is a straight reverse procedure. Always check the condition of the flat spring and clips to avoid subsequent rattling.

6 Rear doors: The trim is removed in a similar fashion as the front doors except that there is a top and bottom lip from which it has to be freed. Also the ashtray, fixed in a similar manner to the arm rest must be removed.

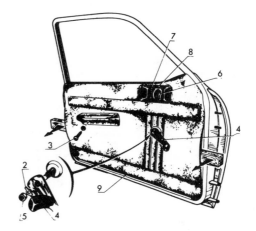

FIG.11.5. FRONT DOOR TRIM PANEL REMOVAL

1 Length of wood	6 Door catch
2 Stop washer	7 Embellisher screw
3 Self tapping screw	8 Cover plate
4 Window winder	9 Trim panel
5 Nut	

9 Window glass and winder mechanism

1 Front doors: Wind the window down so that the glass is 3 3/8 inches (85 mm) from the top of the door frame. Remove the door trim as described in Section 8.

2 See Fig. 11.6 and remove securing nuts (10). Press hard on the shaft (11) to push the whole mechanism inside the door shell. Withdraw the winder mechanism upwards and rearwards to disconnect the two rollers (12) from the slides at the bottom of the window glass holding channel.

3 Remove the window glass and channel together, first front down and then up and through (14).

4 Replacement is a reverse procedure but will require a certain amount of juggling. Once the glass is in the window frame, place it at the same place as in paragraph 1. Before finally tightening everything, check that all operates fully and smoothly.

5 Any attempt at replacement of the weatherstrips and glass channels is difficult. Consult a Renault franchise parts store on availability and the placement of parts. Obviously replace everything which comes out!

6   Rear doors: Rear doors prove a little more difficult. Remove the door trim, see paragraph 6.

7   On the trailing edge of the door, see Fig. 11.7, remove screws (11) and (12) then unclip the compensator spring (13) from inside the door frame. Remove the window bottom channel coupling clips (20) through the hole (14). Lower the window glass slightly and remove the aluminium channel cover and channel (21) and (22). The winding mechanism (19) and its sealing washer (R) can then be removed after screws (15) have been released in a similar manner to that of the front door.

8   Replacement is a straight reverse procedure but again check for correct movement before finally tightening up.

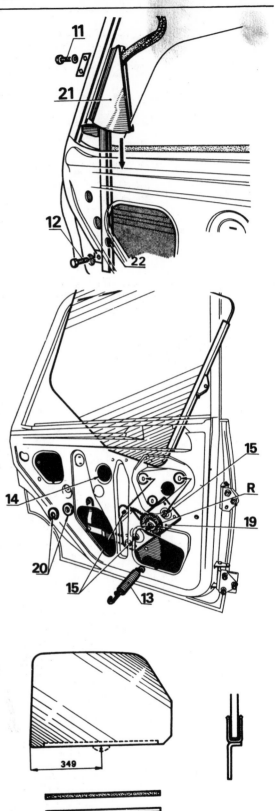

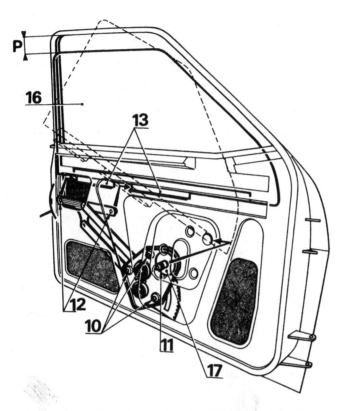

Fig.11.6. Front door window glass and winder mechanism removal
(see numbers in text)

10 Door locking mechanisms

1   Front doors: Remove the door trim (Section 8) and raise the window glass fully.

2   Release the remote control housing fixed by two screws. Push the control rod centre clip into the door to release it.

3   Undo the outer door handle by unscrewing the two fixing screws through the inner frame of the door. Now release the two lock screws visible on the trailing edge of the door. The total mechanism can now be fed through the door frame, through the rear upper aperture.

4   Replacement is a reverse procedure. Adjust the locking mechanism to suit.

5   Rear doors: This is undertaken in a very similar fashion to the front doors just described.

6   The rear door child-proof lock is no hindrance in removal. Its operation will be obvious once removed.

7   For bonnet, boot and tailgate locks see the appropriate Section.

FIG.11.7. REAR DOOR WINDOW GLASS AND WINDER MECHANISM REMOVAL

Dimension on glass (349 mm) indicates position of glass on the centre point of the support channel

11 Doors and door hinges - checking, removal and adjustments

1   Both front and rear doors can be removed by either removing the circlip and punching out the hinge pins or by removing the interior trim panel and undoing the hinge securing screws on the door pillar. Both methods require an assistant to stop the door dropping. Its heavier than it looks! Always use new hinge pins on replacement.

2   The door position is adjustable at the striker at the lock by the use of mounting points with large holes. The striker has adjustment achieved by slackening their fixing screws, moving them, and retightening.

3   Before making any adjustment mark round the edge of the striker, with pencil, so that the original position and the amount moved can be seen.

4   The striker may need to be moved in, or up, to compensate for wear in the lock. After long periods, the hinges wear, so more weight is taken by the striker. This makes the door difficult to close. But the striker must not be lowered, or the bottom of the door will rub on the body.

5   The hinges should be oiled regularly. The key locks to the doors should also be oiled, particularly in winter to keep out the damp, and prevent their freezing.

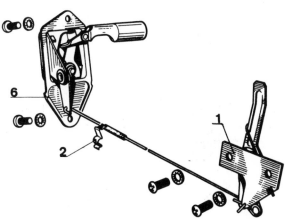

FIG.11.8. BASIC DOOR LOCKING MECHANISM

1   *Catch bracket*
2   *Rod steady clip*
6   *Door catch and lock*

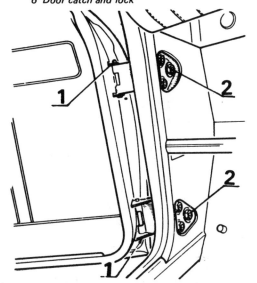

12 Door rattles - tracing and rectification

Door rattles are due either to loose hinges, worn or mal-adjusted catches, or loose components inside the door. Loose hinges can be detected by opening the door and trying to lift it. Any play will be felt. Worn or badly adjusted catches can be found by pushing and pulling on the outside handle when the door is closed. Once again any play will be felt. To check the window mechanism open the door and shake it with the window first open and then closed.

13 Bonnet, boot lid and tailgate

1   Bonnet: Open the bonnet and have an assistant hold it open. Scribe round the hinges and unscrew the four hinge fixing screws in turn. The hinges are fixed by one hinge/pin/bolt. These can be removed once the two headlamp embellishers have been removed.

2   Replacement is simple but adjustment must take place. The fixing screw holes are elongated for this. The bonnet locking mechanism components are shown in Fig. 11.10.

3   In an emergency should the bonnet release cable fail (this cable is replaced in a similar fashion to the choke cable. See Chapter 3), it will be necessary to get under the vehicle and pass a rod up through the engine compartment from below and press the release lever. This should unlock the bonnet.

4   Adjustment of both the hinge positions and the locking mechanism positions may be necessary to obtain proper operation and a proper fitted bonnet position.

5   Boot lid: Boot lid removal is similar to bonnet removal. Removal of the hinges is straight forward although there is one counterbalance spring. This must be removed first.

6   The boot lid lock is not easily removed without a Renault special tool Car. 473, but by using a screwdriver through the aperture on the underside to release the three locking tangs, it is possible. The lock components are shown, the lock barrel is attached to the pivot latch by a roll pin.

7   Tailgate: The tailgate is easily removed with another person. Disconnect any wiring (heated rear window and number plate light). Open it fully and remove the stay from the tailgate, this is obvious. Each hinge is fixed to the tailgate by two studs and nuts. Undo all four and carefully lift it away. Be careful not to damage the studs in the tailgate.

8   Replacement is a straight reverse procedure.

9   The tailgate lock is very similar in operation, as well as removal and replacement, to that of the boot lid. See paragraph 6.

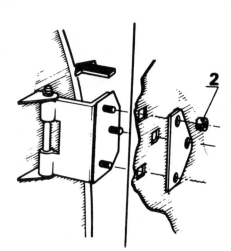

FIG.11.9. DOOR HINGE REMOVAL

1   *Hinge pin*   2   *Pillar hinge connections*

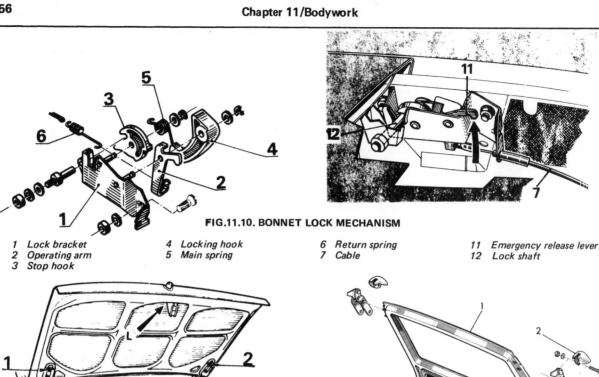

FIG.11.10. BONNET LOCK MECHANISM

1 Lock bracket	4 Locking hook	6 Return spring	11 Emergency release lever
2 Operating arm	5 Main spring	7 Cable	12 Lock shaft
3 Stop hook			

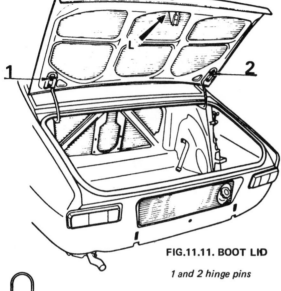

FIG.11.11. BOOT LID

1 and 2 hinge pins

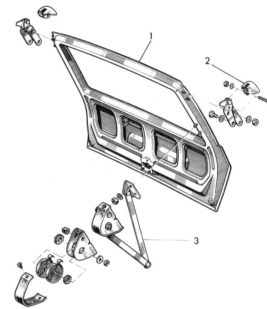

FIG.11.13. TAILGATE COMPONENTS

1 Tailgate
2 Hinge
3 Counterbalance

14 Bumpers

Figures 11.14 and 11.15 show the complete front and rear bumper fixings of the saloons and the estate. There are no special problems associated with their removal and replacement. Always soak all nuts and bolts with penetrating oil some time before their intended removal.

15 Exterior trim

1   Scuttle grille panel: This panel runs across the car under the front windscreen. On it sit the windscreen washer jets. To remove it, unscrew these jets and then remove all the visible sheet metal screws. To prevent distortion carefully lever it up progressively round the panel. Note the exact position of all weatherstrips, which should number five; the bonnet rear weatherstrip, the windscreen lower crossmember, the weatherstrip under the grille and the two side blanking off pieces.
2   Front panel embellisher: This consists of the centre grille and 'U', the two headlamp surrounds and the split moulding which runs along their lower edge. All are individually removable. The grille and headlamp surrounds are held by locating tangs

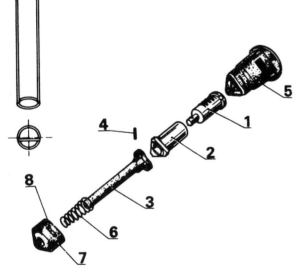

FIG.11.12. BOOT LID LOCK

1 Barrel	5 Casing
2 Push bottom	6 Spring
3 Pivot latch	7 Cover block
4 Roll pin	8 Retaining clips

(bottom) and sheet metal screws. The lower edge moulding is held by bent over tabs.

3 Bonnet moulding: The bonnet has a clipped on leading edge moulding to 'finish' off the grille. The clips are held by rivets to the bonnet and the moulding is pressed onto the clips. Be patient.

4 'Removing trim': All trim strips are clipped to the bodyshell, holes having been drilled into the panel. Slide the trim along the clip and gently pull away at the interior cut-outs.

5 Identification badges: All badges are pressed through the bodyshell and either glued or fastened by a sort of circlip. It is difficult to remove these without breakage or paint damage.

6 Rear ventilation panels: These are fixed by four sheet metal screws and are easily removed.

NOTE: All trim is expensive and fragile. Go slowly and gently - gain your own knowledge of its fixing without unnecessary damage and expense.

16 Interior fittings and fascia panel

1 Most of the floor coverings are located by 'press stud' fittings, and consequently easy to remove and replace. These studs locate through the underside of the bodyshell, therefore must always be fitted to avoid water coming into the car through the floor.

2 Trim and soundproofing felt that has not already been discussed is likely to be stuck to the bodyshell. If not it should pull away. Its removal and replacement requires skill but is not unduly difficult. Use a proprietary adhesive on replacement. The seat adjustment is given in the drivers' handbook supplied with the vehicle.

3 Removal and replacement of the headlining is not easy and should not be undertaken lightly. It is both sprung across and stuck at each long end. Seek advice from a coachbuilder first.

4 The glove compartment is fixed by sheet metal screws. Removal and replacement is straightforward. Obviously all trim panels, such as the front door pillar panels will need removal first, as will the fixing screws of the heater bulkhead casing.

5 Although the facia panel is in two parts, the front and the top framework, it must be removed in total, with the controls. R1177 fascia panels differ from the other versions but the removal/replacement sequence is similar. Remove the instrument panel. See Chapter 9.

6 Remove the top ventilator grille securing screws including those to the side veneers. Remove both grille and veneers. Remove the heater control plate and on - off valve, as described in Chapter 2.

7 Disconnect the two wiring harness junction blocks underneath and then the wiring to the cigar lighter, the wiper switch, unscrew the speedometer cable, (wiring to tachometer - R1177), and any other connected switches.

8 Undo the two nuts fixing the outer ends of the fascia under the ventilator grille panel on the bulkhead and then turn the fixing screws, between the windscreen lower crossmember and the fascia, one quarter of a turn. The fascia should now release.

9 Be very careful with the instruments. See Chapter 9 for instrument removal and Chapter 2 for heater details.

10 Replacement is a reverse sequence of removal.

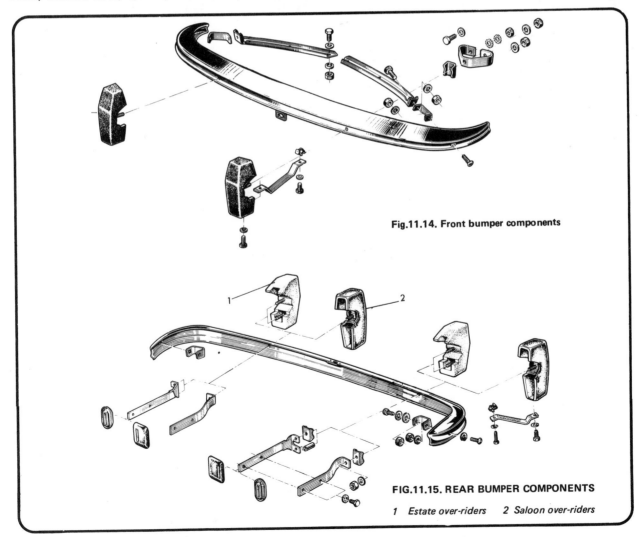

Fig.11.14. Front bumper components

FIG.11.15. REAR BUMPER COMPONENTS

1 Estate over-riders   2 Saloon over-riders

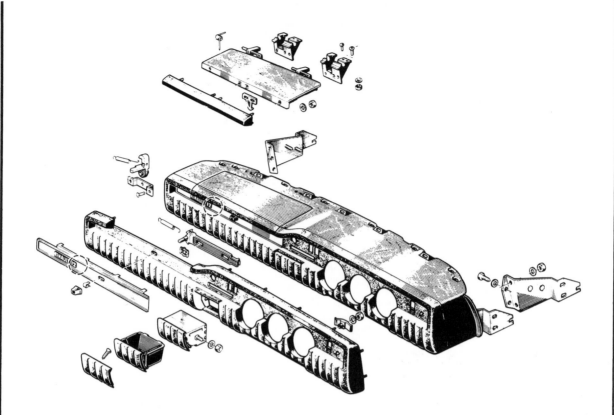

Fig.11.16. Fascia panel/dashboard components (illustrated is that for the TL/L saloon and estates. The TS is different but not significantly)

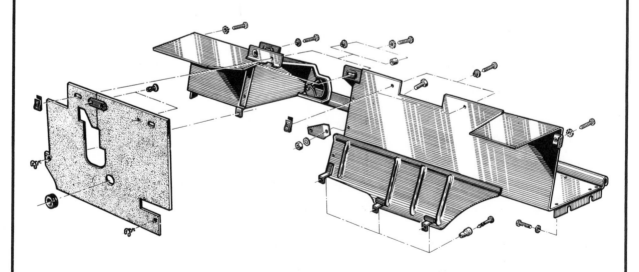

Fig.11.17. The front parcel shelving and trim

Chapter 12 Supplement

Contents

1 Introduction

1 This Chapter details the principal modifications that have been made to the Renault 12 range of vehicles since 1974.
2 The various paragraphs in this Chapter should be read in conjunction with the corresponding Chapter on that subject.
3 Due to the modifications that have been made to certain components over the years, it may be that old and new parts are not interchangeable and therefore it is of the utmost importance to quote the vehicle and engine numbers when ordering replacements.

2 Specifications

The specifications listed below are those items which differ from the original specifications as listed in the relevant Chapter, and in general they are applicable to later models (1974 on).

Engine
Compression ratio:

Model 12L	8.5:1
Models 12TL, 12TL Estate, 12TS and 12 Auto	9.5:1

Maximum power (DIN):

12L	50 BHP at 5000 rpm
12TL and 12TL Estate	54 BHP at 5250 rpm
12TS and 12 Automatic	60 BHP at 5500 rpm

Maximum torque (DIN):

12L	63.6 lbf ft at 3000 rpm
12TL and 12TL Estate	65.1 lbf ft at 3000 rpm
12TS and 12 Automatic	67.2 lbf ft at 3500 rpm

Cylinder head depth:

	8.5:1 CR	9.5:1 CR
Nominal	73.40 mm (2.890 in)	72.00 mm (2.835 in)
Minimum repair size	72.9 mm (2.871 in)	71.5 mm (2.815 in)

Combustion chamber volume:

8.5:1 C/ratio	37.81 cc (2.037 cu in)
9.5:1 C/ratio	33.81 cc (2.063 cu in)

(Cylinder head identical for both types but pistons differ).

Valve seat outside diameter:

Inlet	34.5 mm (1.358 in)
Exhaust	31.3 mm (1.232 in)

Pushrods:

	8.5:1 CR	9.5:1 CR
Length	176 mm (6.937 in)	173 mm (6.812 in)
Diameter	5 mm (0.197 in)	5 mm (0.197 in)

Cooling system

Thermostat — opening temperature (all models)	89°C (192°F)
Thermostat — closes by-pass port (all models)	100°C (212°F)

Fuel system
Solex 32 EISA 2/3/4

		Mark		
	473 and 501	519	513*	592*
Accelerator pump jet	35	35	40	40
Initial throttle opening	0.7 mm (0.028 in)	0.7 mm (0.028 in)	0.7 mm (0.028 in)	0.7 mm (0.028 in)
Main jet	145	147.5	132.5	127.5
Cut compensator jet	155	170	165	130
Idle jet	42.5	45	47.5	42
Needle valve	1.5	1.5	1.5	1.5
Econostat	50	50	70	60
Accelerator pump stroke	1.4 mm (0.055 in)	2.0 mm (0.079 in)		

Note that the mark 513 and 592 model Solex 32 EISA-4 carburettors have an integral air compensator/emulsion tube jet. This is a preset interference fit in the carburettor and must not be removed.

Solex 32 PDIS 5

	Mark	
	583	625
Accelerator pump jet	40	40
Initial throttle opening	1 mm (0.039 in)	1 mm (0.039 in)
Main jet	132.5	132.5
Air compensator jet	140	165
Idle jet	47.5	45
Needle valve	1.5	1.5
Econostat	—	105
Accelerator pump stroke	—	0.138 in (3.5 mm)

Carter 32 RBS

Float level	12.7 mm (0.50 in)
Pump stroke	4 mm (0.16 in)
Initial throttle opening	1 mm (0.039 in)

Zenith 32 IF 8

Initial throttle opening:	
Choke flap at mid cold position	0.80 mm (0.32 in)
Choke flap at extreme cold position	1.05 mm (0.041 in)
Accelerator pump stroke	22.80 mm (0.898 in)
Throttle butterfly angle	4.62 mm (0.182 in)
Auxiliary tube height (to top of body)	15.50 mm (0.609 in)
Accelerator pump tube height (to bottom flange)	67.50 mm (2.656 in)
Main jet	A127
Air compensator jet tube	No. 4
Diffuser (choke tube)	24
Normal idler jet	57.5
Auxiliary idle jet	45
Needle valve	1.5 mm

Zenith 32 WIM

Mark C - 7000 - 12

Main jet	130
Choke tube	25
Needle valve	1.5 mm
Idle jet	60
Air compensator jet	60
Float level	14.5 to 15.5
Enricher	55
Initial throttle opening	0.80 to 0.90 mm (0.032 to 0.035 in)
Accelerator pump	40

Weber 32 DIR 21

Mark 2302 - 2303 - 2304

	1st Barrel	2nd Barrel
Main jet	120 or 117.5	110
Choke tube	23	24
Idle jet	70	60
Air compensation jet	135	100
Float level	7 mm (0.28 in)	7 mm (0.28 in)
Float travel	8 mm (0.312 in)	8 mm (0.312 in)
Needle valve	1.75 mm	1.75 mm
Throttle opening (initial)	0.80 mm (0.032 in)	1 mm (0.039 in)

Weber 32 DIR 39

Mark 4500

	1st Barrel	2nd Barrel
Main jet	122	115
Choke tube	23	24
Idle jet	70	60
Air compensation jet	160	120
Float level	7 mm (0.28 in)	7 mm (0.28 in)
Float travel	8 mm (0.312 in)	8 mm (0.312 in)
Needle valve	175	175
Throttle opening (initial)	1 mm (0.039 in)	1 mm (0.039 in)

Idle speed settings — all carburettors

12L and TL models	700 rpm
12 TS	775 ± 25 rpm
Automatic models	625 ± 25 rpm

Automatic transmission

Torque wrench settings

	lbf ft	Nm
Oil pan bolts	7	9.5
Oil pump cover	10	13.5
Lower closure plate	7	9.5
Transmission case to final drive	15	20
Half-casing bolts (at edge)	17	23
(inboard)	22	30
(studs)	13	18
Stator support bolts	15	20
Brake bellhousing bolts (cast iron)	15	20
Brake bellhousing bolts (aluminium):		
for hydraulic distributor	5	7
for freewheel support	15	20
Torque converter to driveplate bolts	25	34

Oil capacity

Dry transmission	9 pints (5 litres)
At oil change	4.5 pints (2.5 litres)
Converter capacity	4.5 pints (2.5 litres)

Braking system
Rear brakes
Wheel cylinder diameter:

Models L, TL, TS	20.6 mm (0.812 in) or 22 mm (0.867 in)
Early and late model Estates	22 mm (0.867 in)

Drum diameter:

L, TL, TS models	180.25 mm (7.096 in)
Maximum regrind diameter	181.25 mm (7.096 in)
Estate models	228.5 mm (9.00 in)
Maximum regrind diameter	229.5 mm (9.035 in)
Lining thickness (all models)	5 mm (0.203 in)

Master cylinder
Diameter — TS and late model Estates   ...   .   20.6 mm (0.812 in)
Stroke:

TS and late Estate (2nd assembly)	38 mm (1.50 in)
TS and late Estate (intermediate assembly)	31 mm (1.218 in)
L, TL and late Estate (1st assembly)	28 mm (1.093 in)
L, TL and late Estate (2nd assembly)	30 mm (1.187 in)

Electrical system
Starter motor
Make/type   ...   .   Paris-Rhone Type D9E12
(Specification for this starter motor otherwise as per Type D8E81)

Alternator
Make/type	Paris-Rhone A12R1
Voltage	12V
Current	35A
Make/type	Paris-Rhone A13R115
Voltage	12V
Current	50A

Regulator for above alternators
Make/type   ...   .   Paris-Rhone AYB218

Windscreen wiper motor   ...   .   Femsa 2 speed

Flasher unit
Without side repeater lamps:

Cartier 161	42/84W
Klaxon 30860 A 860	42W
Scintex 30630-6	42/84W

With side repeater lamps:

Klaxon A893-308931	46W
Cartier 163	46/92W
Bulbs for the above types	221W (4W wing repeater)

Without side repeater lamps (Hazard warning incorporated):

Klaxon 55834	42/84W
Cartier 161	42/84W
Scintex 30630-6	42/84W

With side repeater lamps (Hazard warning incorporated):

Cartier 163	46/92W
Bulbs for the above types	421W (4W wing repeater)

Suspension and steering
Anti-roll bars —Automatic transmission models:

Rear (diameter)	16 mm (0.630 in)
Front (diameter)	17 mm (0.670 in)

Toe-out (front wheels) ...   .   1 to 4 mm (0.046 to 0.156 in)

Turning circle:

Manual versions (between kerbs)	10.10 m (32ft 9¾in)
(between walls)	10.78 m (35ft 3¼in)
Automatic versions (between kerbs)	11.00 m (36ft 1 1/16in)
(between walls)	11.70 m (38ft 4 5/8in)

Ground clearance to lower side member   ...   .   128.5 mm (5.063 in) less than wheel centre height

Bodywork
Dimensions — Saloon:

Overall length	434.8 mm (14ft 0 15/16in)
Overall width	161.6 mm (5ft 3 13/16in)

Overall height (unladen)	...	...	...	...	...	...	143.5 mm (4ft 8¼in)
Wheelbase	...	...				...	244.1 mm (8ft 0in)
Front and rear track	...	...	...	...	...	...	131.2 mm (4ft 3 9/16in)

Dimensions — Estate:

Overall length	...	...	...	...	...	...	437.1 mm (14ft 4 1/8in)
Overall width	...	...	...	...	...	...	161.6 mm (5ft 3 3/16in)
Overall height (unladen)	...	...	...	...	...	...	145.5 mm (4ft 9 5/16in)
Wheelbase	...	...	...	...	...	...	244.1 mm (8ft 0in)
Front track	...	...	...	...	...	...	131.2 mm (4ft 3 11/16in)
Rear track	...	...	...	...	...	...	131.4 mm (4ft 3¾in)
Tailgate aperture height	...	...	...	...	...	760.0 mm (2ft 5 15/16in)
Tailgate aperture width - top	...	...	...	...	1040.0 mm (3ft 4 15/16in)
Tailgate aperture width - bottom	...	...	...	...	1100.0 mm (3ft 7 5/16in)

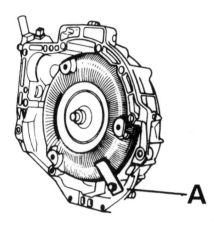

Fig. 12.1 Retaining plate (A) fitted to hold torque converter

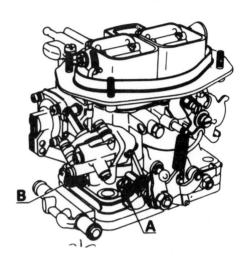

Fig. 12.2 The Weber and Carter carburettor adjustment screws

A Throttle speed adjustment screw   B Fuel mixture screw

3 Engine

Engine removal — automatic transmission models

1 The procedure given in the engine removal section of Chapter 1 is generally identical for automatic transmission models except for the following additional points, which must also be implemented.

2 Having removed the starter motor, disconnect the governor operating cable (see the automatic transmission section of this Chapter).

3 Disconnect the vacuum feed cable from the vacuum capsule.

4 Detach the wiring harness connections from the transmission.

5 When the remaining engine ancillary and associated fixings have been removed, unscrew and withdraw the transmission-to-engine bolts at the top. Unscrew and remove the two fixing studs, using a suitable stud remover, or by locking two nuts together on the stud and unscrewing the innermost nut to extract each of the studs.

6 Remove the converter shield and, using a universal coupling and socket, unscrew each of the three bolts securing the torque converter to the drive plate.

access to each of the bolts. The alignment holes are unequally spaced and it is not necessary therefore to mark the relative position of the drive plate to converter since they only fit one way.

7 Support the transmission underneath, using suitable blocks or a jack, and then unscrew and remove the lower transmission-to-engine retaining bolts.

8 When the engine is being parted from the transmission ensure

that the converter is not disturbed or withdrawn. As soon as possible, fit a retaining plate (see Fig. 12.1) to the converter housing to ensure that the converter is not accidentally disturbed.

9 To re-connect the engine to the automatic transmission, reverse the removal procedure but note the instructions given in paragraphs 22 and 23 of Section 6 of this Supplement.

10 If the engine and automatic transmission are to be removed as a combined unit then follow the instructions given in Section 5 of Chapter 1 and in addition remove/disconnect the following:

    (a) The rear transmission crossmember.

    (b) The selector control: to disconnect this, position the selector lever in 1st gear, then unscrew the clamp bolt retaining the rod to the computer/selector lever. Detach the rod.

11 Installation of the engine and automatic transmission is a reversal of the removal procedure but the following must be adjusted (see automatic transmission Section of this Chapter):

    (a) the accelerator cable.

    (b) the governor control cable.

12 Refill the transmission with oil on completion as described in the automatic transmission (Maintenance) Section of this Chapter.

4 Fuel System

Carburettors — general

1 Varying types and makes of carburettor have been fitted over the production period according to vehicle and engine type and

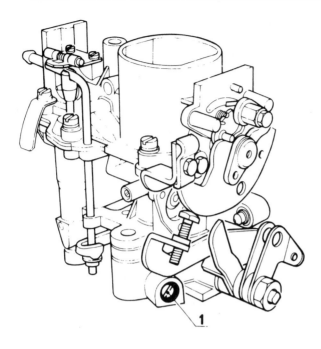

Fig. 12.3 The Zenith 32 IF8 carburettor showing the idle adjustment screw (1)

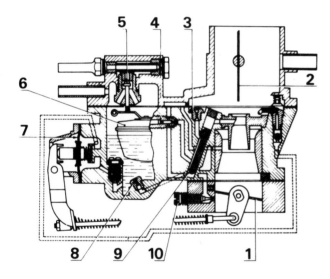

Fig. 12.4 Cross-sectional view of the Solex 32PDIS carburettor

1 *Throttle butterfly*
2 *Choke flap*
3 *Air compensator jet*
4 *Idle speed jet*
5 *Needle valve*
6 *Float*
7 *Accelerator pump*
8 *Main jet*
9 *Emulsion tube*
10 *Fuel screw*

date of manufacture. It is therefore of vital importance to quote your engine number and carburettor type/number when ordering spare parts. The identification mark for the various carburettors will be found as follows:

Solex/Zenith/Carter carburettors — beneath the float chamber fixing screws.
Weber — on the base flange.

Idle speed adjustment — all models

2 The adjustment of the idle speed for the Weber, Carter and Solex carburettors remains the same as that given in Chapter 3, but check the specified idle speeds.

3 On Zenith carburettors there is a single idle speed setting screw, there being a dual-circuit idling system incorporated into its design. Simply turn the screw as desired to achieve the specified idle speed. Fuel mixture screws on these carburettors are generally sealed and should not be tampered with unless a CO meter is available to check the exhaust gas.

Carburettor overhaul — general

4 The carburettor is a finely adjusted, precision-built piece of equipment and it therefore warrants respect from the operator/mechanic. In most instances, any problems associated with or involving the carburettor are best left to your Renault dealer or local carburettor specialist. Special tools and knowledge are required to repair and adjust the comparitively delicate components. Amateur fiddling (and in some cases butchery!) with these components can often lead eventually to additional expense.

5 In case your carburettor is giving you problems and you are unable to get it to a specialist, we have listed below a number of the more simple checks and adjustment procedures for the various carburettor models. Remember when adjusting or working on carburettors that they are delicate and must be handled with care. Use the correct size and type of tool for the job and never overstress any fixings. Where possible always renew the gaskets/seals. Wash any dismantled parts in clean petrol and blow or wipe dry using a non-fluffy cloth before reassembly.

Solex 32 PDIS — description and adjustments

6 The Solex 32 PDIS is similar to the 32 EISA type Solex but it incorporates an accelerator pump which is attached to the float chamber and is operated by the action of the throttle butterfly, whose pivot is interconnected to the pump via a pump lever. The following adjustments can be made on this type of carburettor.

Initial throttle opening

7 To check the initial throttle opening it will be necessary to acquire or fabricate a suitable gauge rod of the thickness quoted in the specifications for the initial throttle opening. If possible use special Renault gauge rod number MS532 or an equivalent diameter twist drill.

8 Check that the choke flap is fully closed, then insert the gauge rod between the flap and the inner body. If adjustment is necessary either way to conform to the specified clearance, bend the connection link (Fig. 12.5) accordingly.

End-of-pump-stroke throttle opening check

9 To check the throttle opening the carburettor must be removed from the manifold so that it can be inverted for accessibility.

10 Insert a gauge rod of the specified diameter between the main bore of the carburettor and the butterfly as shown in Fig. 12.6. Check that the pump is at the end of its stroke and, if adjustment is required, press the pump lever against its stop and then turn the adjustment nut so that it is just in contact with the lever.

Carter 32 RBS carburettor — adjustments
Initial throttle opening

11 There are two adjustments necessary to set the initial

throttle opening. Refer to Fig. 12.7, and set the choke flap in the medium cold position, that is with the hole 'T' and the detent ball aligned. Proceed as follows:

12 Check that the throttle lever adjustment screw is in alignment with the line marked R on the operating cam; if it is not, adjust by bending the connection rod L between the choke flap swivel and the cam to the required amount so that the adjustment screw is in line.

13 Now check the initial throttle opening using a gauge rod of the specified thickness. If possible use Renault special gauge rod number MS532 or an equivalent diameter twist drill. To adjust the opening, unscrew the locknut and turn the adjustment screw accordingly. When set at the correct opening retighten the locknut.

Float level check

14 Remove the carburettor and the float chamber. Invert the carburettor and, holding it level, check the clearance between the cover joint face and the uppermost point of the 'pip' on the float. If adjustment is necessary bend the float tongue accordingly but do not apply any pressure on the needle valve.

Accelerator pump stroke check

15 Refer to Fig. 12.9 and fully open the choke flap. Now check the piston travel distance between the fully open and idle positions. If the distance is not as specified, adjust by bending the accelerator pump-to-throttle-lever connection rod accordingly.

Zenith 32 IF8 carburettor — description and adjustments

16 A single Zenith downdraught carburettor is fitted on some models and, although similar in action to the Solex, it incorporates a dual-circuit idling system and an accelerator pump.

17 The dual-circuit idling system enables a constant mixture supply when idling. Adjustment of the idling is made by turning the single adjusting screw accordingly.

Initial throttle opening check/adjustment

18 Set the choke flap cam at the medium cold position. To do this refer to Fig. 12.10 and align the detent ball and hole, then with the throttle lever in the closed position insert a gauge rod (or twist drill) of the specified diameter (Renault tool MS532 if available), between the inner carburettor body and the butterfly as shown on the progression hole side of the aperture.

19 If adjustment is necessary, loosen the locknut and turn the adjusting screw accordingly to obtain the correct clearance. A further check can be made by positioning the choke control so that it is in the extreme cold position, i.e. with the detent ball opposite hole '12'. Now check the clearance between the butterfly and the inner wall and it should be as specified. If not, further adjustment may be necessary as given above.

Accelerator pump — travel check and adjustment

20 Unscrew and remove the delivery valve - refer to Fig. 12.11. Fully open the choke flap and retain the throttle butterfly in the closed position. Now check the clearance 'A' between the valve contact face and the piston bottom. This should be as given in the Specifications, but if adjustment is necessary rotate the adjustment nut accordingly.

21 A further check to make is that the defuming valve (Fig. 12.12) is fully closed as soon as the accelerator pump has finished its operation stroke. If it is not fully closed at this point, bend the valve stem just sufficiently to achieve this.

Auxiliary jet and accelerator pump outlet tubes — check and adjustment

22 The set positions of these tubes are of critical importance to the efficient operation of the carburettor. Therefore if the carburettor is giving problems it is essential that the tubes be checked and/or correctly positioned on reassembly.

23 To check or reset the auxiliary jet outlet tube, calculate the measurement X between the top of the carburettor and the top of the tube. When correctly set it should be 15.5 mm (39/64 in).

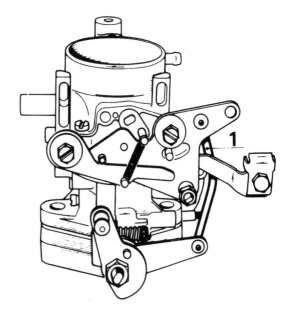

Fig. 12.5 The connecting link (1) on the Solex 32PDIS

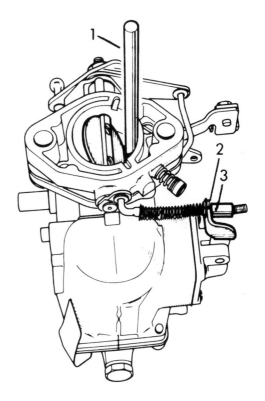

Fig. 12.6 Checking the pump stroke (Solex 32PDIS)

1 Gauge rod in position
2 Pump lever
3 Adjustment nut

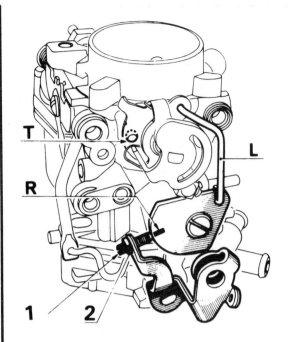

Fig. 12.7 Carter 32 RBS carburettor showing adjustment check points (refer to text)

L   Connecting rod   1 and 2 Adjustment screw and locknut
T   Medium detent hole
R   Alignment check mark

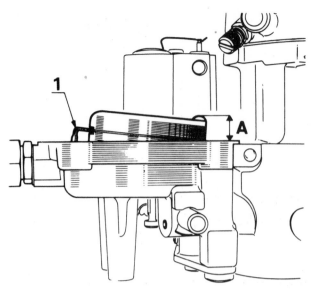

Fig. 12.8 Check the Carter 32 RBS float level at point 'A' which should equal ½ in (12.7 mm)

1   Float tongue

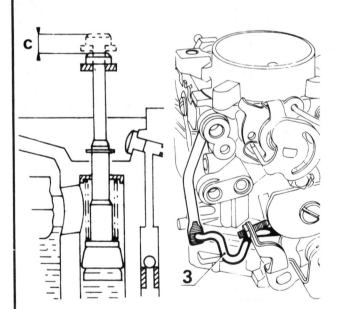

Fig. 12.9 The accelerator pump stroke check (C) which should be 5/32 in (4 mm). Adjustment rod (3) also shown (Carter 32 RBS)

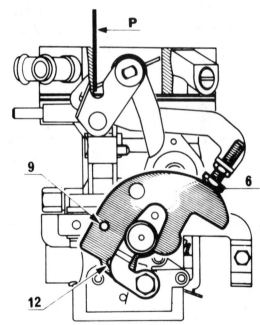

Fig. 12.10 The Zenith 32 IF8 carburettor throttle opening check points

P   Gauge
6   Adjustment screw/locknut
9   Detent alignment hole
12 Extreme cold alignment hole

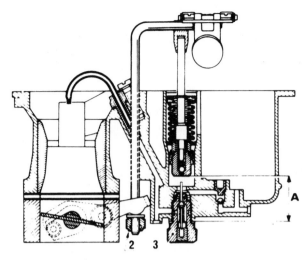

Fig. 12.11 The Zenith 321F8 pump cross-section view showing delivery valve (3) and check point 'A'. Adjustment nut (2) is also shown

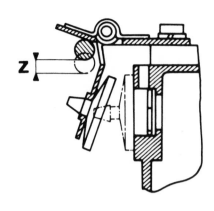

Fig. 12.12 The Zenith 321F8 defuming valve in the float chamber - check that it fully closes
Z = 5/64 in to 1/8 in (2 to 3 mm)

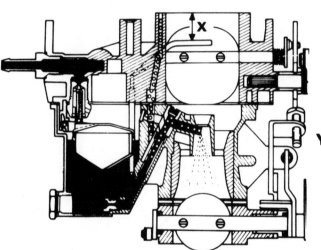

Fig. 12.13 The Zenith 321F8 carburettor - auxiliary jet outlet tube height adjustment check
X = 39/64 in (15.5 mm)

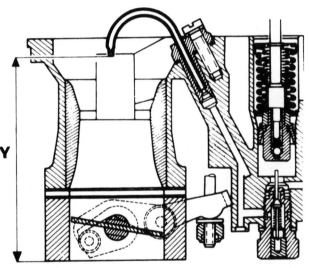

Fig. 12.14 The Zenith 321F8 carburettor - accelerator pump outlet tube height check
Y = 2 21/32 in (67.5 mm)

Bend the tube as required to achieve this height but take care not to distort the tube.

24 The accelerator pump outlet tube is shown in Fig. 12.14. It is most important that the jet of the tube is located between the venturi and the choke tube, and the distance between the tip of the tube and the lower face of the carburettor flange should be 67.5 mm (2 21/32 in). Bend (but do not distort) the tube to achieve this specification if necessary.

Carburettor/engine breather hose

25 The breather pipes via the carburettor and inlet manifold must be in good condition at all times and their connections checked regularly.

26 If a breather hose has to be renewed, ensure that a new calibration jet is fitted as shown in the accompanying illustrations. Failure to do this will result in a weakening of the

mixture causing uneven running, especially on idling.

5 Ignition system

Distributor — description

1 A Femsa distributor is fitted to some engines, the details of this being given in the Specifications. Adjustment and overhaul procedures are as for the Ducellier type distributor — see Chapter 4.

Distributor — cassette type contact breaker unit (SEV-Marchal)

2 Some models are being fitted with a new type of distributor which uses a cassette type contact breaker unit.

3 The principal components of this distributor are shown in

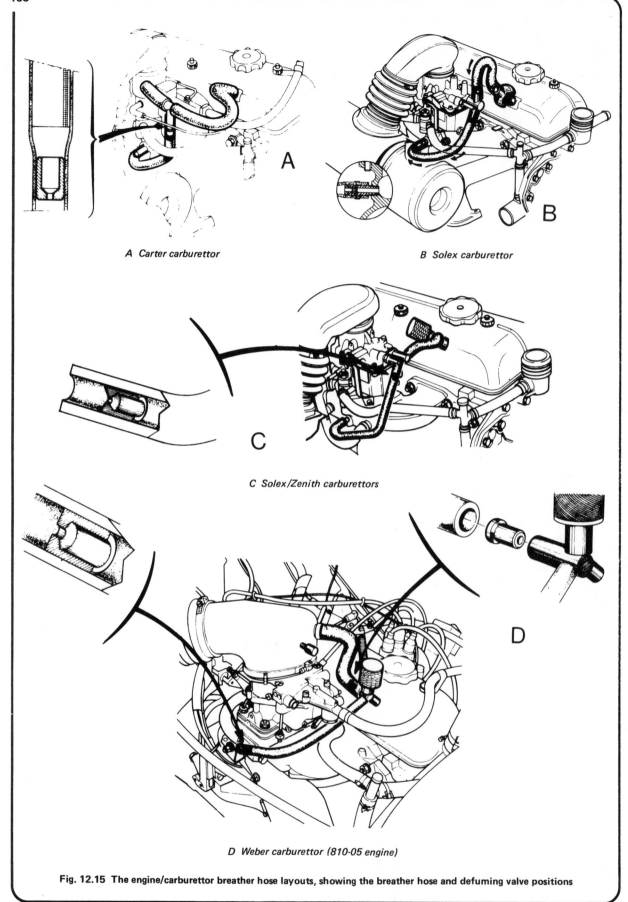

A Carter carburettor

B Solex carburettor

C Solex/Zenith carburettors

D Weber carburettor (810-05 engine)

Fig. 12.15 The engine/carburettor breather hose layouts, showing the breather hose and defuming valve positions

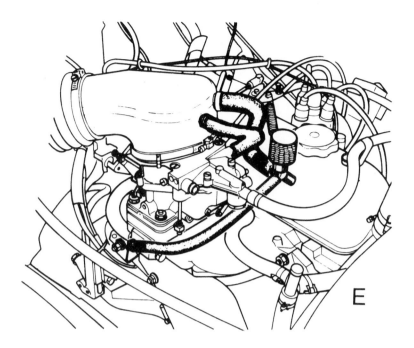

E Weber carburettor (810-06 engine)

Fig. 12.17. The main advantage of this type of distributor is that
the contact breaker points are adjusted (with the aid of a 3 mm
Allen key) from the outside, without removing the cap and with
the engine running.

4 Another advantage is that, whereas with the old type
distributor, when the spindle side play increased, the spark
voltage would vary because of the variation in distance between
the distributor cap plug lead segments and the rotor arm, on this
latest type, the spark from the rotor arm to the cap segments is
vertical and therefore the distance remains the same irrespective
of the side play in the spindle.

5 Checking the gap adjustments of the contact points is best
performed with a dwell meter which will give the correct dwell
or cam angle reading and these should be as follows:

    Dwell = 63% ± 3%
    Cam angle = 57° ± 3°

If adjustment to the dwell percentage or angle is necessary, use a
3 mm Allen key inserted through the hole in the side of the
distributor body, and locate in the knurled points adjuster in the
cassette. To increase the dwell turn the key clockwise, and vice
versa. This operation is carried out with the engine idling.

6 If you do not have a dwell meter, then the contact points can
only be checked for adjustment by removing the cassette (see
below) and passing a piece of bar through the drive spindle
aperture. The bar must be 16.96 mm (0.6677 in) diameter which
is the corresponding cam diameter. The contact points should be
set to give a clearance of 0.40 mm (0.016 in) and this can be
checked using a feeler gauge in the normal manner.

7 If the points need to be renewed then the complete cassette
must be replaced. To remove it, detach the distributor cap,
withdraw the rotor arm and disconnect the vacuum advance tube
from the capsule. The cassette is now simply lifted out of the
distributor body and clear of the spindle. Use a screwdriver and
lever the connector from the condenser to release the cassette.

8 Insert the new cassette, sliding it into the condenser/vacuum
capsule securing lugs. When fitting the cassette unit over the
spindle cam, align the condenser support with its body recess and
before pushing into position, check that the contact point heel
and cam apex are not in line with each other (otherwise the heel
may be damaged) then press home the cassette. Reposition the

Fig. 12.16 Femsa type distributor components

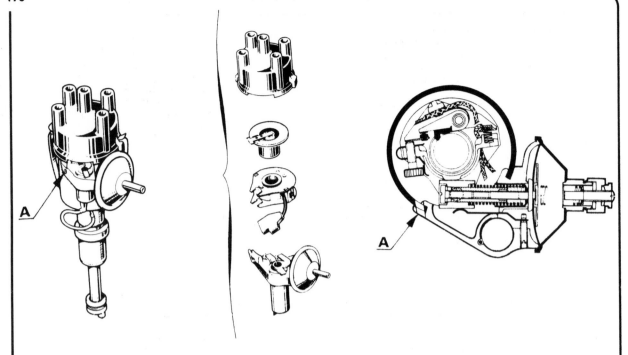

Fig. 12.17 SEV-Marchal distributor showing principal components. A Hole for Allen key

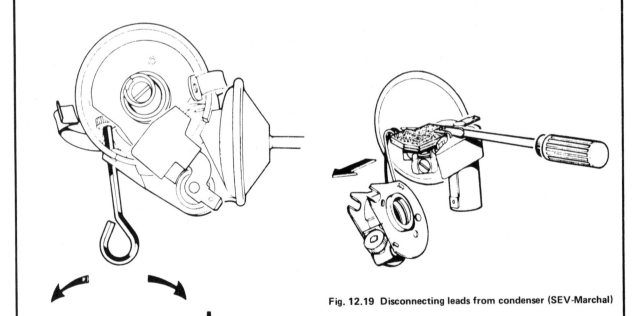

Fig. 12.19 Disconnecting leads from condenser (SEV-Marchal)

−　＋

Fig. 12.18 Using Allen key to adjust dwell angle (SEV-Marchal distributor)

rotor arm over the drive spindle and ensure that it is fully located. Replace the cap and check the electrical connections. Refit the vacuum advance tube to the capsule nozzle (if detached) and start the engine. If a dwell meter is available, check the dwell angle as described previously.

6 Automatic transmission

Introduction

1 In April 1974 an automatic transmission became available fitted to the TR model which was otherwise similar to the TL version. In October 1975 the TR became known as the 12 Automatic.

The operating principles and general service adjustments are given below. Any repairs and adjustments should be restricted to those described. Major internal 'surgery' should be entrusted to your Renault dealer who has the specialised knowledge and equipment necessary to undertake any of the more involved operations.

General description

2 A Renault type 4139 automatic transmission system is employed, which enables either fully automatic gear changes without the use of a clutch pedal or over-riding selection controlled by the driver.

3 The transmission major assemblies comprise a torque converter, the gearbox containing the epicyclic gear train, and the relative electric and hydraulic controls. The differential unit is also incorporated into the system, being situated between the torque converter and the gearcase. Refer to Fig. 12.21 for a general cutaway view of the transmission components.

4 The torque converter comprises an impeller, turbine and stator. Its function is to boost the torque when accelerating from rest, and it also acts as an automatic clutch.

5 The epicyclic gears are of a helical type and they give the respective ratios as decided by the hydraulically fed clutch and brake receivers — E1, E2, F1 and F2 in Fig. 12.21.

6 The engine driven oil pump feeds oil to the converter, the transmission generally for lubrication, and also to the brake and clutch receivers. The pump is located in the rear of the unit.

7 Electrically operated solenoid ball valves open or close channels to enable gear changes through the range (up or down), as dictated by the computer.

8 In order that the hydraulic clutch and brake receivers can be regulated to suit the engine torque, a vacuum capsule is fitted and this activates the pressure regulation in the hydraulic distributor as dictated by the inlet manifold vacuum.

9 The computer, which transmits the electrical impulses to the solenoid ball valves, is operated by the AC current from the governor, according to engine speed and/or torque and also the selector lever location.

Maintenance — lubrication

10 The transmission oil level must be checked at regular intervals of 3000 miles (5000 km). Proceed as follows:

11 The oil used in the automatic gearbox/transmission unit provides the requirements of the gearbox, converter and final drive and must therefore be of specified grade and maintained at the correct level.

12 When checking oil level, position the vehicle on flat ground and place the hand control in 'P'. Start the engine and run it for two minutes to allow the converter to fill up.

13 Allow the engine to tick over and, with the lever still in 'P', check the oil level on the dipstick.

14 Dependent on whether the car has just finished a run and the engine/gearbox is thoroughly hot, or whether it has been started from cold check as follows:

COLD - Minimum 1 or Maximum 2.
HOT - Minimum 2 or Maximum 3.

As a rough guide the quantity requirement between marks 1 and 2 is about ½ pint (0.25 litre).

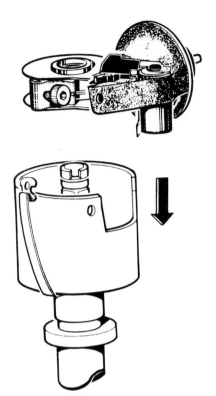

Fig. 12.20 Refitting the cassette (SEV-Marchal distributor)

15 If topping up is necessary, this is achieved via the dipstick location tube — use a funnel to prevent spillage. Do not allow the oil level to drop below the minimum mark and never overfill as this may cause overheating.

16 Oil changing is recommended at 18 000 miles (30 000 km) intervals after the first two vehicle services on a new vehicle. The oil must be drained (hot) by removing the drain plug as shown in Fig. 12.23 and allowing the oil to drain for up to five minutes. Refit the plug and refill the transmission using only automatic transmission oil to Renault specification which is Elf-Renaultmatic or Mobil ATF 200.

The amount of oil required to top up will depend on the amount drained. The full capacity of the transmission and converter units is 9 pints (5 litres), but it will probably only be necessary to refill using about 6 pints (3.5 litres). Recheck the level with the engine running.

Operations possible with transmission in position in vehicle.

17 The following can be carried out with the gearbox/transmission unit in position in the car, and are fully described in the sections that follow:

Renewing the governor
Renewing the electronic computer unit.
Renewing the vacuum capsule
Renewing the differential sunwheel oil seals
Renewing the oil pump cover gasket
Rectifying lower housing oil leak
Renewing the lower cover plate gasket

The Governor — adjustment

18 When the governor or operating cable has been removed or renewed, then the following setting procedure must be carried out. Removal and replacement of the carburettor, accelerator control, cylinder head and rocker box will also necessitate

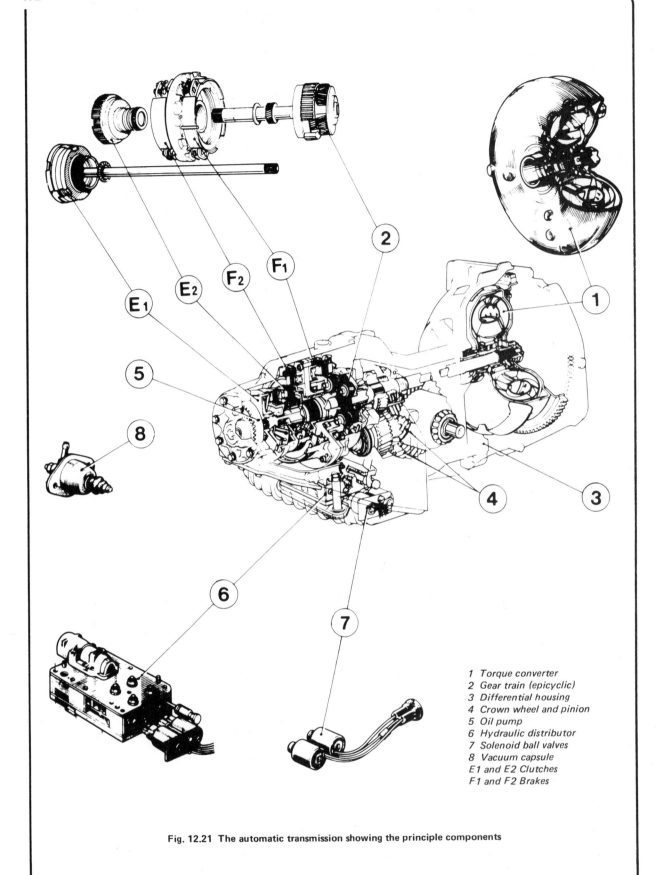

E₁

E₂

F₂

F₁

2

5

8

6

7

1

4

3

1 Torque converter
2 Gear train (epicyclic)
3 Differential housing
4 Crown wheel and pinion
5 Oil pump
6 Hydraulic distributor
7 Solenoid ball valves
8 Vacuum capsule
E1 and E2 Clutches
F1 and F2 Brakes

Fig. 12.21 The automatic transmission showing the principle components

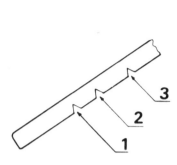

Fig. 12.22 Dipstick markings

1 Min   2 Max (COLD)
2 Min   3 Max (HOT)

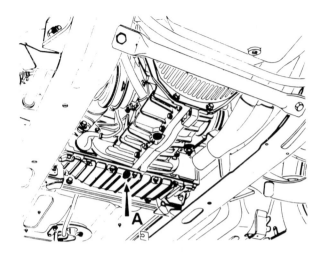

Fig. 12.23 Drain plug (A) on automatic transmission

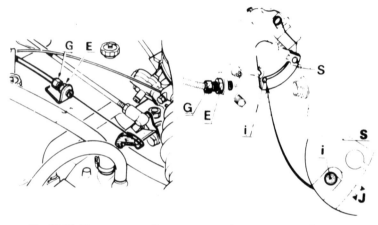

Fig. 12.24 The governor adjustment points (auto transmission)

J   Clearance points = 0.008 to 0.028 in (0.2 to 0.7 mm)   S   Quadrant
I   Index   G and E Adjuster and stop

checking of the governor control cable setting.

19 Adjust the cable stop (G) so that its threaded length is positioned equally either side of its retaining bracket.

20 Attach the control cable to the control segment (S).

21 Attach the other end of the operating cable to the cam at the side of the carburettor.

22 Press the accelerator right down and stretch the cable taut by removing the outer cable from its connection. Now tighten the inner cable connection to the carburettor cam. There should not be any play in the inner cable run at this stage. Refit the outer cable.

23 Release the accelerator pedal and then screw in the outer cable stop (G) about one turn and check the free travel at the end of the cable travel. When cable adjustment is correct, there should be free play between segment (S) and the pointer (1) within the scale cut-out, of 0.2 to 0.7 mm (0.008 to 0.028 in). When adjustment is correct, tighten the locknut (E).

Governor — removal and refitting

24 Disconnect the battery connections.

25 Working underneath the vehicle (it must be securely jacked up or on ramps), detach the governor control cable and feed wires.

26 Unscrew and remove the governor unit retaining screws.

27 Pass a universal joint wrench through the aperture in the left-hand front wheelhousing and locate on the uppermost retaining screw to remove. Alternatively remove the battery and its support to gain access to the retaining screw. The governor can now be withdrawn.

28 To refit, locate the new gasket which must be smeared with a coating of jointing compound. Slide the governor into position, rotating the speedometer gear slowly whilst simultaneously exerting slight pressure on the governor unit.

29 When in position, refit and tighten the retaining screws and attach the wiring.

30 Re-locate and adjust the governor control cable as described previously.

Gear selector control — adjustment

31 To adjust the selector control mechanism first move the selection lever to the 'P' (Park) position.

32 The quadrant securing bolts (Fig. 12.26) are now slackened and the quadrant adjusted accordingly.

33 Tighten the quadrant securing bolts on completion.

34 To check that the transmission-to-selector control coupling adjustment is correct, refer to Fig. 12.27 and measure the

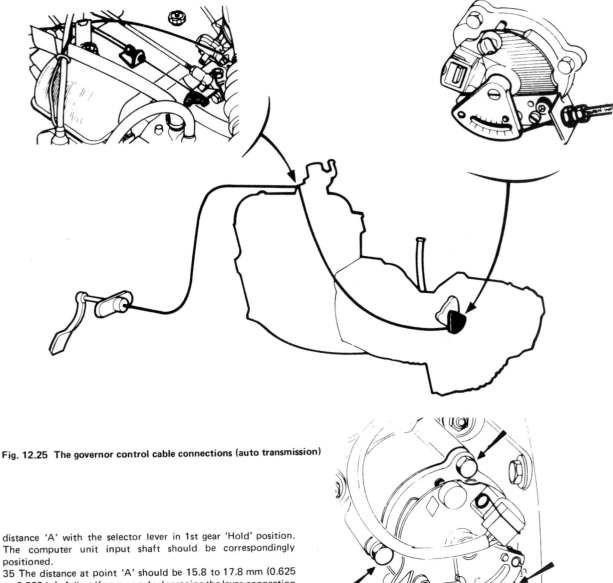

Fig. 12.25 The governor control cable connections (auto transmission)

distance 'A' with the selector lever in 1st gear 'Hold' position. The computer unit input shaft should be correspondingly positioned.

35 The distance at point 'A' should be 15.8 to 17.8 mm (0.625 to 0.703 in). Adjust if necessary by loosening the lever connection securing bolt and adjusting the distance accordingly. Retighten the retaining bolt.

36 Check that the starter solenoid switch is operational only when the selector lever is engaged in the 'P' (Park) or 'N' (Neutral) positions.

Kickdown switch — adjustments

37 When the accelerator pedal reaches the limit of its normal travel, additional foot pressure will operate the kick-down switch which will have the action of changing the automatic gearbox to the next low ratio provided that the road speed is not above the maximum pre-set level at which the lower gear ratio can be engaged. The lower gear will only be held for as long as the speed does not exceed the maximum permitted revs for this ratio, or the accelerator pedal is released, in which case the gear will return to its original (higher) ratio.

38 It is imperative to maintain correct adjustment of the kickdown switch and this should be carried out as follows:

39 First check the serviceability of the kickdown switch by connecting a 12 volt test bulb between the switch and the battery + terminal. When the accelerator pedal is fully depressed, the test bulb will light proving the switch is in order.

40 Ensure that the choke is fully off (released) and that the accelerator cable has a little play when fully depressed, to provide 3 to 4 mm (1/8 to 5/32in) movement of the spring pad of the kickdown switch (B in the sectional view). Where the adjustment is incorrect, then carry out adjustment of the accelerator cable, the governor control cable and the kickdown switch simultaneously as their tolerances and adjustment are inter-dependent.

Electric computer unit — removal and refitting

41 First disconnect the computer wiring harness together with the junction block support.

42 The sealed multiple plug protection shield can now be removed, and the two screws that retain the computer unit unscrewed and extracted.Remove the computer.

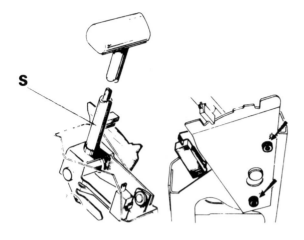

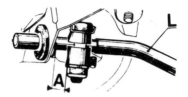

Fig. 12.27 Transmission coupling adjustment point
A = 15.8 to 17.8 mm

Fig. 12.26 The selector lever 'S' and quadrant retaining bolts
(arrowed) - Auto transmission

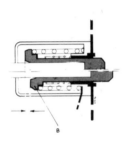

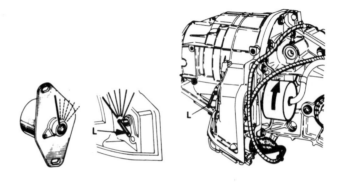

Fig. 12.29 The computer unit (auto transmission)

Fig. 12.28 Kickdown switch testing and spring pad
movement (auto transmission)
B = 3 to 4 mm

43 To reinstall, first rotate the control shaft on the computer unit fully in a clockwise direction so that it is in the 1st gear 'Hold' position.

44 Place the selector lever into the 1st gear 'Hold' position.

45 Reposition the computer unit (using new spacers) and locate the securing screws, but tighten them using only finger pressure. When fitting the unit turn the lever 'L' and the computer unit correspondingly in the direction shown (arrowed) but do not force. This procedure is necessary to align the manual valve.

46 Do not overtighten the retaining screws or the plastic distance pieces will distort. Re-attach the wires and check that the terminals are located in the two blocks, then refit the multiple plug shield to seal.

Vacuum capsule — removal and refitting

47 Detach the vacuum hose.

48 Unscrew and remove the capsule retaining bolts.

49 Remove the capsule. It should be noted that it is not possible to repair it, and therefore the capsule should be discarded and a new replacement fitted.

50 When fitting the new capsule, smear the oil seal with gasket cement and then secure the capsule in position and reattach the hose.

51 Check the transmission oil level and top up if necessary due to any loss of fluid when the capsule was removed.

52 The transmission oil pressure is preset at the factory and should not therefore be in need of further adjustment. Any

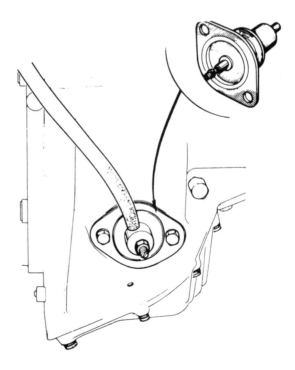

Fig. 12.30 The vacuum capsule (auto transmission)

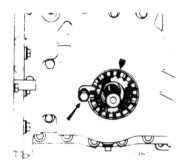

Fig. 12.31 Differential adjustment nut locktab and bolt

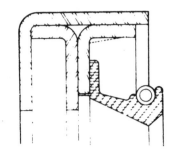

Fig. 12.32 Oilseal in position with felt washer

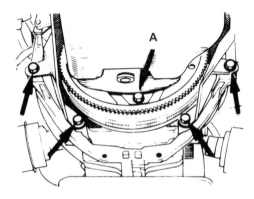

Fig. 12.33 A torque converter/drive plate bolt (A) also arrowed
are the lower attachment bolts

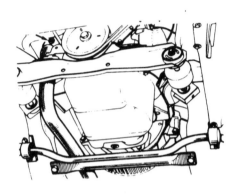

Fig. 12.34 Removing the anti-roll bar and tubular crossmember

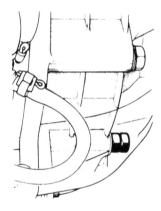

Fig. 12.35 Removing the studs using two locknuts

Fig. 12.36 Torque converter oil seal removal

adjustments must be made only by a Renault dealer, who will be
able to carry out a pressure test to ensure that the setting is
correct.

Differential sunwheel oil seal — renewal

53 Drain the transmission oil.
54 Disconnect the brake caliper, the upper suspension balljoint
and then the steering arm balljoint (see Chapter 10).
55 Withdraw the driveshaft from the sunwheel as described in
Chapter 7.
56 Dot punch the relative position of the differential bearing

adjustment nut to the gearbox casing.
57 Unscrew and remove the nut locking tab and unscrew the
bearing adjustment nut taking note of the number of turns
required to free it. Remove the oil seal O-rings and the lip type
seals.
58 Renew both the O-rings and oil seals. When fitting, take care
that the oil seal is fitted the correct way round and use a piece of
suitable tubing as a drift to ease assembly and ensure that it is
correctly aligned. Take care not to damage the seals during
assembly.
59 Reassembly is now a reversal of the dismantling procedure,

but take care to readjust the ring nut the exact number of turns and lock in position with the tab washer and lockbolt.

60 Reconnect the driveshaft/s and the steering/suspension components.

Automatic transmission unit — removing and refitting

61 This section describes removal of the gearbox/transmission unit leaving the engine in position in the vehicle. If it is wished to remove the engine and transmission unit combined, refer to Chapter 1 and disconnect the engine attachment fittings (except those to the gearbox). To disconnect the automatic transmission proceed as given below but omit the instructions given in paragraphs 65, 66, 75 and 77. If the transmission is to be detached from the engine on removal, adhere to the cautionary notes in paragraph 81.

62 Drain the transmission and remove the torque converter housing cover.

63 Disconnect the battery connections, and the automatic transmission wire connections.

64 Jack up and support the front of the car using axle stands or blocks. Remove the two front roadwheels.

65 Unscrew and remove the starter motor retaining bolts (3) and extract the starter unit.

66 Disconnect the torque converter from the drive plate by removing the three retaining bolts. These are best removed using a universal joint socket drive. Turn the engine over by hand by applying a spanner to the crankshaft pulley nut and rotate so that each retaining bolt in turn is accessible for removal.

67 Insert a suitable spacer (special tool T.AV.509 if available) between the lower suspension arm hinge pins and the shock

absorber lower fixing pins.

68 Drift out the driveshaft roll pins using a suitable size punch (see Chapter 7 Section 2, paragraph 3).

69 Refer to Chapter 8 and disconnect the brake caliper units. Note that it is not necessary to disconnect the hose, but on removal support the caliper — do not allow it to hang free.

70 Refer to Chapter 10 and disconnect the steering arm balljoints and upper arm balljoints.

71 Withdraw the driveshafts from the sunwheels. Tilt the stub axle carriers to ease this operation.

72 Refer to Chapter 10 and remove the anti-roll bar.

73 Unscrew the retaining bolts and remove the tubular cross-member.

74 Detach the exhaust downpipe from the manifold and also from the transmission mounting, and tie it back out of the way.

75 The upper engine-to-transmission retaining bolts can now be removed. The fixing stud can be removed using a suitable stud remover or two nuts locked together on the exposed stud thread, unscrewing the innermost nut to remove the stud.

76 Place a jack securely in position under the transmission and just support its weight.

77 Unscrew and remove the transmission lower retaining bolts.

78 Unscrew the retaining bolts and remove the transmission rear cross-member, then slightly lower the supporting jack.

79 Detach the vacuum capsule pipe and the governor cable.

80 Detach the selector control by engaging 1st gear (hold) and then disconnecting the rod from the computer and selector lever end by unscrewing the clamp.

81 The transmission is now ready for removal, but first check that all fittings and associated transmission fixtures are free

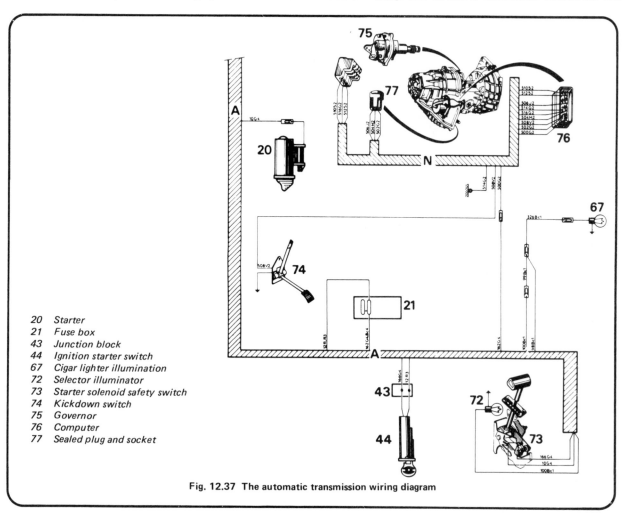

20   Starter
21   Fuse box
43   Junction block
44   Ignition starter switch
67   Cigar lighter illumination
72   Selector illuminator
73   Starter solenoid safety switch
74   Kickdown switch
75   Governor
76   Computer
77   Sealed plug and socket

Fig. 12.37 The automatic transmission wiring diagram

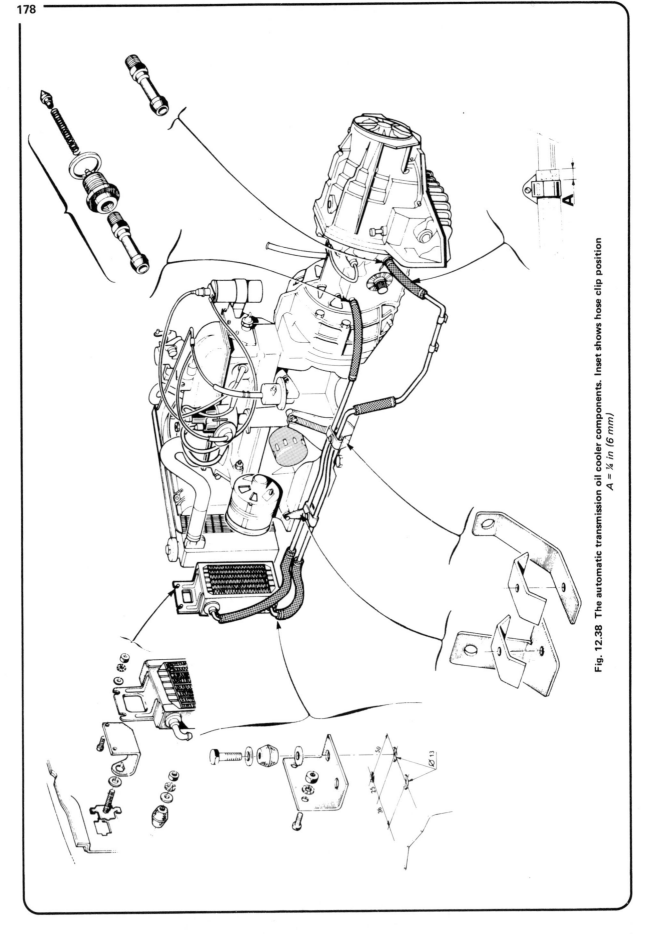

Fig. 12.38 The automatic transmission oil cooler components. Inset shows hose clip position

A = ¼ in (6 mm)

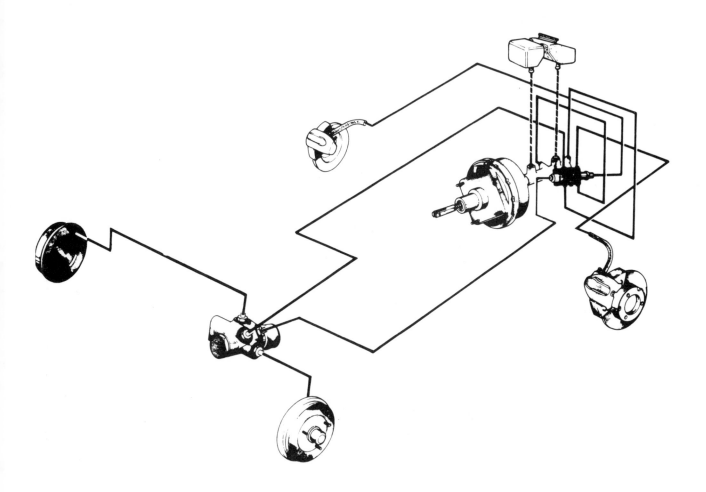

Fig. 12.39 The latest brake system layout showing the tandem master cylinder and ICP by-pass unit

before withdrawing. Disconnect the oil cooler pipes and temperature gauge connections if fitted. When removing the transmission, ensure that the torque converter is not dislodged and on removal fit a temporary retaining clip bolted to the housing to ensure that the converter is not disturbed whilst the transmission is out of the vehicle - see Fig. 12.35.

82 Refitting is the reversal of the removal process but the following points must be observed.

83 Before tightening up the engine-to-transmission bolts the three drive plate holes must be aligned with the converter boss holes. The holes are not evenly spaced and therefore the drive plate can only be coupled to the converter boss one way. Insert but do not tighten the three bolts, then rotate the converter so that the spot of blue paint close to the centre is positioned at the bottom. The bolts can now be tightened to 25 lbf ft (34 Nm).

84 Readjust the selector control and governor cable on completion and check that all wiring connections are clean and secure on reassembly.

Torque converter oil seal — renewal

85 Remove the gearbox/transmission unit as described in the preceding Section.

86 Carefully pull the converter from the driveshaft. Check the condition of the converter centralising ball, the oil seal bearing

surface, the white metal converter sleeve, the starter ring gear, the fan, and converter threaded securing bosses for cracks or stripping of the threads. Renew as required.

87 Carefully prise the oil seal out, noting the depth to which it is fitted in its recess.

88 Use a suitable diameter tubular drift and fit the new oil seal in position. Lubricate the seal bearing surfaces.

89 Reassemble the torque converter and the gearbox/transmission unit as described previously.

Automatic transmission — oil cooler

90 An oil cooler is fitted to some models equipped with automatic transmission, usually when the vehicle is to be used for towing. An oil temperature gauge is (or should be) fitted as well in this instance, and the oil temperature must never be allowed to exceed 284°F (140°C) at any time.

91 The layout of the oil cooler and connecting pipes, together with the respective connections, is shown in the accompanying diagram (Fig. 12.37).

92 The oil capacity of the automatic transmission with an oil cooler fitted is obviously increased, and an allowance for this must therefore be made when draining and refilling the automatic transmission.

93 No additional maintenance is required with an oil cooler

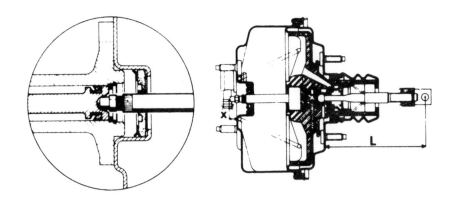

Fig. 12.40 The 19 mm bore master cylinder/servo unit as fitted to the Estate and TS models

L = 5 5/32 in (131 mm)   X = 23/64 in (9 mm)

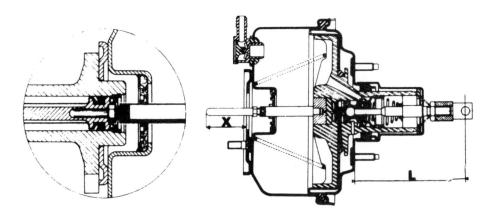

Fig. 12.41 The 20.6 mm bore master cylinder/servo unit as fitted to the following Estate and TS models:

	Vehicle fabrication Nos.
R1330 (Estate)	*94 410 to 94 600*
	95 001 to 95 600
	96 001 to 96 600
	96 652 to 96 800
	97 001 to 97 021
R1177 (TS models)	*51 301 to 52 600*
	52 800 to 54 836

L = 5 5/32 in (131 mm)
X = 1 9/32 in (32.5 mm)

installed but a close inspection should be made periodically to ensure that the pipes and their connections are secure and show no signs of leakage. Also check that the pipes are not chafing against surrounding fittings and components.

94 When removing the automatic transmission, the oil cooler, gauge pipes and securing clips will need to be disconnected in addition to those items specified in the relevant Section. Check on reassembly that the pipes and their connections are secure, and on starting the engine look for any signs of leaks. After an initial period, recheck the oil level in the transmission.

95 If a hose is to be replaced at any time, position the retaining clips so that there is a free length of ¼ in (6 mm) between the end of the hose and the clip, (Fig. 12.38 - inset).

7 Braking system

General description

1 A tandem master cylinder and dual-circuit braking are fitted to all later models. The various overhaul procedures for this system are given below.

Tandem master cylinder — removal and refitting

2 Clean the master cylinder cap and reservoir, then remove the cap. The brake fluid must be drained from the reservoir, and this is best performed with a syringe if available. If not, disconnect an outlet feed pipe from the cylinder, taking care not to distort

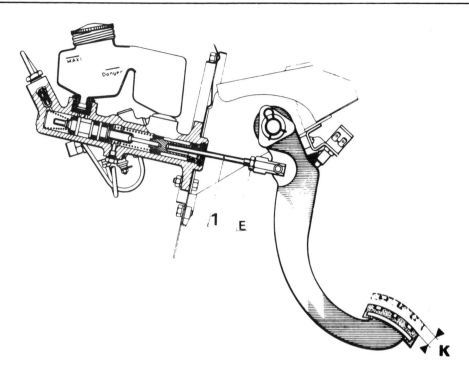

Fig. 12.42 A tandem master cylinder cross-sectional view showing the 'max' and 'danger' fluid levels on the reservoir body. Also shown are the adjustment points

1 Push rod   E Adjustment nut   K Pedal free movement — 13/64 in (5 mm)

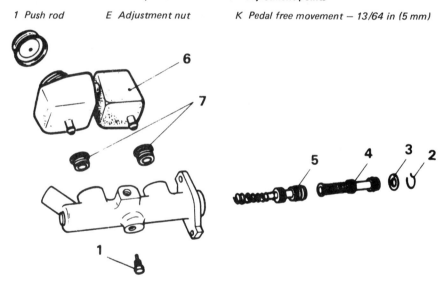

Fig. 12.43 The tandem master cylinder components

1 Stop screw   3 Stop washer   5 Secondary piston   7 Rubber sleeves
2 Snap-ring   4 Primary piston   6 Reservoir

it, and plug the end of the pipe to prevent the ingress of dirt and leakage of fluid. Drain the fluid from the cylinder into a container - don't spill any on the surrounding fittings or paintwork.

3 Unscrew the other pipe connections and plug them.

4 Unscrew and remove the low pressure indicator retaining bolt.

5 Unscrew the servo unit/pedal bracket retaining bolts and carefully withdraw the servo unit.

6 Disconnect the master cylinder pushrod from the brake pedal by removing the clevis pin.

7 Refitting is a direct reversal of the removal sequence but take care when reinserting the pushrod. On reassembly the brake

system must be bled as described in Chapter 8, Section 10. Check and adjust the pedal clearance as described in Section 12 of Chapter 8, and on models fitted with a servo unit, the master cylinder pushrod to master cylinder face clearance must be checked and adjusted accordingly (see below).

Tandem master cylinder — dismantling and reassembly

8 Position the master cylinder in a soft-jawed vice to secure.

9 Ease the reservoir unit from the cylinder by pulling up whilst tilting from right to left to free it from the rubber retaining sleeves.

10 Using a suitable soft drift (a piece of wood dowelling is ideal)

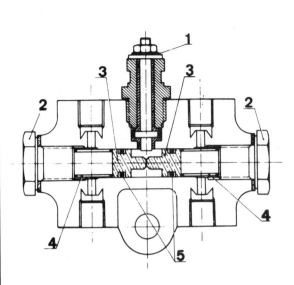

Fig. 12.44 The pressure drop indicator

1 Terminal   4 Springs
2 End plugs   5 Seals
3 Piston

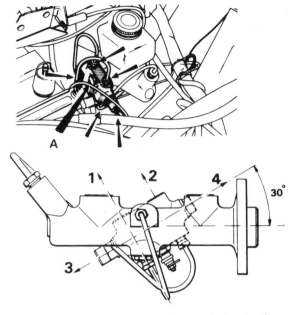

Fig. 12.45 The pressure drop indicator unit showing the respective connections and retaining bolt (A). Note also the angle of fitting in relation to master cylinder

1 RH front outlet   3 LH front outlet
2 Rear wheels outlet   4 Additional circuit outlet

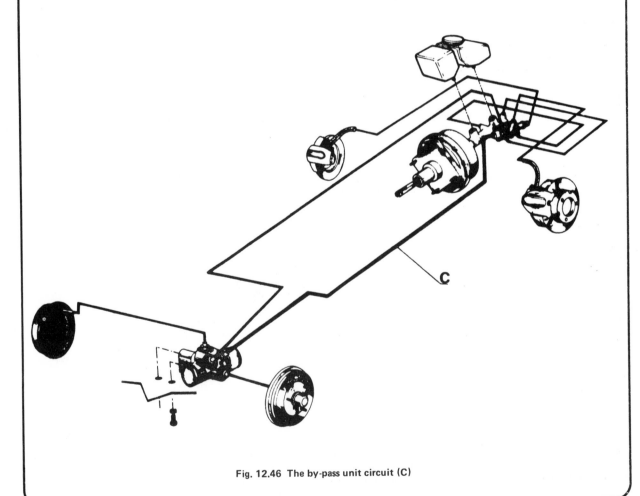

Fig. 12.46 The by-pass unit circuit (C)

push each piston in about 5 mm (0.20 in). Unscrew and remove the stop screw from its location in the cylinder wall.

11 Applying pressure to the piston spring, release the snap-ring and remove the stop washer, then withdraw the primary and secondary pistons taking note of their respective directional positions in the cylinder. If they are reluctant to be withdrawn apply some compressed air through the front aperture. Air from a hand pump is sufficient.

12 The primary and secondary piston assemblies cannot be repaired and should never be dismantled. Renew them if they are damaged or suspect.

13 Clean the respective components using clean methylated spirit and inspect the various parts for signs of wear, damage or distortion. In particualr inspect the cylinder bore for signs of scoring or scratches, in which case it must be renewed as must any other defective components.

14 Reassemble the cylinder components in the reverse order but dip each in some clean hydraulic brake fluid prior to fitting.

Servo unit — removal and refitting

15 Remove the servo unit as described in Chapter 8.

16 Refitting is a reversal of the removal process but the master cylinder operating clearance must be checked and adjusted if necessary — see Figs. 12.40 and 12.41.

17 To adjust, turn the pushrod nut to set the clearance at that specified.

Pressure drop indicator (single ICP unit) — description

18 A pressure drop indicator is now incorporated into the dual-circuit brake system and its object is to give an indication of a failure in the brake circuit. Any imbalance in the circuit pressure will actuate the electrical contact within the unit, causing the warning light on the instrument panel to light. The most probable defects are likely to be:

(a) Fluid leak in the system
(b) Defective tandem master cylinder
(c) Air locks in the system, which is in need of bleeding

19 Should the pressure drop indicator ever become defective it must be renewed as it is not repairable.

20 The brake warning light is combined with the 'handbrake on' warning light, and to test the bulb simply operate the handbrake with the ignition switched on.

Indicator unit — removal and refitting

21 First drain the hydraulic fluid from the master cylinder reservoir. Then unscrew the connecting pipes from the indicator unit and also detach the electrical connecting wire.

22 Prior to removal of the indicator retaining bolt, note the angle of the indicator unit in relation to the master cylinder unit which is 30°. Unscrew the retaining bolt and remove the indicator unit.

23 Refitting is a direct reversal of removal, but position the indicator unit at 30° in relation to the master cylinder (Fig. 12.45) as shown. Bleed the brake system on completion.

ICP by-pass unit — description

24 This unit is designed to direct additional pressure to the rear brakes in the event of a failure in the front circuit. Acting independently, it diverts the pressure flow to the rear via an additional circuit which by-passes the limiter to the rear brakes. This action is initiated only by a drop in pressure to the front brakes, which will open a by-pass valve in the unit to re-route the pressure flow direct to the rear brake wheel cylinders.

25 When bleeding the brakes, this independent circuit must also be bled, but only after the respective wheel cylinders have been bled first. The bleed screw is incorporated into the unit as shown in Fig. 12.46.

Disc brake calipers

26 On some models, the bolts retaining the caliper brackets in the front disc brake assembly, are not fitted with washers and are consequently slightly shorter in length. If, when dismantling for repair, you find this type of bolt fitted, clean the threads

prior to assembly using a wire brush and smear them with Loctite Frenoloc which is an adhesive solution for locking threads. Alternatively fit longer bolts (Part. No. 5003 001 104) and lockwashers to suit.

Rear self-adjusting drum brakes — removal, inspection and reassembly

27 Raise the rear of the car and support with a chassis stand. Remove the roadwheel on the side concerned and release the handbrake. Place the car in gear and chock the front wheels to prevent the car rolling. If the drum will not pull easily, the shoes are probably holding it. Carry out the following work.

28 To slacken off the brake shoes from the drum you will need a rod 5 mm (3/16 in) in diameter which is inserted through an access hole in the brake drum (Fig. 12.47). On some models there is a hole in the brake backplate instead of in the drum, and

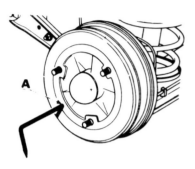

Fig. 12.47 Access hole position 'A' through brake drum

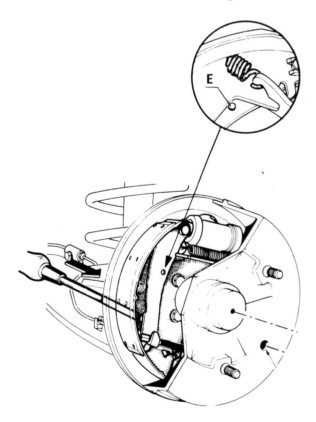

Fig. 12.48 Access hole in backplate - press screwdriver in direction of arrow to release from peg 'E'

RH. drum

Fig. 12.49 Rod to engage with sector 'D' of lever 'C'

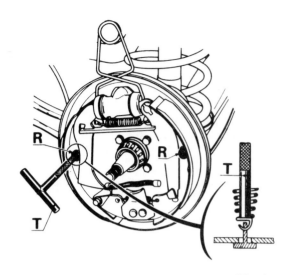

Fig. 12.50 Insert tube 'T' into shoe steady springs 'R' and turn
to release

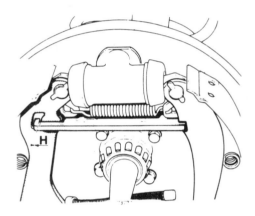

Fig. 12.51 Check the clearance between the shoe and link rod
'E' at 'H' (self-adjusting rear brakes).
H = 1 mm

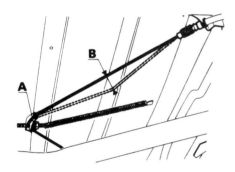

Fig. 12.52 Handbrake cable check (self-adjusting brakes),
showing the adjuster 'A' and clearance check 'B'

a normal flat-bladed screwdriver is all that is needed to release
the shoes from the drum (Fig. 12.48).

29 Where the hole is in the drum, prise the seal plug free, and
rotate the drum so that when the rod is inserted through the
hole it engages with the sector of the toothed lever to release the
shoes.

30 Where the access hole is in the backplate, remove the seal
plug and insert the screwdriver, engaging it with the handbrake
actuating lever by passing it through the hole in the brake shoe.
Push on the screwdriver to release the peg from the brake shoe as
shown in Fig. 12.48 and then push the lever rearwards to back
off the adjustment.

31 The brake drum on both types can now be withdrawn in a
similar manner to that described in Chapter 8, Section 3. The
inspection procedures are also the same.

32 To remove the brake shoes, unhook the upper brake shoe
return spring (just below the wheel cylinder), detach the handbrake cable and using a suitable hollow tube, insert it into the
respective shoe steady springs and turn to release (Fig. 12.50).

33 Press the toothed lever in towards the hub and ease the shoes
away from the backplate. Disconnect the link plate and release
the leading shoe, then with the adjuster sector set in the initial

position remove the leading shoe, tilting it outwards by 90°.
Unhook the lower return spring and remove both shoes.

34 Do not under any circumstances press the brake pedal whilst
the shoes are removed or the wheel cylinder will be operated and
the pistons ejected, with the resultant loss in brake fluid. If this
happens the cylinder will have to be reassembled, the system
topped up, and the brakes will need bleeding. As a precaution tie
some string around the cylinder to retain the pistons in position.

35 If a replacement is required for a brake drum which incorporates an access hole, you will have to drill this hole in the new
drum before fitting. The hole is 5 mm (13/64 in) in diameter and
is drilled at a radius of 85 mm (3 11/32 in) in the drum; the hole
position in the old drum can be used as a guide. This hole must
be drilled to enable the drum to be removed (when necessary) as
previously explained.

36 Installation of the brake shoes is a reversal of the removal
procedure, but note the following:

(a) When the brake shoe steady spring attachments are
located rotate them 90° to secure.

(b) When the shoes are installed the self-adjusting tension
spring setting must be checked. Referring to Fig. 12.51
measure the clearance between the primary shoe and link rod

at 'H'. This should be approximately 1 mm (3/64 in). If the clearance is incorrect then the link spring must be renewed together with the shoe upper and lower return springs.
(c) Before refitting the brake drum apply some bearing grease to the hub.
(d) On completion apply the footbrake a few times and check for correct operation of the rear brake/s. Readjust the handbrake as described below.

Handbrake adjustment — self-adjusting brakes

37 Where self-adjusting rear brakes are fitted, the handbrake adjustment is normally taken up automatically. The only time it is necessary to adjust the handbrake is after the rear brake unit/s have been dismantled for inspection and/or overhaul. Proceed as follows.
38 Checking and adjustment is carried out with the vehicle standing normally and not jacked up, although for accessibility it is preferable if this check/adjustment can be undertaken with the vehicle parked over an inspection pit. Chock the wheels and release the handbrake.
39 Referring to Fig. 12.52 the secondary cable must be checked for tension. It must not be slack or taut. Check the clearance at point B from the floor which must be 20 mm (25/32 in). If it is not, turn the adjuster nut accordingly and recheck the cable tension and clearance from the floor.
40 Operate the handbrake lever a few times and recheck in the 'off' position. The handbrake lever travel from 'off' to fully 'on' should be 12 to 13 notches.

8 Electrical system

Combination light switch — removal and refitting
1 First raise the bonnet and disconnect the battery leads.
2 Carefully remove the bottom cover from the switch unit and disconnect the wires from their connections but take note of their respective positions.
3 The switch is now retained by three screws, and when these are removed the switch unit can be withdrawn.
4 Refit in the reverse order but ensure that the wires are reconnected to their respective terminals. Check the operations of the switch on reconnecting the battery.

Headlights — Quartz-halogen bulb renewal (TS models)
5 First remove the light unit as described in Chapter 9, and then detach the connection from the rear of the bulb.
6 Unclip the bulb retaining spring clips and release the bulb, but when withdrawing it from the reflector take care not to handle the glass section of the bulb (unless of course it is known to be defective anyway).
7 Insert the replacement bulb and retain with the spring clips. Reverse the removal procedures to complete and then check the bulb operation.
8 If the bulb is inadvertently handled, clean the glass of the bulb with methylated spirit before switching on.

Headlight beam deflection (LHD/RHD)
9 On some models a rotator is built into the headlight unit which enables a simple conversion to be made from right-hand to left-hand drive or vice versa. This of course is designed to simplify the headlight beam adjustment when a change to driving on the left or right (according to country) is made, thus complying with local regulations with the minimum of fuss.
10 To do this, first remove the bulb as described in Chapter 9 and turn the rotating lever to the left for driving on the right or to the right if driving on the left (Fig. 12.54).

Instrument panel and instruments
11 Although the instrument panel and instrument layout has been revised, the removal instructions remain the same as for those of the earlier types (see Chapter 9, Section 15). However, the wiring connections to the instrument panel will probably

differ from that shown in Fig. 9.14, so for later models refer to the respective wiring diagram in this Supplement.

Heated rear screen
12 A heated rear screen is now fitted to all models and is operated electrically via an element in the glass. It is operated from a dashboard mounted switch incorporating a warning light which acts as a reminder to the driver that the screen heater is on. The rear screen heater should only be used for short periods to initially clear the glass of frost or mist.
13 This equipment rarely gives problems, but if it should fail to operate, check the switch and wire connections to the rear window using a continuity tester or test light before assuming the element to be the culprit.
14 If the element is defective have it checked by your Renault dealer before deciding on a course of action.
15 If a replacement screen is to be fitted, the removal and installation instructions are identical to those given in Chapter 11, Section 7 on windscreen and fixed glass replacement.

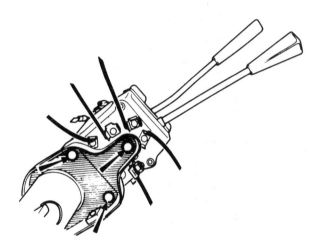

Fig. 12.53 The combination switch showing the terminal connections and the three retaining screws (arrowed)

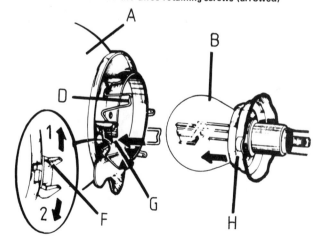

Fig. 12.54 The RH drive to LH drive headlight rotator assembly

A Reflector
B Bulb (note stepped flange)
D Retaining clip
F Rotator lever
G Bulb lug slot for 'H'
1 and 2 Rotate accordingly for right-or left-hand drive

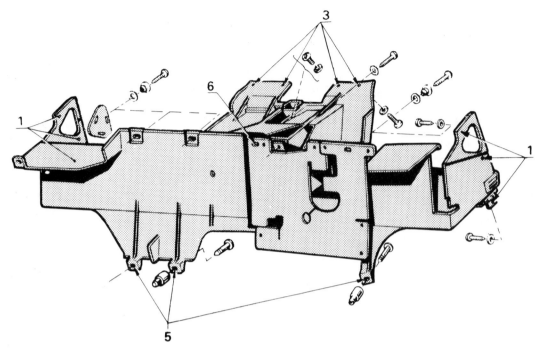

Fig. 12.55 The parcel shelf retaining screw positions

1 Front pillar linings   3 Dash board   5 Scuttle plastic screws   6 Nut

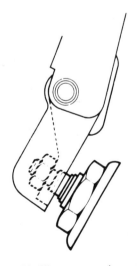

Fig. 12.56 Wiper arm attachment nut

Windscreen wiper motor — removal and refitting (R1177 models from 1976)

16 On the above models fitted with the later style dashboard it is not necessary to completely remove the dashboard and instruments in order to extract the wiper motor; proceed as follows.

17 Having first disconnected the battery, unscrew and remove the console retaining screws and then detach the clock earth wire.

18 Move the front seats back fully and manoeuvre the console round the gear lever.

19 Unscrew and detach the combination light and indicator switch cowling covers.

20 The parcel shelf must now be lowered. To do this unscrew and extract the six front pillar lining screws, the four dashboard retaining screws, the three plastic scuttle screws, and also the nut.

21 Unscrew and remove the two heater control panel retaining screws and free the panel.

22 Detach the windscreen wiper motor junction block and unscrew and remove the second mounting plate nut.

23 Detach the windscreen wiper arms and unscrew and remove the spindle bearing retaining nuts. The windscreen wiper motor can now be removed.

24 To assemble, reverse the removal sequence but check that the wiper motor is in the 'parked' position before refitting the wiper arms. Check all electrical connections for security before reconnecting the battery.

Windscreen wiper arms — later models

25 The windscreen wiper arm on later models is retained in position on the spindle by a nut. To gain access to the nut, hinge back the base section of the arm, then unscrew the nut to free the arm. Refit in the reverse order, aligning the arm in the 'parked' position.

Fuses (R1330 and R1177 versions)

26 Later vehicles have the fusebox located inside the glove compartment in front of the driver.

27 The fuse ratings and the circuits protected are as follows:

No. 1	16A	Instruments, stop lamps, rear lamps
No. 2	5A	Automatic transmission
No. 3	5A	Direction indicators
No. 4	8A	Heater fan
No. 5	8A	Interior lamp, luggage boot lamp
No. 6	8A	Windscreen wiper, windscreen washer

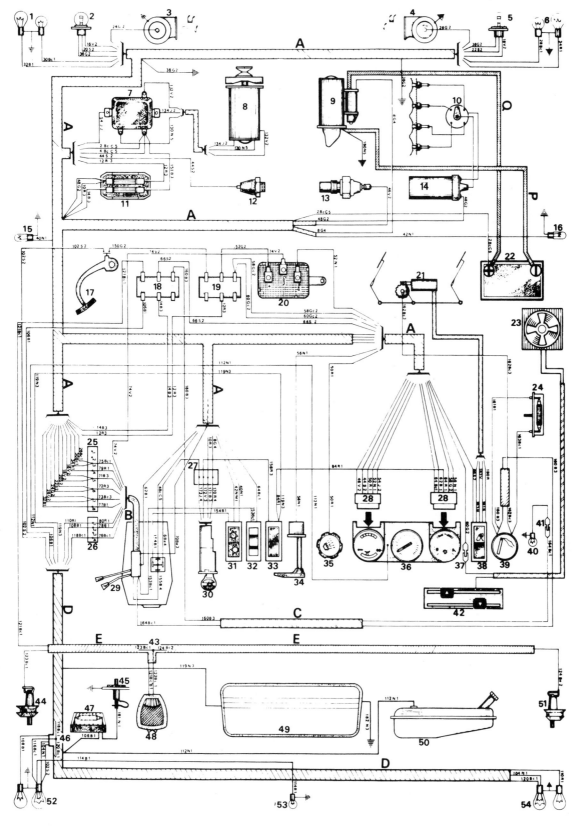

Fig. 12.57 Wiring diagram for 1970 and 1971 R1170 and R1171 models

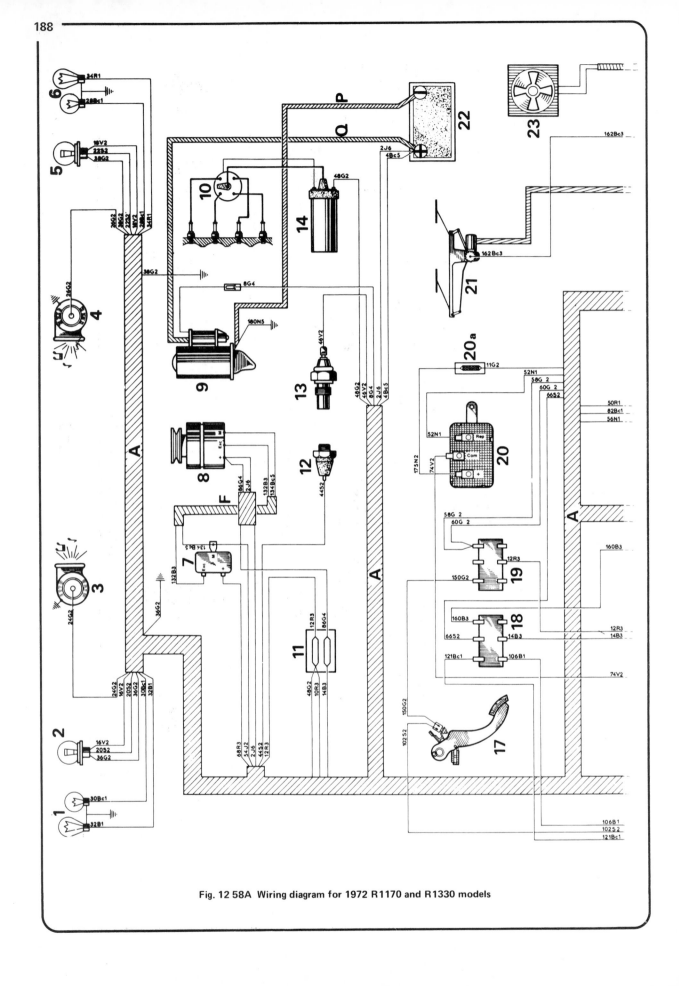

Fig. 12 58A Wiring diagram for 1972 R1170 and R1330 models

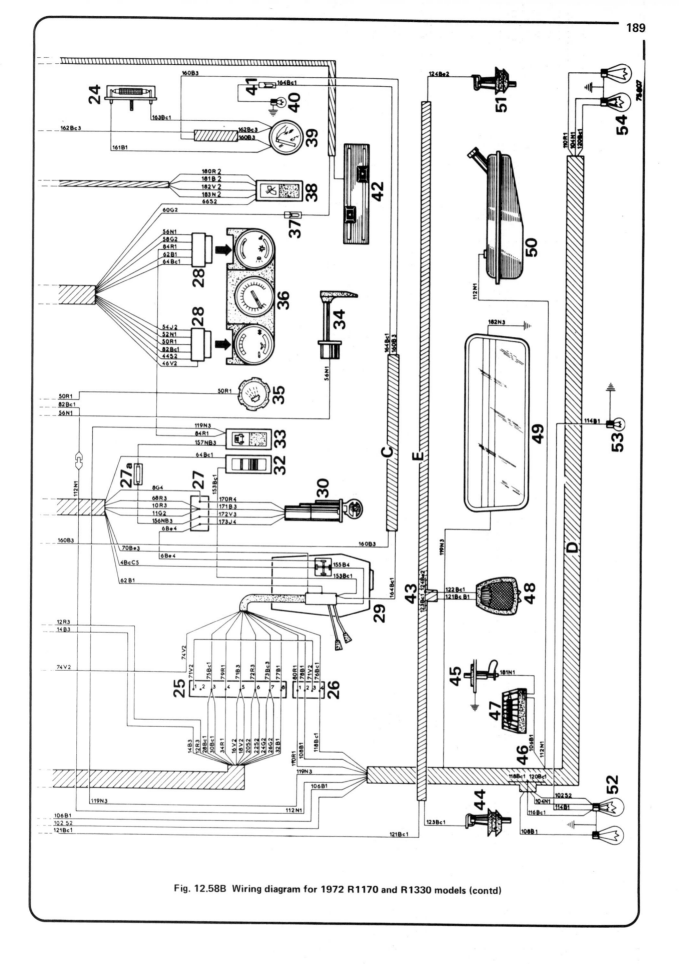

Fig. 12.58B Wiring diagram for 1972 R1170 and R1330 models (contd)

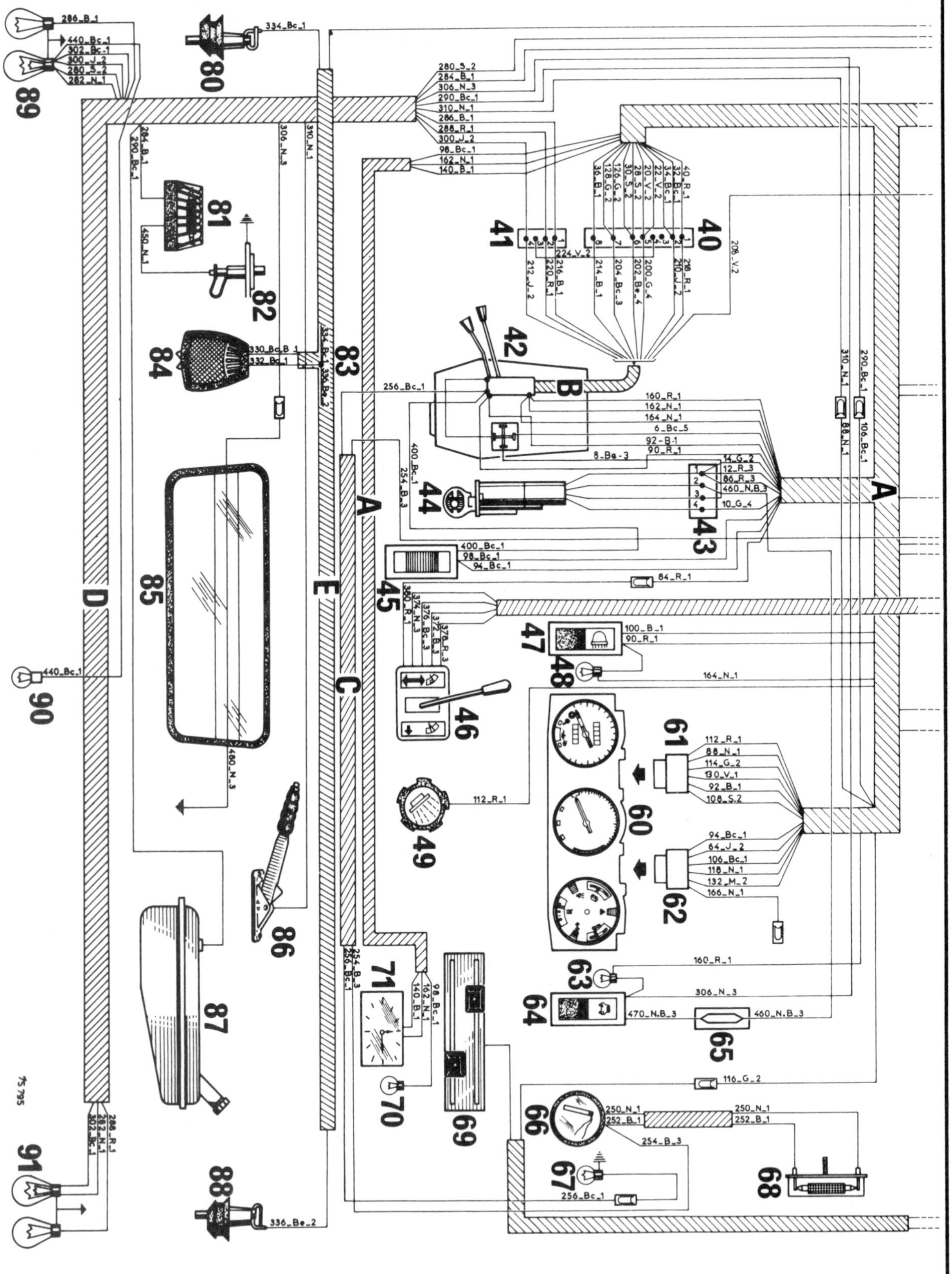

Fig. 12.59A Wiring diagram for 1972 R1177 model

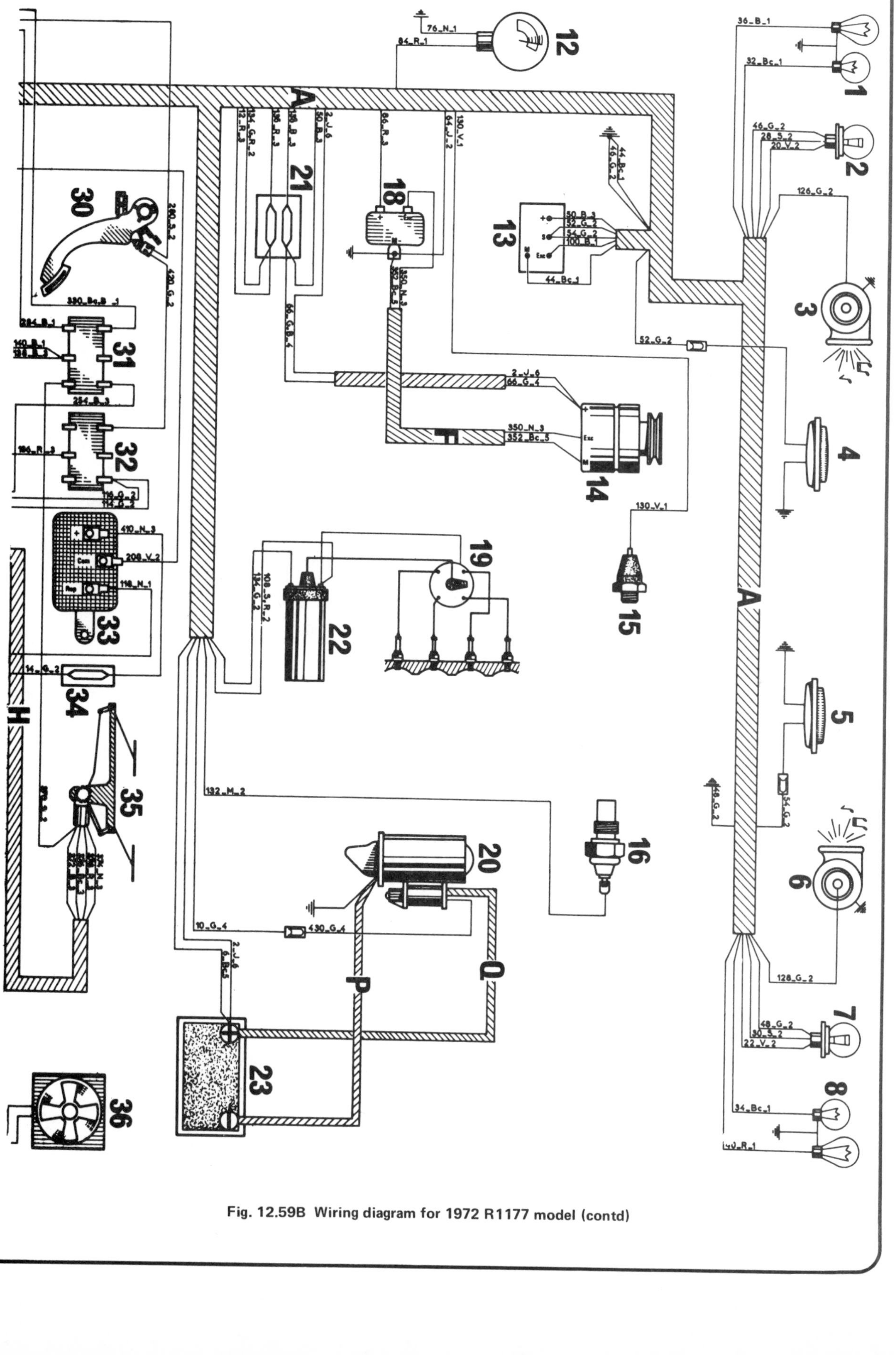

Fig. 12.59B Wiring diagram for 1972 R1177 model (contd)

Wiring code for wiring diagrams 12.57, 12.58 and 12.59

1 LH front side and flasher lights
2 LH front headlight
3 LH horn
4 RH horn
5 RH front headlight
6 RH front side and flasher lights
7 Regulator
8 Generator
9 Starter motor
10 Distributor
11 Fuses
12 Oil pressure switch
13 Water temperature switch
14 Ignition coil
15 LH park light
16 RH park light
17 Stop light switch
18 Ignition switch junction plate (before switch)
19 Ignition switch junction plate (after switch)
20 Flasher unit
20a Flasher unit fuse
21 Windscreen wiper
22 Battery
23 Heating ventilation fan
24 Glovebox light
25 Loom to combination light switch junction
26 Loom (rear) to combination light switch junction
27 Ignition/starter switch to front loom junction

27a Rear screen heater fuse
28 Front loom to instruments junction
29 Combination switch
30 Ignition/starter switch
31 Park light switch
32 Panel light rheostat
33 Rear screen heater switch
34 Handbrake warning light
35 Choke 'on' switch
36 Instrument panel
37 Terminal and socket - fan motor
38 Windscreen wiper motor switch
39 Cigar lighter element
40 Cigar lighter illumination
41 Push-on terminal and socket
42 Heater/fan control
43 Interior light wire junction
44 LH front door pillar switch
45 Boot switch
46 Rear lights wire junction
47 Boot light
48 Interior light
49 Heated rear screen
50 Fuel tank gauge unit
51 RH front door pillar switch
52 LH rear light
53 No. plate light
54 RH rear light

Cable colour code — (wire and sleeve)

Be - Beige
Bc - White
B - Blue
C - Clear
G - Grey
Y - Yellow

N - Black
S - Pink
R - Red
V - Green
M - Maroon

Wiring code for wiring diagrams 12.60 and 12.61

1 and 8   Front side and indicator lights
2 and 7   Headlights
3 and 6   Horns
4 and 5   QI driving lights
12   Windscreen washer pump
13   QI driving lights relay
14   Alternator
15   Oil pressure switch
16   Water temperature switch
18   Regulator
19   Distributor
20   Starter motor
21   Fusebox
22   Ignition coil
23   Battery
24   Reverse light switch
30   Stoplight switch
31   Ignition switch junction (before)
32   Ignition switch junction (after)
33   Flasher unit
35   Windscreen wiper
36   Heater/fan motor
40   Front loom to combination light switch junction
41   Rear loom to combination light switch junction
42   Combination switch
43   Junction - front loom to ignition/starter
44   Ignition starter switch
45   Panel light rheostat
46   Windscreen wiper/washer switch

47   QI driving light switch
48   QI driving light switch warning 'on' light
49   Choke 'on' light
50   Junction - front to rear loom
53   Hazard warning system terminal
54   Hazard warning system switch
55   Hazard warning system to indicators junction
56   Junction block
60   Instrument panel
61 and 62   Instrument panel LH and RH junctions
63   Windscreen wiper switch identity plate
64   Rear screen heater switch
66   Cigar lighter
67   Cigar lighter illumination
68   Glove compartment light
69   Heater/fan control
70 and 71   Clock and light
80 and 88   Door pillar switches
81   Boot light
82   Boot light switch
83   Interior light wire junction
84   Interior light
85   Heated rear screen
86   Handbrake 'on' warning light switch
87   Fuel gauge sender unit
89 and 91   Rear light assemblies
90   Number plate light
92 and 93   Terminals/sockets for reverse lights

Cable colour code — (wire and sleeve)

Be - Beige
Bc - White
B - Blue
C - Clear
G - Grey
Y - Yellow

N - Black
S - Pink
R - Red
V - Green
M - Maroon

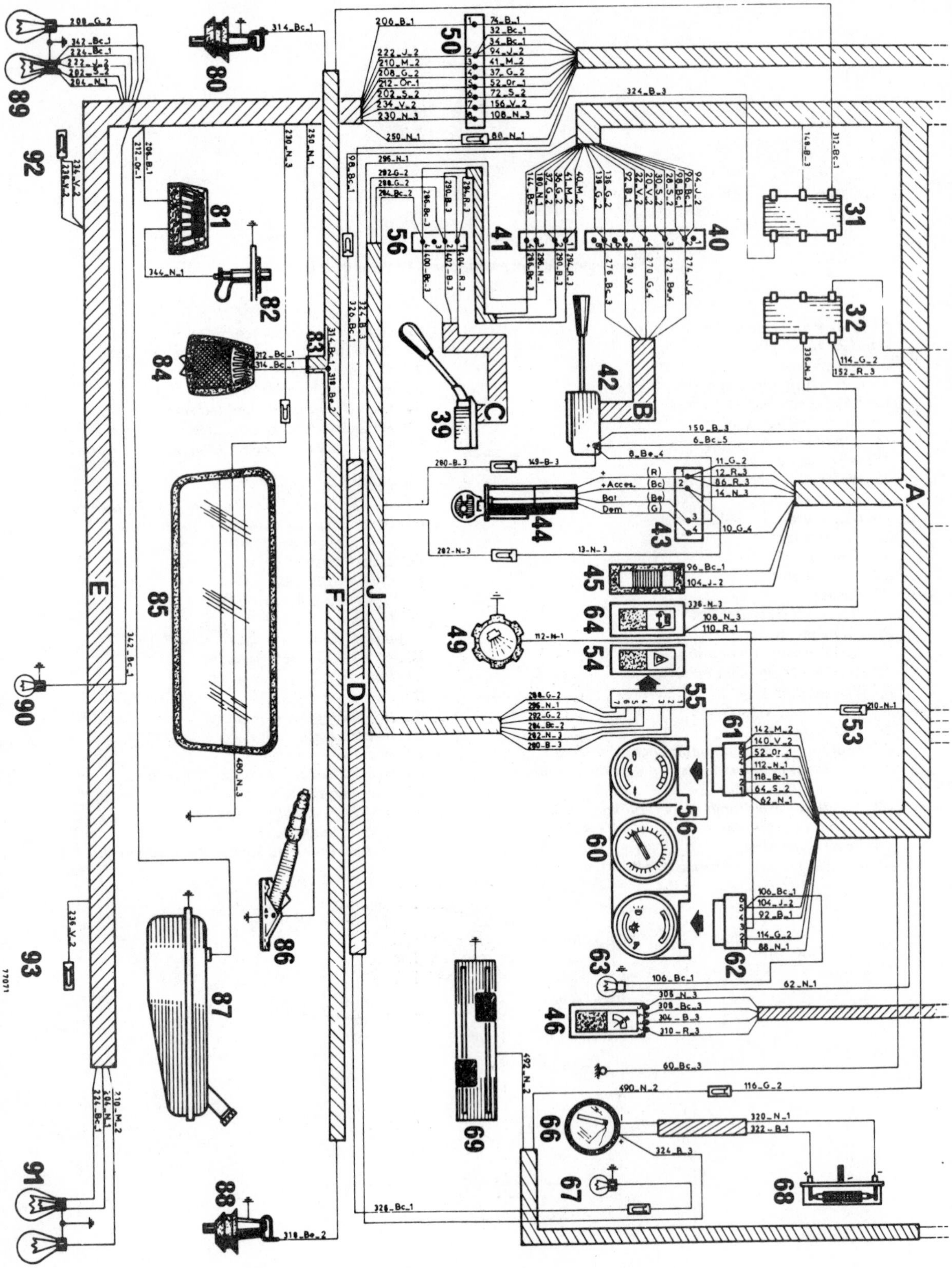

Fig. 12.60A Wiring diagram for 1975 model R1170

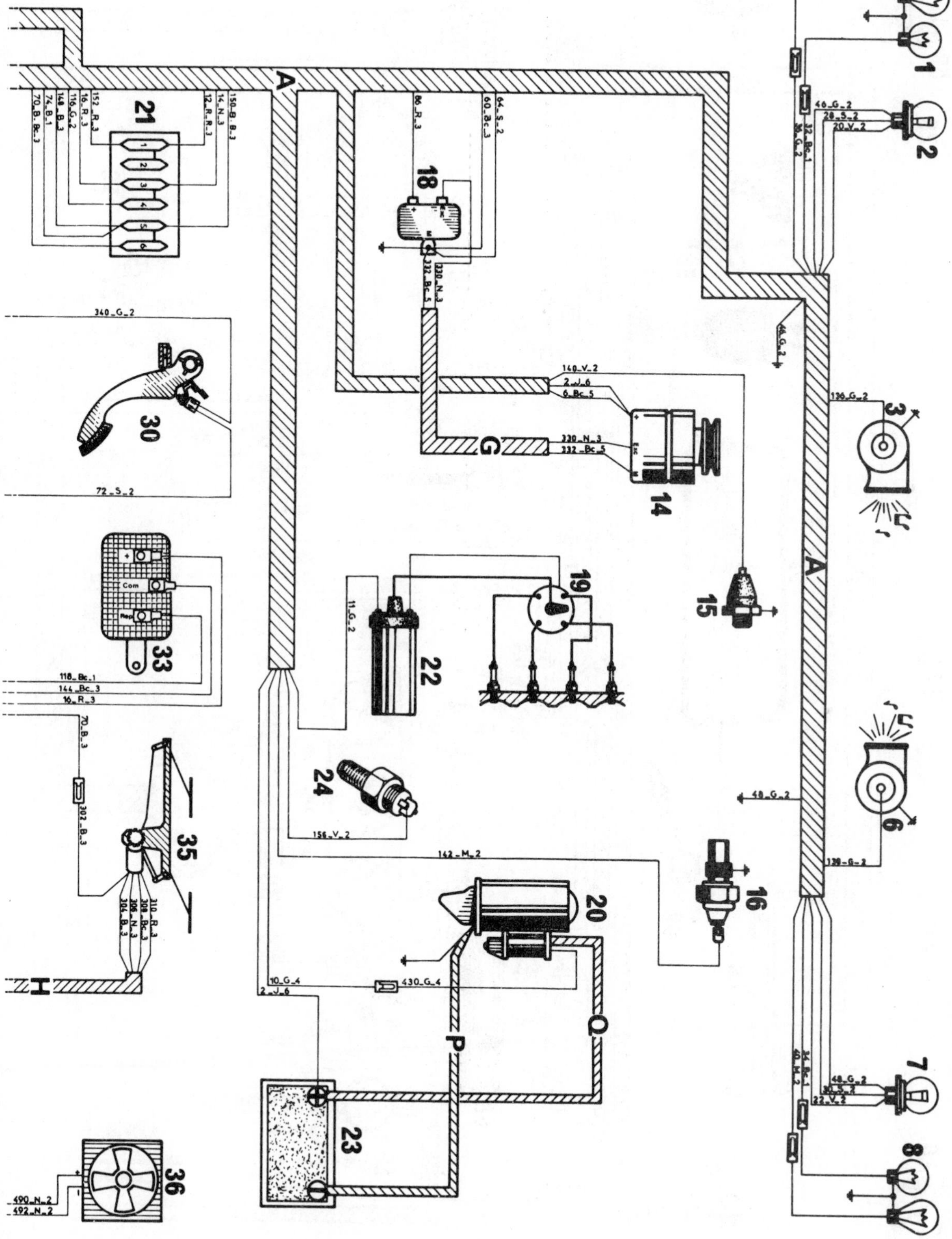

Fig. 12.60B Wiring diagram for 1975 model R1170 (contd)

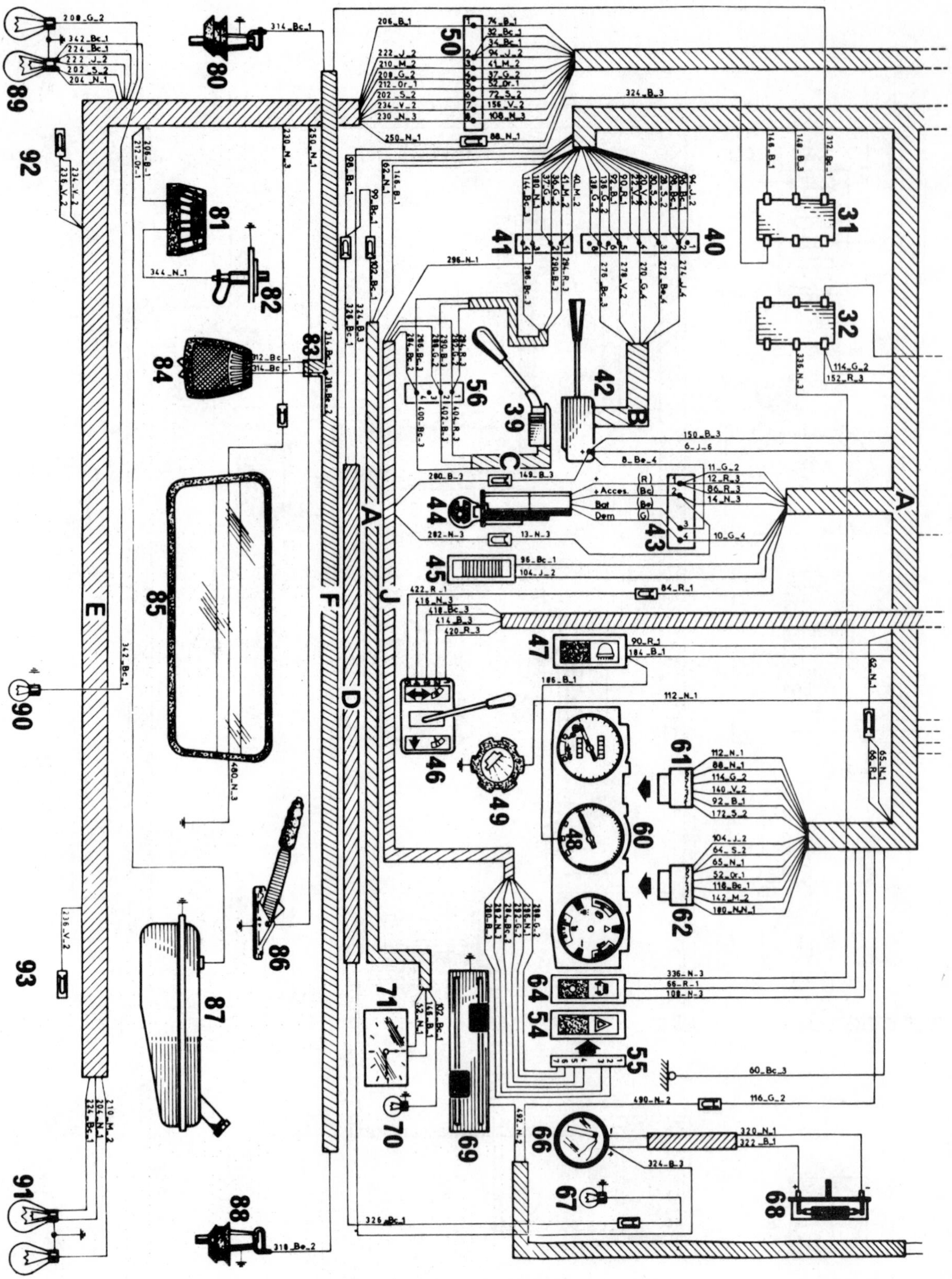

Fig. 12.61A Wiring diagram for 1975 model R1177

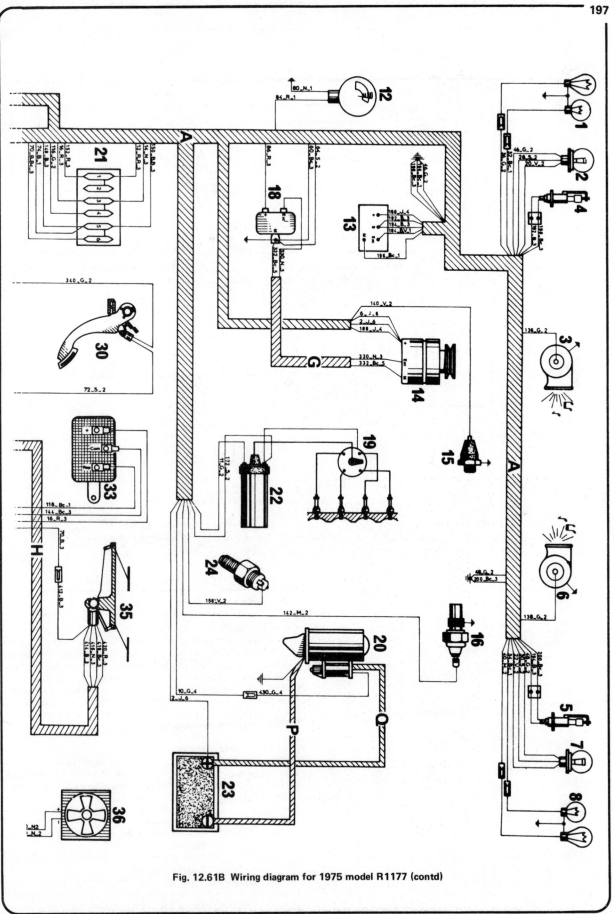

Fig. 12.61B Wiring diagram for 1975 model R1177 (contd)

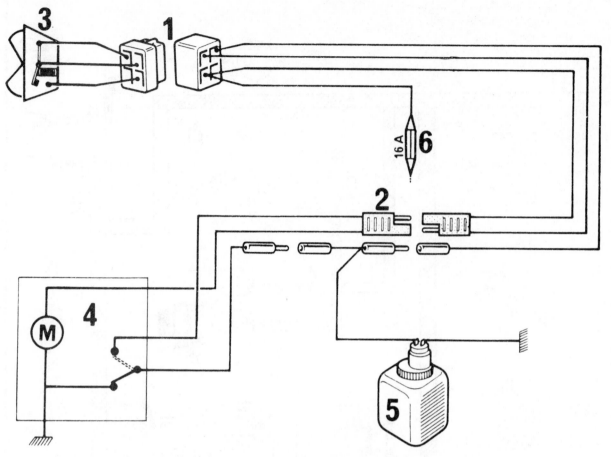

Fig. 12.62 The Estate rear screen washer/wiper wiring diagram

1   Junction - washer/wiper switch   4   Rear screen wiper motor
2   Rear harness to screen wiper motor plug/socket   5   Rear screen washer pump unit
3   Switch to washer/wiper   6   No. 1 fuse

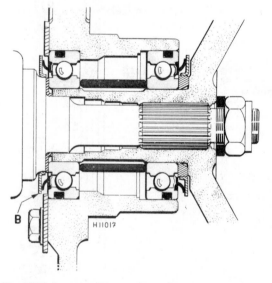

Fig. 12.63 Late type front stub axle/hub seal and bearing

9 Suspension and steering

Front coil springs

1   The front coil springs are available with alternative numbers
of coils to suit different models and road conditions. The springs
can have 6, 7, 8 or 9 coils and, if replacing a spring, the new one
must be identical to the old one for obvious reasons. Both front
coil springs may be changed for an alternative type, but consult
your Renault dealer prior to removal of the old ones, so that he
can advise you on which type you need, and of course the
availability of the replacements.

Front stub axle assembly

2   On the latest models, the front stub axle/hub unit is fitted
with a modified type of bearing and seal. The following items are
all new parts and are not directly interchangeable with their
earlier counterparts, but only as an assembly.
New parts: Drive shaft deflector
                     Bearing spacer
                     Bearing thrust washer (and deflector)
                     Bearing closure plate
                     Inner and outer bearings (with lip seal)
                     Stub axle carrier
3   The bearings and hub assembly are overhauled in the same
manner as that given in Chapter 7, Section 4, but note that when
fitting a new assembly to the old type, the deflector must be

changed and must be positioned as shown in Fig. 12.64, allowing a gap of 3.7 mm (0.145 in) between it and the anti-squeak face.

Steering arm (track rod) — identification

4   Later model steering arms have a boss which must always face the front of the vehicle. Left-hand arms may also be identified with a small hole.

---

10   Bodywork

Jacking and towing

1   The jack supplied with the tool kit should only be used for emergency wheel changing.

2   To lift the vehicle for repair and overhaul work, use a substantial hydraulic, screw or trolley jack.

3   Locate the jack at the points indicated and always supplement the jack with axle stands before working under the vehicle.

4   On cars with automatic transmission, it is recommended that the front of the car is raised for a suspended tow in order to avoid damage to the transmission assembly.

5   Always keep the doors closed when jacking the vehicle to prevent body flexing and distortion.

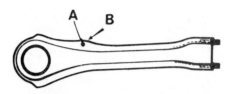

Fig. 12.65 A late type steering arm (track-rod)

A *Small hole*   B *Boss*

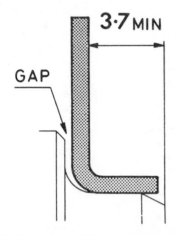

Fig. 12.64 Front hub deflector positioning diagram (Late type bearing seal assembly)

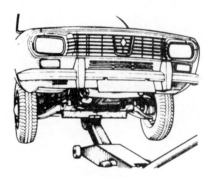

Fig. 12.66 Jacking front end with baulk of timber under both side frame members

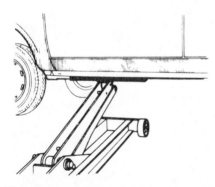

Fig. 12.67 Raising one side with jack placed just behind sill at centre of front door

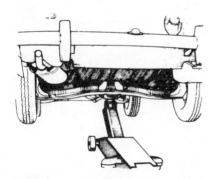

Fig. 12.69 Raising rear end with jack and wooden block under rear panel bottom edge (Estate)

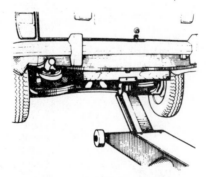

Fig. 12.68 Raising rear end with jack positioned under centre of rear axle crossmember (Saloon)

Metric conversion tables

Inches	Decimals	Millimetres	Millimetres to Inches		Inches to Millimetres	
			mm	Inches	Inches	mm
1/64	0.015625	0.3969	0.01	0.00039	0.001	0.0254
1/32	0.03125	0.7937	0.02	0.00079	0.002	0.0508
3/64	0.046875	1.1906	0.03	0.00118	0.003	0.0762
1/16	0.0625	1.5875	0.04	0.00157	0.004	0.1016
5/64	0.078125	1.9844	0.05	0.00197	0.005	0.1270
3/32	0.09375	2.3812	0.06	0.00236	0.006	0.1524
7/64	0.109375	2.7781	0.07	0.00276	0.007	0.1778
1/8	0.125	3.1750	0.08	0.00315	0.008	0.2032
9/64	0.140625	3.5719	0.09	0.00354	0.009	0.2286
5/32	0.15625	3.9687	0.1	0.00394	0.01	0.254
11/64	0.171875	4.3656	0.2	0.00787	0.02	0.508
3/16	0.1875	4.7625	0.3	0.01181	0.03	0.762
13/64	0.203125	5.1594	0.4	0.01575	0.04	1.016
7/32	0.21875	5.5562	0.5	0.01969	0.05	1.270
15/64	0.234375	5.9531	0.6	0.02362	0.06	1.524
1/4	0.25	6.3500	0.7	0.02756	0.07	1.778
17/64	0.265625	6.7469	0.8	0.03150	0.08	2.032
9/32	0.28125	7.1437	0.9	0.03543	0.09	2.286
19/64	0.296875	7.5406	1	0.03937	0.1	2.54
5/16	0.3125	7.9375	2	0.07874	0.2	5.08
21/64	0.328125	8.3344	3	0.11811	0.3	7.62
11/32	0.34375	8.7312	4	0.15748	0.4	10.16
23/64	0.359375	9.1281	5	0.19685	0.5	12.70
3/8	0.375	9.5250	6	0.23622	0.6	15.24
25/64	0.390625	9.9219	7	0.27559	0.7	17.78
13/32	0.40625	10.3187	8	0.31496	0.8	20.32
27/64	0.421875	10.7156	9	0.35433	0.9	22.86
7/16	0.4375	11.1125	10	0.39370	1	25.4
29/64	0.453125	11.5094	11	0.43307	2	50.8
15/32	0.46875	11.9062	12	0.47244	3	76.2
31/64	0.48375	12.3031	13	0.51181	4	101.6
1/2	0.5	12.7000	14	0.55118	5	127.0
33/64	0.515625	13.0969	15	0.59055	6	152.4
17/32	0.53125	13.4937	16	0.62992	7	177.8
35/64	0.546875	13.8906	17	0.66929	8	203.2
9/16	0.5625	14.2875	18	0.70866	9	228.6
37/64	0.578125	14.6844	19	0.74803	10	254.0
19/32	0.59375	15.0812	20	0.78740	11	279.4
39/64	0.609375	15.4781	21	0.82677	12	304.8
5/8	0.625	15.8750	22	0.86614	13	330.2
41/64	0.640625	16.2719	23	0.90551	14	355.6
21/32	0.65625	16.6687	24	0.94488	15	381.0
43/64	0.671875	17.0656	25	0.98425	16	406.4
11/16	0.6875	17.4625	26	1.02362	17	431.8
45/64	0.703125	17.8594	27	1.06299	18	457.2
23/32	0.71875	18.2562	28.	1.10236	19	482.6
47/64	0.734375	18.6531	29	1.14173	20	508.0
3/4	0.75	19.0500	30	1.18110	21	533.4
49/64	0.765625	19.4469	31	1.22047	22	558.8
25/32	0.78125	19.8437	32	1.25984	23	584.2
51/64	0.796875	20.2406	33	1.29921	24	609.6
13/16	0.8125	20.6375	34	1.33858	25	635.0
53/64	0.828125	21.0344	35	1.37795	26	660.4
27/32	0.84375	21.4312	36	1.41732	27	685.8
55/64	0.859375	21.8281	37	1.4567	28	711.2
7/8	0.875	22.2250	38	1.4961	29	736.6
57/64	0.890625	22.6219	39	1.5354	30	762.0
29/32	0.90625	23.0187	40	1.5748	31	787.4
59/64	0.921875	23.4156	41	1.6142	32	812.8
15/16	0.9375	23.8125	42	1.6535	33	838.2
61/64	0.953125	24.2094	43	1.6929	34	863.6
31/32	0.96875	24.6062	44	1.7323	35	889.0
63/64	0.984375	25.0031	45	1.7717	36	914.4

1   Imperial gallon = 8 Imp pints = 1.20 US gallons = 277.42 cu in = 4.54 litres

1   US gallon = 4 US quarts = 0.83 Imp gallon = 231 cu in = 3.78 litres

1   Litre = 0.21 Imp gallon = 0.26 US gallon = 61.02 cu in = 1000 cc

Miles to Kilometres		Kilometres to Miles	
1	1.61	1	0.62
2	3.22	2	1.24
3	4.83	3	1.86
4	6.44	4	2.49
5	8.05	5	3.11
6	9.66	6	3.73
7	11.27	7	4.35
8	12.88	8	4.97
9	14.48	9	5.59
10	16.09	10	6.21
20	32.19	20	12.43
30	48.28	30	18.64
40	64.37	40	24.85
50	80.47	50	31.07
60	96.56	60	37.28
70	112.65	70	43.50
80	128.75	80	49.71
90	144.84	90	55.92
100	160.93	100	62.14

lbf ft to kgf m		kgf m to lbf ft		lbf/in^2 to kgf/cm^2		kgf/cm^2 to lbf/in^2	
1	0.138	1	7.233	1	0.07	1	14.22
2	0.276	2	14.466	2	0.14	2	28.50
3	0.414	3	21.699	3	0.21	3	42.67
4	0.553	4	28.932	4	0.28	4	56.89
5	0.691	5	36.165	5	0.35	5	71.12
6	0.829	6	43.398	6	0.42	6	85.34
7	0.967	7	50.631	7	0.49	7	99.56
8	1.106	8	57.864	8	0.56	8	113.79
9	1.244	9	65.097	9	0.63	9	128.00
10	1.382	10	72.330	10	0.70	10	142.23
20	2.765	20	144.660	20	1.41	20	284.47
30	4.147	30	216.990	30	2.11	30	426.70

Index

PURCHASED.

SERVICED

POINTS.   37900
G/BOX   OIL   38800

ENG.   OIL   38900
        OIL FILTER   45
        AIR FILTER   (3⁴⁴⁶⁰⁰
                         "

                   42646.

Printed by
Haynes Publishing Group
Sparkford Yeovil Somerset
England